Understanding Political Science Research Meth

This text starts by explaining the fundamental goal of good political science research—the ability to answer interesting and important questions by generating valid inferences about political phenomena. Before the text even discusses the process of developing a research question, the authors introduce the reader to what it means to make an inference and the different challenges that social scientists face when confronting this task. Only with this ultimate goal in mind will students be able to ask appropriate questions, conduct fruitful literature reviews, select and execute the proper research design, and critically evaluate the work of others.

The authors' primary goal is to teach students to critically evaluate their own research designs and others' and analyze the extent to which they overcome the classic challenges to making inference: internal and external validity concerns, omitted variable bias, endogeneity, measurement, sampling, and case selection errors, and poor research questions or theory. As such, students will not only be better able to conduct political science research, but they will also be more savvy consumers of the constant flow of causal assertions that they confront in scholarship, in the media, and in conversations with others.

Three themes run through Barakso, Sabet, and Schaffner's text: minimizing classic research problems to making valid inferences, effective presentation of research results, and the nonlinear nature of the research process. Throughout their academic years and later in their professional careers, students will need to effectively convey various bits of information. Presentation skills gleaned from this text will benefit students for a lifetime, whether they continue in academia or in a professional career.

Several distinctive features make this book noteworthy:

- A common set of examples threaded throughout the text give students a common ground across chapters and expose them to a broad range of subfields in the discipline.
- "When Things Go Wrong" boxes illustrate the nonlinear, "non-textbook" reality of research.
- "Inferences in the Media" boxes demonstrate the often false inferences and poor social science in the way the popular press covers politics.
- "Ethics of Conduct" boxes encourage students to think about ethical issues at various stages of the research process.
- Robust end-of-chapter exercises.
- A companion website that gives students additional opportunities to fine tune their understanding of the book's material.

Understanding Political Science Research Methods

The Challenge of Inference

Maryann Barakso
Daniel M. Sabet
Brian F. Schaffner

Routledge
Taylor & Francis Group

NEW YORK AND LONDON

Publisher: Craig Fowlie
Editor: Michael Kerns
Development Editor: Elizabeth Mills
Marketing Manager: Paul Reyes
Editorial Assistant: Darcy Bullock
Cover Design: John Maloney
Production Editor: Alf Symons
Composition: Apex CoVantage, LLC

First published 2014
by Routledge
711 Third Avenue, New York, NY 10017

and by Routledge
2 Park Square, Milton Park, Abingdon, Oxon OX14 4RN

Routledge is an imprint of the Taylor & Francis Group, an informa business

© 2014 Taylor & Francis

The right of Maryann Barakso, Daniel M. Sabet, and Brian F. Schaffner to be identified as authors of this work has been asserted by them in accordance with sections 77 and 78 of the Copyright, Designs and Patents Act 1988.

Library of Congress Cataloging-in-Publication Data

Barakso, Maryann.
  Understanding political science research methods : the challenge of inference /
Maryann Barakso, Daniel M. Sabet, Brian Schaffner.
     pages cm
  1. Political science—Research.   I. Title.
  JA86.B28   2013
  320.072—dc23   2013022170

ISBN: 978-0-415-89520-0 (pbk)
ISBN: 978-0-203-80125-3 (ebk)

Typeset in Adobe Garamond

Printed and bound in the United States of America by Sheridan Books, Inc. (a Sheridan Group Company).

"For Sarah and Ellie, with our hope that you always have a passion for science."

—Brian and Maryann

"For those who first inspired a love of learning, Jeanne and Sabet Abdou Sabet."

—Dan

Contents

Preface

Although we are each involved in numerous other scholarly projects, when approached to write our own book on "doing political science" we jumped at the chance. Our enthusiasm for this book arises from our belief that the best way to help newcomers to political science research is to make sense of the research process by emphasizing the end goal: to discover something about a political phenomenon that is of value to scholars and others with an interest in the topic.

In fact, the exciting prospect of expanding our collective knowledge about the political world, perhaps even upending conventional wisdom about a subject, is what drives political scientists through the highs and lows of the scholarly research process. Yet, we argue, this target is unreachable without fully appreciating the many challenges to drawing accurate, reliable inferences.

If you were to skim through a series of academic journal articles or books, the many judgment calls scholars make in the research process would not be immediately apparent. It often seems that the research question and hypotheses arise clearly from the literature, the methodology appears best suited to answer the question, and the findings emerge quite naturally from the author's data. In truth, however, the research process is rarely as tidy as its final iteration in a published study lets on. An important goal of this book is to draw back the veil on political science research, revealing the many decisions or educated guesses scholars must make in conducting their studies.

Given that scholars do have to make so many choices as they pass from determining the research question all the way to drawing the final conclusions, opportunities abound for introducing error. Therefore, in order to ensure that the final conclusions, or inferences, that we draw are sound, it is essential to understand the many challenges we confront along the way.

For instance, if you reviewed those published journal articles a bit more closely, you might notice that the authors' choice of research questions isn't simply presented as an obvious area of inquiry. Rather, scholars justify their questions based on how they have *interpreted* the prior scholarship related to their topic. The researchers don't simply state a thesis that answers their question, but they evaluate and present various plausible alternative theories, again, based on their *interpretation of and extrapolation from* the extant research. From this evaluation, the authors glean expectations about which theories or prior findings are more or less likely to shed light on their research question. Prior literature, theory, and data help researchers develop a testable model, which is simply a hypothetical framework that intends to explain how the world works in terms of a particular research question. The model includes the key factors, or variables, that scholars *believe* (infer) work together to produce a certain outcome or that describe a certain relationship.

Since our goal as political science researchers is to make an intellectual contribution to the field, and because our success depends upon our ability to make sound decisions at every stage of the research process, in this book we focus on how students can best navigate the challenges of conducting research and arriving at reliable and accurate inferences. In this book, then, we explain how students can overcome the classic challenges to making inference: measurement error, error in sampling or case selection, omitted variable bias, and reversal causality, among others. With this background, students will not only be better able to conduct political science research, but they will also be more savvy consumers of the constant flow of causal assertions that they confront in scholarship, in the media, and in conversations with others. These twin goals are our primary objective and where we hope our textbook adds to the plethora of extant works.

In support of our focus on overcoming the challenges to inference, this book on research methods distinguishes itself from others in several important ways. For example, research methods textbooks often gloss over what is perhaps the most critical aspect of a good research design: a good question. Good research questions have the potential to build upon a body of knowledge, whereas questions poorly chosen or framed may only accumulate more information on a topic while failing to extend our understanding. In addition teaching students how to focus and move from a broad topic to a specific research question helps clarify the rest of the research process.

Second, in this book, we believe that in order to help students understand how to execute or evaluate political science research, they need substantial guidance as to why they or a given researcher might choose one approach over another. Students need a foundation in understanding how to design their research projects in order to produce the best answers to the questions they pose. In particular, we emphasize how the types of questions students are interested in might lend themselves to different approaches. In other words, new researchers do not simply need a menu of methodological choices, but they must also understand why they might choose one item from this menu in lieu of another. This skill is equally if not more important in evaluating the studies that they encounter in their coursework.

In addition, we also discuss how to convey the substance of one's research to others in a clear way since we believe this is at least as important as producing those findings in the first place. We discuss how to present research in the most effective and intellectually honest way. Since the ultimate goal of a research project is to convey information to others, students should also be instructed on how to best present each stage of their research project to their audience. Ultimately, students should not only be able to tell either an expert or lay audience what their research shows, but also to relate how confident they can be in their findings and what aspects of their research design lead to this level of confidence. Emphasizing the presentation of results *during* the research process—and not simply afterwards—can help students uncover inconsistencies, omissions, and new issues that deserve further inquiry, in addition to highlighting interesting relationships. Furthermore, the ability to concisely, clearly, and conscientiously convey research conclusions is, of course, a key skill many students will find applicable in their future careers, whether as academic researchers or in the numerous other fields political science students can apply their degrees.

And finally, political science research texts traditionally take students through the research process sequentially, treating each earlier stage as if it were relatively unaffected by later stages. Yet, most scholars know that the "textbook" research process is rarely followed in practice. The development of a research question is informed at least partly by the type of research design that can reasonably be employed and those questions may be revised based on the types of preliminary findings that the student encounters. Likewise, one's theory is not just a function of the question asked, but may also be adjusted and revised based on what one encounters later in the research process. When learning the research process sequentially, students often lose perspective on how one stage of the process relates to every other stage. Furthermore, such an approach fails to recognize how elements often outside of the researcher's control frequently frustrate even the most well-designed studies. Thus, this book presents students with a more practical view of the research process, one that clearly demonstrates how each stage of the process is related to every other stage. Recognizing the limitations of each of the research methods, we challenge students with real and hypothetical research examples to consider what might go wrong in a given project at all stages of the process and—importantly—explore potential avenues for fixes.

Acknowledgments

As an editor, Michael Kerns is a force—he is sharp, thoughtful, and profoundly knowledgeable about political science as a field. We couldn't have asked for a better guide on this journey. We also want to acknowledge the excellent editorial assistance of Jillian D'Urso and Elizabeth Mills.

The authors would also like to thank those who contributed to our development as researchers and our thinking about the research process. Naturally our approach to the research process is heavily influenced by other scholars, including those who have more recently influenced our work in addition to our own intellectual histories as undergraduates and graduate students.

First, this book clearly owes a debt to Gary King, Robert O. Keohane, and Sidney Verba's *Designing Social Inquiry: Scientific Inference in Qualitative Research*, a text that introduced each of us to the challenge of inference in graduate school, and continues to inform how we approach the research process today.

Maryann Barakso thanks Professors Esther Fuchs, Michael Delli Carpini, and the faculty of the Department of Political Science at Barnard College for their having guided her, for having inspired her deep enthusiasm for the field, and for feeding her passion for asking questions as an undergraduate. Esther Fuchs was Barakso's first female professor and mentor, and is the reason she decided to attend graduate school. Barakso also owes a tremendous debt of gratitude to Professors Stephen Ansolabehere, Suzanne Berger, Dan Kryder, Richard Locke, Richard Samuels, Charles Stewart, Rick Vallely, and the faculty of the Department of Political Science at MIT for creating an exciting and extraordinarily agile intellectual environment during her doctoral studies that continues to inform her research and thinking about political science and the academic project. As exemplars, teachers, and mentors Jane Mansbridge,

Kay Lehman Schlozman, and Theda Skocpol also profoundly and directly influenced Barakso's development as a political scientist.

Daniel Sabet thanks his first professor of research methods, Elinor Ostrom, whose work is frequently mentioned throughout this book. Several other professors helped further build on this foundation, including Robert Huckfeldt, Robert Rohrschneider, Jack Bielasiak, Burt Monroe, and particularly Kenneth Bickers. He thanks the many study participants who have taught numerous research lessons in countless hours of interviews, focus groups, surveys, and observation.

Brian Schaffner is grateful to professors at Indiana University who helped him think critically about research methods, including John Williams, Pat Sellers, Burt Monroe, and Jerry Wright. He is also grateful to those who have helped further refine his understanding of inference since receiving his PhD. In particular, the opportunity to serve as a program director at the National Science Foundation provided a much broader and deeper understanding of the research process. Schaffner is particularly indebted to Brian Humes, Frank Scioli, and Harold Clarke, who made that time at NSF so rewarding. Schaffner is also grateful for the opportunity to frequently offer courses in quantitative analysis at the University of Massachusetts, Amherst and the Summer School in Social Science Data Analysis at the University of Essex.

Finally, perhaps our greatest debt of gratitude is owed to our students. Teaching about the research process has substantially deepened our own understanding of that process and will no doubt continue to influence our own evolution as researchers and educators. Our eye-opening experiences in teaching both undergraduates—including sophomores—as well as graduate students the principles of academic research and guiding them through their processes of discovery has convinced us that students very much *want* to understand what their professors do and how they do it. Furthermore, they want to do it themselves. This knowledge has inspired our interest in finding better ways to explain how to tackle the challenge of inference and why it is so important to do so.

Introduction

THE ROLE OF THE LOGIC OF INFERENCE IN POLITICAL SCIENCE RESEARCH

In 2008, Barack Obama became the first African American to win a presidential election. Many political reporters and analysts reacted to this breakthrough by wondering whether the event signified that the country had made significant progress on race relations. Specifically, many journalists and analysts optimistically concluded that Obama's victory proved that he had not been penalized by voters because of his race. Social scientists tend to be skeptical of sweeping claims made without the benefit of clear evidence. Yes, Obama won, but can we be sure race played no role in the 2008 election? If race did play a role, how much impact did it have?

It is strange but true that the research papers students are asked to write throughout their college careers in the social sciences often bear only a passing resemblance to the scholarship that their own professors produce. For example, perhaps the most common college research assignment involves asking students to state a thesis and then track down facts from a variety of sources to bolster their argument. The research resulting from such a process certainly has the potential to contribute to the sheer amount of *information* in the world on a particular topic. However, what it can never do is fulfill the primary objective of the social scientist: to advance our collective *knowledge* about a subject. To fulfill this lofty objective, the scholar begins, not with an argument, but instead with a question. For example, following the 2008 election, pundits debated whether President Obama's election signified the "end of race," whereas scholars asked whether racial prejudice depressed white support for Obama.

The second critical difference between the typical student paper and that of a scholarly paper is that the scholar's research question develops not only out of her particular interests or her anecdotal observations of the world around her, but also—perhaps primarily—out of her interaction with the research of others on the subject. In other words, scholars view themselves not as isolated producers of information, but instead as participants in an ongoing conversation with other scholars' ideas and research.

For instance, scholars investigating the role of race in the 2008 presidential election were not simply responding to an important political event. They were also guided by and hoping to contribute to one or more of the existing scholarly discussions about the impact of race on how people vote. This previous body of literature not only provides insight into how race can affect electoral behavior, but it also provides helpful cues as to what aspects of the issue future research on the subject might address and how that research might be conducted.

Being aware of how scholars interact with each other through their research and how they build on prior studies makes a researcher's job more manageable because we are aware that we need not start from scratch every time we begin a new project. We also gain confidence in how to tackle a new study because we are guided by the communities of researchers before us who have explored questions similar to ours.

Scholars research and write, not to advance their own opinions or to reinforce their personal hunches about how the world should or does work, but to advance our collective understanding. Indeed, **scholarship** in the social sciences can be defined as the published work of individuals who are self-consciously building upon, challenging, and hoping to contribute new insight to research that has both already been produced and that is in progress.[1] By knowing and learning from each other's work on a subject, scholars interested in that topic are able to refine their own ideas, questions, theories, and methods. In this way, scholars position themselves to contribute something valuable to the discourse in their field of study and perhaps others as well.

THE CHALLENGE OF INFERENCE AND THE ADVANCEMENT OF KNOWLEDGE

To facilitate the scholarly project, it is essential that researchers agree on a set of conventions that should be followed as they conduct and evaluate their studies and the studies of others. In this book we focus on the *logic of inference* (a concept we explore in greater detail in Chapters 1), which sets forth general principles that guide inquiry in much of the social sciences. By better understanding the logic of inference we can move from being collectors of information to producers of knowledge.

1 We use the terms "scholarship" and "literature" interchangeably in this book.

In this book, we discuss two types of inference. One, **descriptive inference**, seeks to describe the state of the world. The other, **causal inference**, involves understanding how the world works by deriving empirical conclusions about the existence, extent, and direction of relationships between phenomena. While we are often ultimately interested in making causal inferences, such inferences are typically not possible without first making descriptive inferences. For example, a descriptive inference we can make from exit poll surveys in 2008 is that approximately 43 percent of whites voted for Obama (compared with 41 percent for John Kerry in 2004). A causal inference we may wish to test is whether racial prejudice *caused* any whites to vote against Obama.

While causal relationships are often what we are most interested in as researchers, they are also the most challenging to establish. In order to determine whether race mattered in the 2008 election, it is not sufficient to know that Obama won. What we need to know is whether more white voters would have voted for Obama if he were white. But this question confronts the fundamental problem of establishing causation: we can never know for sure whether a white candidate would have won more (or less) of the vote than Obama did, because we cannot observe that scenario—it didn't happen. Although we cannot know for certain what would have happened in this alternative reality, known as the **counterfactual**, by understanding the challenge of inference when asking research questions, designing studies, and evaluating data, we can make important deductions about the relationships between cause and effect with respect to many important political phenomena.

While it is impossible to be sure how many votes a white Barack Obama would have garnered in 2008, by building on existing literature and armed with an appreciation for the challenges of making causal inferences, several researchers set out to systematically examine whether race mattered in the 2008 presidential vote.[2] These scholars used different sources of data and different approaches to measuring racial prejudice, but overall they reached very similar conclusions. Race did not change the election outcome, but it did appear to matter for some white voters in 2008. Specifically, these studies estimated that Obama lost about 3 to 5 percent of the white vote because he was African American. This research has been invaluable because it not only provides context to Obama's historic victory, but also because it deepens our understanding about the continuing role of race in contemporary American politics. This book is about how you can join scholars in building upon and expanding what we know about the political world.

2 Vincent L. Hutchings, "Change or more of the same? Evaluating racial attitudes in the Obama era," *Public Opinion Quarterly* 73 (2009): 917–942; Josh Pasek, Alexander Tahk, Yphtach Lelkes, *et al.*, "Determinants of turnout and candidate choice in the 2008 US presidential election illuminating the impact of racial prejudice and other considerations," *Public Opinion Quarterly* 73 (2009): 943–994; Brian F. Schaffner, "Racial salience and the Obama vote," *Political Psychology* 32 (2011): 963–988.

PREVIEWING A FEW PRINCIPLES INTRINSIC TO MEETING THE CHALLENGE OF INFERENCE

Over time, empirically minded scholars have developed methodological approaches, research tools, and best practices that, when adhered to, promote the production of research that is likely to produce useful and theoretically well-grounded insights. Furthermore, as we discuss below, when scholars agree to be explicit about our assumptions, our research design, our methods, and our level of uncertainty about our results, others interested in the conversation can more easily learn from our work, correct it, or leverage it to make their own advances.

In the discussion that follows, we lay the groundwork for the rest of this book by calling attention to some of the fundamental premises and practices that political scientists often employ to address the challenge of inference. Fundamentally, we argue that by understanding the logic of inference, students will be better able to understand and critique the descriptive inferences and the assertions of causality that they confront in the media and in academic writing. Furthermore, they will be better equipped to contribute to ongoing conversations among researchers with whom they share substantive interests.

The Role of Theory in Scholarly Research

Scholarship is essentially about developing and testing theories about how the world works. As discussed above, rather than reinvent the wheel, we look to prior scholarship to gain insight into which competing theories may be contenders for further research and testing, to better hone our research questions, and to identify appropriate research design strategies. Becoming knowledgeable about and building on others' theories increases the likelihood that we will be in a position to make well-supported inferences as we embark on our own studies.

For example, one might be able to create a list of at least a dozen possible reasons why women are less likely than men to run for political office. Yet, by reading academic journal articles and scholarly books on the topic, it is likely that a student interested in the subject will be able to hone in on four or five "most likely" explanations for the dearth of women candidates, thereby helping him to design a much more manageable project and one that has a chance to move the ball forward. Similarly, scholars need not naively approach the question of whether race mattered in the vote for Obama; decades of research has explored how prejudice affects support for minority candidates.

Asking Questions That Can Be Answered

Applying the logic of inference drives us to ask questions that are answerable. Note that this does not mean political scientists do not or cannot ask "interesting," "difficult," or "big" questions. The principles of inference simply encourage us to craft those questions such that we may gain some traction on them. For example, a scholar might be tempted to ask a question such as, "What is the best form of government?" This is what we call a **normative question**. It asks about how the world *should* be. In this book, we have a preference for **empirical questions**, or questions that can be answered with real-world evidence. An empirical question might ask: "Are democratic or authoritarian forms of government more likely to produce economic development?"

Generalizability

Finally, a question worthy of study is one that is generalizable. This means that scholars strive to design research studies whose findings will have some theoretical value beyond the particular time period, context, or case that they are focusing on. If the results of the study have too few applications or implications, the research is unlikely to influence the state of our knowledge on a subject. For example, political scientists are not just interested in the effect of race on voting for Barack Obama in 2008; instead, a study of the 2008 election should speak to the broader issue of the effects of race on voting behavior in all elections.

Acknowledging and Minimizing Uncertainty

For most researchers the primary goal of collecting data and conducting a study of any kind is to draw reliable and accurate conclusions. But how does one know whether those conclusions are sound?

Guided by the logic of inference, scholars endeavor to be as explicit as possible about revealing and justifying the many decisions all researchers make during the research process. Scholars have to be able to explain why their question is an important one to study; why they chose to include a given set of theories and not others; why and how they selected this particular set of cases to study; why and how they employed a specific method; how, precisely, their findings do or do not support their initial theories; and finally, how to interpret their findings. Furthermore, scholars are charged with taking seriously and responding to theories, evidence, and findings that appear to undermine their own expectations. In fact, one challenge of inference is that scholars must explicitly engage with alternative theories throughout the research process and consider whether and to what extent competing explanations or contradictory findings in the literature choices may undermine their own conclusions.

Scholars know that even as they do their best to make careful decisions throughout the research process, every choice risks introducing error into their study. Such errors are an inherent characteristic of research in the social sciences, regardless of the particular method one employs. Together with

5

inadvertent errors and omissions, these factors demonstrate why social scientists cannot claim to "prove" that their conclusions are correct. Instead, they acknowledge that a measure of uncertainty remains, no matter how confident they are of their findings.

Advancing Our Collective Knowledge

In our attempts to contribute to the existing scholarship on a subject, we must also be conscious of the need to facilitate future conversations. Many of you may remember painstakingly writing out mathematical proofs in high school or college to demonstrate "how you know what you know"—or the precise steps you took to justify your final answer. While we do not employ proofs very often in political science, adhering to the logic of inference when designing and conducting research makes it much easier for someone else to "check your work," or, at the very least, to feel more confident in your findings. In principle, non-reproducible work is of limited use in advancing knowledge because, by definition, the scholar has chosen not to fully engage in the scholarly conversation. Instead of using the shared language of science, the scholar asks her colleagues to "trust" her judgment, even as her peers are not provided with the tools to evaluate the validity of her findings. Although it is certainly possible that this scholar's work has the potential to contribute valuable information about her subject, irreproducible research cannot advance knowledge until other scholars are able to confirm, refine, or refute her findings.

THE PLAN OF THE BOOK

This book explains how political scientists design their research in order to make descriptive and causal inferences that will advance our knowledge on a topic. Students who grasp the challenge of causal inference will be able to better understand and critique the inferences they are confronted with and conduct their own social science research. This book is not intended to teach students how to conduct a multivariate regression or how to carry out structured interviews in the field, although we discuss these research techniques in light of the inferential challenges different methods pose. Rather, this book asks students to step back from the nuts and bolts of conducting research and to think about the big picture: how good theory can help you craft sound research questions, how different research questions can be addressed using diverse methodologies, and how different research methodologies minimize certain challenges to inference while exposing others.

While we tend to discuss the research process in a somewhat linear fashion, the research process is in fact non-linear. This reality is often obscured by the way academic journal articles follow a tidy sequence from research question to theory, to hypothesis, to methodology, to results. In practice, however, data often inform our theories and available methodologies might affect our hypotheses. The development of a research question, for example, is informed at least partly by the type of research design that can be reasonably tackled by the student, given his resources (time, skills, prior knowledge, funding) and those questions may be revised based on the types of preliminary findings that he encounters. Knowing that the research process does not necessarily proceed sequentially will help you maintain an awareness of how one stage of the research process relates to every other stage. It will also remind you to remain open to adjusting your question, theory, or approach as you gain more information in the research process.

In truth, the research process can feel somewhat daunting at times. Ideally we could follow a set, prescribed methodology much like a cook would follow a recipe. However, every research project is at least slightly different (except for replications of prior studies) and poses different obstacles to overcome. Factors, often outside of the researcher's control, sometimes threaten to derail even the most well-designed studies. Recognizing the limitations of each of the research methods discussed, we present real and hypothetical research examples to illustrate what might go wrong in a given project at all stages of the process and—importantly—explore potential avenues for fixes.

In Chapter 1, we lay out the principles that describe the challenge of inference and explore how our attention to this challenge guides each stage of the research process. In Chapter 2 we turn to the matter of developing the all-important research question. In our experience, students often struggle more in defining their research question than in almost any other area of their projects. Yet, this element constitutes the most critical aspect of a successful research project. A poorly chosen or framed research question could lead to the accumulation of more information on a topic, but it will not allow you to draw meaningful inferences, which is the basis of advancing knowledge. Furthermore, once you are clear about the role of the research question, you will be much better equipped to explain to your audience why your inquiry matters.

Recognizing the centrality of the research question and how it relates to the broader goals of scholarship in the social sciences will clarify many other stages of the research process for you. For example, another frequently confounding but necessary element of scholarly research is the literature review. Students typically wrestle mightily with the concept of a literature review, but if you understand the challenges of inference, the connection between your question and your research design, the logic and purpose of this component of your study will make more sense. Chapter 3 focuses on the best way to think about and complete a review of the literature: not as an attempt to discover everything that has ever been written on a particular topic, but rather as a way of identifying the building blocks for your own theory and research.

In the second section of this book, we turn to the matter of which method to choose to execute your research design. We emphasize the different benefits and drawbacks associated with three different approaches: experimental studies, large-n observational studies, and small-n observational studies. The overarching message of this section of the book is how important it is to choose a method best suited to answering the particular question you are asking. We examine how different research approaches can be used to address similar questions, while also demonstrating the instances where a particular method is not well suited for the question being posed. We do not simply provide a menu of methodological choices, but explain why you might choose one item from this menu in lieu of another.

Finally, conveying the substance of one's research to others in a clear way is at least as important as producing those findings in the first place. And meeting the challenge of inference is most rewarding when you can effectively convey your work to others. Throughout this section of the book, we guide you through the critical steps of evaluating, describing, and presenting your results accurately and effectively. The goal is for you to be able to explain not only what your research shows, but also to relate how confident you can be in your findings and what aspects of your research design lead to this level of confidence. Emphasizing the presentation of results during the research process—and not simply afterwards—can help you uncover inconsistencies, omissions, and new issues that deserve further inquiry, in addition to highlighting interesting relationships. Furthermore, the ability to concisely, clearly, and accurately convey research conclusions is, of course, an important skill applicable in many other contexts beyond the university.

KEY TERMS

causal inference 3	empirical questions 5
counterfactual 3	normative question 5
descriptive inference 3	scholarship 2

Establishing the Framework

The Challenge of Inference

There is no doubt that political observers believe that there has been a fundamental change in the nature of U.S. politics over the past few decades. David Broder noted in 2006 that "the terms 'gridlock' and 'polarization' have become staples of the political vocabulary."[1] Ezra Klein wrote in 2012, "We use 'polarization' as an epithet. It's what's wrong with America's politics. It's what's wrong with America's political parties. It's what's wrong with America's politicians. It's what's wrong, finally, with America."[2] But to what extent has America actually become more polarized in recent years? You may be surprised to learn that there is actually some debate over this question among political scientists. Stanford University professor Morris Fiorina wrote a book shortly after the 2004 presidential election posing the question, "Culture War?" Fiorina takes issue with the notion that the public has become more ideologically polarized over the past several decades, arguing that this is actually an elite phenomenon that is not duplicated at the mass level:

> Americans are closely divided, but we are not deeply divided, and we are closely divided because many of us are ambivalent and uncertain, and

1 David Broder, "Behind the Gridlock," *Washington Post*, November 2, 2006, p. A17.
2 Ezra Klein, "Olympia Snowe is right about American politics. Will we listen?" *Washington Post*, February 28, 2012. Accessed July 4, 2013. www.washingtonpost.com/blogs/wonkblog/post/olympia-snowe-is-right-about-american-politics-will-we-listen/2011/08/25/gIQA3K kwgR_blog.html.

consequently reluctant to make firm commitments to parties, politicians, or policies. We divide evenly in elections or sit them out entirely because we instinctively seek the center while the parties and candidates hang out on the extremes.[3]

According to Fiorina, Americans are mostly moderate, caught somewhere in between the polarized parties. Fiorina's view is contested by other political scientists, however. Alan Abramowitz and Kyle Saunders find evidence that the most politically engaged and active citizens take very polarizing positions.[4] In essence, they argue that those who identify with a political party have become more polarized in recent decades:

> There are sharp divisions between supporters of the two major parties that extend far beyond a narrow sliver of elected officials and activists. Red state voters and blue state voters differ fairly dramatically in their social characteristics and political beliefs. Perhaps most importantly, there is a growing political divide in the United States between religious and secular voters. These divisions are not the result of artificial boundaries constructed by political elites in search of electoral security. They reflect fundamental changes in American society and politics that have been developing for decades and are likely to continue for the foreseeable future.

In other words, the existing research points us in two different directions.

The debate over polarization is by no means the only thing that political scientists argue about. Indeed, for almost every research study produced by a political scientist, there are at least some scholars who question the validity of that study's findings. The fact that political scientists engage in spirited debates is testament to how challenging it is for us to generate knowledge in the first place and how seriously we take the enterprise.

In this chapter, we introduce some of the key reasons why making inferences, even those as basic as whether or not the public is polarized, can be so challenging for political scientists. By calling attention in this first chapter to the challenges a researcher faces when attempting to make sound inferences, we can then use subsequent chapters to help you understand how to overcome those challenges. We begin with some examples of the challenges that political scientists have faced in answering a diverse set of research questions.

---

3 Morris P. Fiorina, Samuel J. Abrams, and Jeremy Pope, *Culture war?* (New York: Pearson Longman, 2005).
4 Alan Abramowitz and Kyle Saunders, "Why can't we all just get along? The reality of a polarized America," *Forum* 3 (2005): 1–22.

THREE ADDITIONAL EXAMPLES

Does Campaign Advertising Work?

Early attempts to answer this question found that campaign advertising did not seem to have much impact. From the 1940s through the 1980s, most studies on American elections relied heavily on survey research. Public opinion surveys were invaluable for studying how Americans thought about politics and what influenced them to vote the way they did. However, public opinion surveys were quite limited as an instrument for studying the effects of campaign advertising. During this period, scholars would typically test whether campaign advertisements had influenced vote decisions by asking individuals whether they recalled seeing any of the candidates' advertisements during the campaign and then seeing whether those who could recall seeing advertisements voted differently than those who did not see any.

This approach faced a significant inferential challenge, however. To measure exposure to campaign advertising, studies during this period relied on survey questions asking individuals whether they recalled seeing advertisements aired by the candidates. Yet, *seeing* an advertisement and *recalling* that you saw an advertisement are by no means equivalent. In fact, one set of experiments run by two political scientists discovered that about half of all individuals who had been exposed to a campaign advertisement did not recall having seen that advertisement just thirty minutes later.[5] Furthermore, individuals who recall seeing advertisements tend to be more interested in politics, more supportive of a particular party, and more loyal to a particular candidate.[6] These are precisely the types of individuals who are the least likely to be susceptible to advertising effects.

Thus, studies of advertising effects that relied exclusively on survey data appear to have understated the effects of campaign advertisements since the types of voters who fail to recall seeing political advertisements are the ones who are most likely to be persuaded by those advertisements. The problem confronting these early studies was a measurement problem. In recent decades, scholars have turned to new techniques and approaches that have overcome some of these inferential challenges and generated different conclusions about the influence of campaign advertising. We describe these techniques in much more detail in Chapters 5 and 6.

5 Stephen Ansolabehere and Shanto Iyengar, *Going negative* (New York: Free Press, 1995).
6 Shanto Iyengar and Adam F. Simon, "New perspectives and evidence on political communication and campaign effects," *Annual Review of Psychology* 51 (2000): 149–169.

Do Ethnic Divisions Cause Civil Wars?

Conventional wisdom posits that civil wars are the product of ethnic and religious division, and early scholarship echoed this sentiment. One could point to salient cases such as the Holocaust in Europe, conflict between the Hutus and the Tutsis in Rwanda and Central Africa, and civil war in the former Yugoslavia between Serbs, Bosnians, Croatians, and other groups. Based on these prominent cases, it is tempting to conclude that ethnic divisions are the key drivers of conflict.

As data on civil wars, conflict, and ethnic and religious division have developed and improved, however, more recent scholarship has been better able to test this relationship. By comparing civil wars from 1945 to 1999, for example, Fearon and Laitin find that more ethnically or religiously diverse countries are no more likely to experience civil war.[7] These findings have been echoed by other scholars, including Bates, Collier, and Hoeffler.[8] While the instances of ethnic conflict mentioned above are so prominent in our collective conscience, there are far more civil wars that are driven by conflicts over resources or opportunistic political entrepreneurs. Furthermore, there are many more diverse societies that are entirely peaceful. In the language used in the discussion that follows, previous studies of ethnicity and conflict suffered from sampling, or case selection, problems—they studied cases that were more likely to be driven by a theory that ethnic divisions caused civil wars.

Is Privatization or Government Intervention Necessary to "Govern the Commons?"

In his influential article on governance of common-pool resources (e.g. pastures, water resources, forests, fisheries, irrigation systems), Garrett Hardin coined the term "the tragedy of the commons."[9] He described a pasture open to all and observed that an individual herder gains the benefits of his own animals grazing and shares the cost of overgrazing on the pasture with everyone else who is using the commons. He noted that it is in the herder's short-term, best interest to increase his own herd and absorb more of the benefits of the pasture while only bearing a share of the costs. If all herders increase their own herd and capture the benefits of the pasture, however, the pasture will quickly become overgrazed and usable to no one, hence the tragedy of the commons. Subsequent authors proposed two solutions to governing common-pool

---

7 James D. Fearon and David D. Laitin, "Ethnicity, insurgency, and civil war," *American Political Science Review* 97 (2003): 75–90.
8 Robert H. Bates, *When things fell apart* (Cambridge, UK: Cambridge University Press, 2008); Paul Collier, Anke Hoeffler, and Catherine Pattillo, "Flight capital as a portfolio choice," *World Bank Economic Review* 15 (2001): 55–80.
9 Garrett Hardin, "The tragedy of the commons," *Science* 162 (1968): 1243–1248.

resources: either the government could take over the commons and manage it, or the land could be divided up and privatized.

In her influential work on governing the commons, however, Elinor Ostrom argues that Hardin's theory and the policy prescriptions that emanated from it were not empirically tested.[10] For example, subsequent research revealed that nationalization of land in order to protect it often led to disastrous consequences. To provide a more accurate understanding of how the commons are and should be governed, based on social goals, Ostrom and her colleagues collected and coded thousands of case studies on different common-pool resources throughout the world upon which to draw more accurate inferences. Surprisingly, Ostrom found that, in many cases, users of the resource were able to avoid the tragedy of the commons without privatization or government nationalization. This work was so important and path breaking that it ultimately earned Ostrom the Nobel Prize.

SOME BASIC TERMINOLOGY

As these examples suggest, making valid and reliable inferences is a challenge for political scientists. In this chapter, we introduce some of the more common challenges or threats to inference; however, it would be "challenging" to go much further in this book without first introducing some of the most basic terminology that political scientists employ. As we introduce this terminology, keep in mind that at such an early stage in the book it is difficult to fully contextualize this information; your understanding of these concepts will increase as we continue our discussion here and in subsequent chapters.

Nearly every research project starts with a **research question**. However, generating a good research question is actually quite challenging, as scholars and students are often tempted to study a wide range of questions rather than focus on a specific one. Furthermore, it is common for research questions to evolve or even change quite dramatically as one proceeds with a research project. The formulation of the research question is so crucial to a successful research project that we devote the entirety of the next chapter (Chapter 2) to this enterprise. For now, it is sufficient to note that a research question generally identifies some (political) phenomenon we wish to understand. For example, the previous section lists several potential research questions. Does campaign advertising work? Do ethnic divisions cause civil wars? Is privatization or heavy government intervention necessary to "govern the commons?" We might also refer back to the introduction for a research question: Does a candidate's race affect his/her electoral success?

---

10 Elinor Ostrom, *Governing the commons: The evolution of institutions for collective action* (Cambridge, UK: Cambridge University Press, 1990).

After formulating a good research question, we generally move on to constructing a **theory**. Broadly speaking, a theory is an idea about how we think the world works. More narrowly, a theory is typically a discussion of what we expect to be the most likely answers to our research question and, especially important, *why* we expect these answers to be correct over other possibilities. For example, in considering whether the race of a candidate affects his/her electoral success, we might construct a theory that explains that racial prejudice still exists among some white voters and that this prejudice would cause them to refuse to support a candidate of color whose political ideology they might have otherwise supported.

Theory building is also an essential part of the research enterprise because it provides significant guidance to how we should construct our empirical tests and which possible alternative explanations need to be ruled out. Despite the centrality of theory in every aspect of a research project, theory building is another aspect of the research process that students find challenging. Chapter 3 focuses directly on best practices for building theory in a research project and the remainder of this chapter will often refer back to the importance of this step for making strong inferences about the world.

Using our theory we can derive testable **hypotheses**. If a theory is a broad discussion of how the world works, a hypothesis is a specific statement based on our theory that we can test in the real world. For example, our theory above links racial prejudice to vote choice. From this theory we could derive a hypothesis, such as:

> *White voters will be less likely to vote for African American candidates than white candidates.*

Note that hypotheses are specific and testable statements, while theories are more general. Unlike a theory, a hypothesis does not explain why a researcher might expect a relationship to exist; it merely states what relationship is expected.

Typically, hypotheses identify at least one **dependent variable**, or a phenomenon that we want to explain, and at least one **independent variable**, a factor that we think does the explaining. In the example above, the vote choices of white voters is the dependent variable and the race of the candidate is the independent variable.

We use the term **variable** to denote the measurement or **operationalization** of concepts we are interested in studying. For example, we may be interested in gauging electoral support for African American electoral candidates, but this could be measured in a number of different ways, depending on the question. One way of measuring this is to estimate the percentage of the white vote won by all white candidates for a particular office compared with the percentage of the white vote won by all African American candidates.

However, there are other ways to measure support as well. For example, instead of counting votes, perhaps we have access to a public opinion poll that asked respondents whether they had a favorable or unfavorable opinion of a number of different candidates. If we chose this approach, then we would want to adjust our hypothesis to reflect this somewhat different dependent variable. Our hypothesis might now be altered to read:

White voters will evaluate African American candidates less favorably than they evaluate white candidates.

Note that this hypothesis is similar to the first, but we have adjusted the wording to reflect the different dependent variable we would be using. In the first example, our dependent variable was the vote; in our second example, our dependent variable was how favorably voters evaluate candidates.

After the researcher specifies her hypothesis (or hypotheses), the next step is to design a research study that will allow her to test this hypothesis. There are two broad approaches that political scientists can take to studying the world—observational and experimental. An **observational study** is one that collects information on the independent and dependent variables as they exist in the natural state of the world. Observational studies can take many forms, including quantitative studies that analyze a larger number of cases (see Chapter 6) or qualitative studies with a small number of cases (see Chapter 7). An observational study hypothesizing that whites are less supportive of minority candidates might examine the percentage of whites who voted for minority candidates for Congress compared with the percentage who voted for white candidates in the past several election cycles. If the study found that white voters tended to vote at higher rates for white candidates than minority candidates, then the evidence would support the hypothesis.

Experimental studies are different from observational studies in that we do not merely examine the independent variable as it exists in the world; rather, as researchers, we directly control the independent variable. Chapter 5 is dedicated to explaining the experimental approach. To offer an example: suppose we took a sample of white voters and asked them to choose between two fictitious candidates. We might describe the candidates in exactly the same way for each participant in our study, but for half of our respondents we might tell them that the candidate is an African American while for the other half we would describe that same candidate as being white. If participants who were told the candidate was African American were less likely to support that candidate than the participants who were told he was white, then this would again support our hypothesis that race influences support for African American candidates.

Regardless of the design chosen, we would never be able to study every instance in which a white voter casts a ballot for a minority candidate. As a result, we will never be able to definitively prove our hypothesis. We can, however, make inferences.

17

WHAT IS AN INFERENCE?

Gary King, Robert Keohane, and Sidney Verba define **inference** as "the process of using the facts we know to learn about facts we do not know."[11] This definition underscores the basic point that we can never know all of the facts, so the knowledge we construct is always built on inference. On a daily basis, consciously or subconsciously, we are constantly observing the world around us and making inferences based on these observations. We cannot directly know how someone is feeling, but we observe facial features, like a frown or a smile, and make an inference about those feelings. We may not have time to stop and talk to protesters downtown, but we may be able to infer from their signs or chants what is motivating them to protest. We may see a long line outside of a local restaurant and infer that they must serve delicious food.

There are two types of inferences we might formulate about the world—descriptive and causal. An easy way to think about the difference between these two types of inference is to consider the difference between describing something and explaining something. A **descriptive inference** is an inference we make about how the world is (or was)—it is the act of describing some aspect of the world. For example, you may notice that people you know seem to have more intense political disagreements than they used to. Based on this observation, you might infer that Americans are more politically polarized than they used to be. In this case, you would be using the facts you know (the intensity of political disagreements among your acquaintances) to infer something you cannot directly observe (how much Americans disagree about political issues): a descriptive inference.

In many cases, we want to go a step further than merely making a descriptive inference. In addition to knowing something about how the world is, we often want to know *why* the world is that way—we want to explain. For example, if we determine that Americans are more polarized than they used to be, we might want to know *why* they are more polarized. Answering this question will require us to make a different type of inference called a **causal inference**. Causal inferences are inferences we make about why something happens. This is where our theory and hypotheses come into play. If we conduct a study of racial attitudes and vote choice and conclude that racially prejudiced Caucasian voters are less likely to vote for Barack Obama, then we would be making a causal inference.

Descriptive and causal inferences are inherently related. Indeed, it is impossible to make a causal inference without first making a descriptive inference. After all, how can you know *why* Americans are more polarized without first

11 Gary King, Robert O. Keohane, and Sidney Verba, *Designing social inquiry: Scientific inference in qualitative research* (Princeton: Princeton University Press, 1994), p. 46.

knowing that they are in fact more polarized? Most frequently, a descriptive inference is what sparks our research question in the first place. For example, despite Fiorina's arguments against the notion that Americans are more polarized today, observations and evidence to the contrary have motivated dozens of political scientists to ask why this shift occurred or how polarization has influenced American politics and policymaking. To offer another example, several decades ago political scientists observed that nations with democratic governments rarely went to war with each other; this descriptive inference sparked an enormous body of scholarship attempting to explain what has been termed the "Democratic Peace."

THE CHALLENGE OF INFERENCE

Anybody can make inferences about the world—after all, we make inferences every day, often without realizing it. What is challenging is making *accurate*, or valid, inferences. Consider the example above: if we observed an increase in political arguments and inferred that people were more ideologically polarized than in the past, would this be a valid descriptive inference? We cannot know for sure whether our inference is correct; after all, if we knew the truth, we would not have needed to make an inference in the first place. But what we can do is evaluate how we arrived at that inference. The more defensible our method of making the inference, the more likely the inference is to be correct. In this section, we describe some of the common challenges we face when making descriptive and causal inferences. While we preview some of the solutions to those challenges here, the remainder of the book is largely reserved for exploring these challenges and potential solutions in greater detail.

Challenges to Descriptive Inference

It might seem like the process of making a descriptive inference would not be particularly challenging. But extending the example we discussed above will help to illuminate just how difficult the task can be. Here we summarize the inference we made about polarization and the data utilized to make that inference:

Data: Witnessing more intense political arguments among our acquaintances.
Inference: The American public is now more ideologically polarized.

On its face, the inference we drew seems perfectly reasonable in light of the data we have accumulated, but, as social scientists, we are trained to be

Box 1.1: How the Daily Stock Report Reveals the Differences between Journalists and Social Scientists

Most weekday evenings one can tune in to the news and hear a report about how the stock market fared that particular day. Reporters' stories on the stock market's performance almost always provide a straightforward accounting of whether the Dow Jones Industrial Average increased or decreased during the day's trading. But reporters typically do something else in these stories—they make causal inferences by attempting to explain why stocks rose or fell that day. Unfortunately, as political scientist Edward Tufte once wrote, "Explanations of daily changes in aggregate stock market indices are among the most ridiculous, speculative, and uncertain causal inferences made by journalists."[a]

The problem is that journalists generally are not using a systematic approach to making inferences about changes in the stock market. Instead, they first typically note that the stock market has changed, and then they search for something that can explain that change. Often, the causal stories they tell are plausible—perhaps the government released a report showing a decrease in unemployment and on that same day the Dow Jones increased by 100 points. The headline that evening is likely to note, "U.S. Jobs Report Gives Stocks a Lift" (as a February 3, 2012 *New York Times* headline read). But how do we know that the jobs report caused the stock market movement? Indeed, a substantial body of research produced by economists attempts to discern whether events like the releasing of employment reports causes stock market fluctuations. The association between the two is by no means clear. In fact, one study even found that, on average, the stock market performed *worse* when the government announced lower unemployment and *better* when the announcement noted higher unemployment.[b] Other studies have found no significant effect in either direction.[c]

Of course, journalists typically do not have time to carry out systematic research to support the inferences they make in their stories. Unfortunately, these reporters typically fail to convey how this lack of research affects how confident (or doubtful) their viewers should be about the inferences they are making on-air.

a. www.edwardtufte.com/bboard/q-and-a-fetch-msg?msg_id=0000ml. Accessed August 22, 2013.
b. John H. Boyd, Jian Hu, and Ravi Jagannathan, "The stock market's reaction to unemployment news: Why bad news is usually good for stocks," *Journal of Finance* 60 (2005): 649–672.
c. Mark J. Flannery and Aris A. Protopapadakis, "Macroeconomic factors do influence aggregate stock returns," *Review of Financial Studies* 15 (2002): 751–782.

skeptics. A *social scientist should resist the urge to dismiss or accept an inference before evaluating how the inference was arrived at.*

Inferential challenges can come in many forms. First, we can arrive at an unsupported inference simply by failing to properly formulate or operationalize the concepts we are studying. In this case, our key concept is "ideological polarization." How might we define the concept of ideological polarization? The best approach to this task is to draw on previous research. For example, Morris Fiorina and Samuel Abrams suggest: "Movement away from the center toward the extremes would seem to be a noncontroversial definition of polarizing."[12]

Concept definition is just the first step; once a concept is defined, a researcher must decide how to measure it. As discussed above, operationalization is the process of moving from the definition of a concept to determining how to measure that concept. In this case, we have operationalized polarization as the frequency with which we observe our acquaintances having intense political disagreements. Do you see the problem? Our operationalization is not an ideal measurement of our concept. While the frequency of political arguments may be related to political arguments, this is not the same thing as polarization as Fiorina and Abrams define it above. The former is an action and the latter an attitude. To be sure, an increase in political disagreements may be one observable implication of increased polarization, but an increase in political disagreements does not necessarily indicate more polarization.

Even if our measurement was a successful operationalization of our concept, we would face other challenges to making valid descriptive inferences. One such challenge comes in the form of **measurement error**—error we encounter when we actually go about measuring our concepts. In our example, measurement would occur every time we recognize and record an intense political argument among our sample. Consider the various sources of errors we might encounter in doing so. For example, we might miss some arguments or mis-categorize some friendly discussions as arguments.

Another challenge to inference confronting our study is **sampling**, or **case selection**—the way in which we select the cases or observations from which we make inferences. The challenge in case selection is choosing cases that will allow us to make valid inferences about the population of interest: in this case, Americans. Frequently, it is not feasible to collect data for the entire population of interest. For example, it is not possible (and certainly not affordable) to measure the attitudes of every single American. In our case, our inference about polarization was generated from observing people we happened to know.

But what threats to inference might this case selection method create for us? One immediate concern we would expect a skeptical social scientist to raise is that people we happen to know are not likely to be representative of the American public in general. Among other differences, given our interest in politics, our acquaintances are probably much more interested in politics than

12 Morris P. Fiorina and Samuel J. Abrams, "Political polarization in the American public," *Annual Review of Political Science* 11 (2008): 563–588.

Americans in general. As a result, we can say that our sample is likely biased. **Bias** is a term we will use in many contexts when discussing challenges to inference; indeed, there are many potential sources of bias when we attempt to make inferences. But regardless of the context, *bias always refers to systematic, or non-random error*. In this case, we likely have constructed a biased sample of Americans, in that our sample will be systematically more interested in politics than the average American. Since previous research teaches us that people who are more interested in politics also tend to have more extreme opinions than those who are less interested, it is likely that the data we collected from our sample of acquaintances will lead us to infer that there is more polarization than we might see if we had surveyed a more representative sample of Americans.

This example may strike you as a relatively straightforward one, but case selection is another crucial step in a research design. How one selects cases is very important and will differ depending on the goal of the study (whether we want to make descriptive or causal inferences) and the type of study (quantitative or qualitative). Thus, we return to the issue of case selection later in this chapter as well as in Chapters 4 and 7.

It should be obvious by now that there are myriad reasons to question the inference we made about political polarization in the United States based on our casual observations of political disagreements among our friends and neighbors. This does not necessarily mean that our conclusion is wrong—it may indeed be true that political polarization has increased. But it does mean that our approach, or our methodology, is too flawed for us to be confident in our conclusion. So how might we improve this research design to reduce the number of challenges we face in making inferences? Let us briefly consider an alternative design that attempts to address some of the limitations of our original approach.

Recall that our first problem occurred because we operationalized our measure in a way that did not match our concept. To address this issue, we can attempt to measure our concept through a survey rather than observation. For example, we could ask people about their opinions on a variety of political issues. Such an operationalization would more directly capture the concept of ideological polarization.

When it comes to measuring this ideological polarization, we still need to be conscious of measurement error. There will certainly be some measurement error when we ask people about their opinions on the issues. Some individuals may not understand the question and inadvertently give the wrong response. It is also possible that the interviewers might record the information incorrectly. These are examples of **random measurement error**. This is called *random* error because it does not systematically bias our results in any one direction. For example, if we were measuring if someone has moderate or extreme views we might randomly overstate one respondent's extremism and understate another's.

By contrast, a greater concern is **systematic measurement error**, which would cause bias in our estimates. For example, systematic measurement error could occur if some respondents thought it was undesirable to express extreme political views and therefore systematically chose more moderate responses than what truly represented their opinions. In this case, our measure would systematically underestimate the amount of polarization that actually existed.

To address concerns about case selection, we could try to construct a sample that is much more representative of the American population. We could do this by taking a random sample of American adults. We discuss this approach in more detail in Chapter 4, but, under a variety of assumptions, a random sample of approximately 1,000 is typically sufficient to be representative of the population, within some margin of sampling error.

In sum, even with an improved research design, it is important to bear in mind that we face many challenges when we seek to make descriptive inferences about the political world. As we discuss in more detail below, the scientific enterprise does not require us to have a flawless research design, but we must endeavor to make inferences in as sound a manner as possible and to be open and transparent about the decisions we make in producing these inferences so that other scholars can evaluate their quality.

Challenges to Causal Inference

Although we face many challenges when we wish to make descriptive inferences about the political world, we must grapple with many more when our goal is to make causal inferences. Imagine that we were able to infer with a reasonable amount of confidence that the American public was more ideologically polarized now than it had been previously. This may lead us to an important research question: What caused Americans to become more polarized? Indeed, this question has been a source of significant debate among political scientists. One hypothesis is that Americans have become more divided as a reaction to polarization among political elites, such as elected officials. We will elaborate more on the formulation of research questions in Chapter 2 and the derivation of theories and hypotheses in Chapter 3. For the moment, it is sufficient to note that this hypothesis was derived by consulting the existing literature on how individuals formulate their opinions; specifically, many scholars have shown that the public tends to take cues from politicians and formulate their opinions accordingly.[13] Thus, it is reasonable to suggest that if politicians begin to express more extreme political views, the public is likely to follow suit.

Of course, this is merely a hypothesis; to be able to make a causal inference we first need to develop a research design that would allow us to test this

13 John Zaller, *The nature and origins of mass opinion* (Cambridge, UK: Cambridge University Press, 1992).

hypothesis. Then, armed with our results, we would be far more confident in making inferences. For example, we could track the polarization of elites and of ordinary Americans over time and see if polarization of the former precedes the latter. Imagine that we used Abramowitz's measure of political polarization among the public—the percentage of people who took a consistently liberal or conservative position on every issue they were asked about. In 2008, Abramowitz and Saunders estimated that about 33 percent of Americans had consistent ideological opinions across all issues.[14] Now suppose that a similar study was conducted several years earlier. At that time elite polarization was shown to be less, and the study found that only 24 percent of Americans held consistent ideological positions on the issues: a difference of 9 percentage points.

Assuming the studies are comparable, it would be tempting to conclude that the causal effect of the independent variable (the polarization of politicians) is 9 percentage points. Of course, this would only be an estimate because we can never observe two alternate states of the world at the same time; that is, we can never know what issue positions Americans would have taken if politicians had not become more polarized over the past few decades. This is the fundamental challenge of causal inference.[15] King, Keohane, and Verba explain just how serious this challenge is: "no matter how perfect the research design, no matter how much data we collect, no matter how perceptive the observers, no matter how diligent the research assistants, and no matter how much experimental control we have, we will never know a causal inference for certain."[16] This statement may seem off-putting to students at first, but our experience is that the most passionate social scientists see this challenge mostly as an exciting one. We can never know for certain whether a causal effect exists, but we *can* design our studies so that we are as certain as possible.

In thinking about how to design our research so that we can make causal inferences with as much confidence as possible, it is always good to keep in mind the **counterfactual**. The counterfactual is the state of the world that you do not observe. In our running example, the counterfactual would be a world where politicians had not become more polarized over the past few decades. While we can never directly observe the counterfactual, we should use the counterfactual to think about how to design a study that would allow us to make reasonable causal inferences. For example, we might think about how we can replicate as closely as possible an environment like our counterfactual, and then use that as a baseline for estimating the effects of our independent variable.

As we noted above, our theory leads us to expect that when politicians become more polarized the public will also become more polarized in response.

14 Abramowitz and Saunders, "Why can't we all just get along?" p. 544.
15 We are paraphrasing Paul W. Holland, "Statistics and causal inference," *Journal of the American Statistical Association* 81 (1986): 945–960, who referred to this as the fundamental problem of causal inference.
16 King, Keohane, and Verba, *Designing social inquiry*, p. 79.

Let's say that to test this theory we compared the polarization of elites and the public in the 1970s with polarization among both groups in the 2000s. Indeed, scholars who have conducted such a comparison have demonstrated convincingly that politicians have become more polarized over that period. And while there is some debate about whether the public has also become more polarized, there are some indications that such polarization has occurred. Thus, there appears to be a relationship between these two variables—when politicians are polarized, so too is the public. Nonetheless, without knowing the counterfactual, a world where no elite polarization occurred, there are good reasons to be skeptical of this finding.

One issue that is often problematic, particularly for observational research, is that of **reverse-causation**. Reverse-causation occurs when the dependent variable causes the independent variable, either instead of or in addition to the expected causal relationship of the independent variable on the dependent variable. Figure 1.1 shows how this might occur with regard to our example; it is possible that rather than the public reacting to increasing polarization among politicians (as shown in panel A), politicians actually become polarized in response to increasing polarization among the public (panel B). This possibility is theoretically plausible, since we know that politicians need support from the public to win elections—so they might very well polarize in response to the public. It is also possible that the relationship is **reciprocal**—that is, that the independent and dependent variables simultaneously impact each other (panel C).[17] This might happen if, for example, elites began to polarize, which then led the public to become more polarized, which then caused politicians to become even more polarized.

The challenge to inference in this case is significant. Imagine that we took a snap shot of polarization among politicians and the public in the 1970s and then we took another snap shot of polarization among both groups in the 2000s. The problem is that our expected causal relationship (polarization among politicians causes polarization among the public) would yield identical results as the reverse relationship (polarization among the public causes polarization among politicians); regardless of whether politicians caused the public to polarize or vice versa, both would be more polarized in the 2000s than they were in the 1970s. Thus, we cannot confidently say that elite polarization has caused polarization among the mass public if we cannot rule out the possibility that the relationship exists in the opposite direction.

Another challenge to causal inference that we must often confront is called **spuriousness**, a dynamic that occurs when some other factor causes changes in both the dependent and independent variables simultaneously. Indeed, even if two variables move together, this does not always mean that they are directly related to each other. For example, since the 1970s, the mass media

---

17 A reciprocal relationship is also sometimes referred to as a recursive relationship.

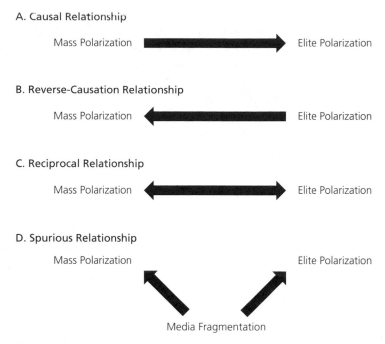

FIGURE 1.1 Different Explanations for Increasing Polarization among Elites and the Public

has become more highly fragmented, leading news outlets to cater to specific ideological outlooks (for example, Fox News for conservatives and MSNBC for liberals). This change in the nature of the modern news media may produce mass polarization by limiting the extent to which ideologues hear opposing viewpoints; at the same time; it may also produce incentives for politicians to take more extreme political views to appeal to these ideological news outlets (shown in Figure 1.1, panel D). In this case, the relationship we thought we detected between elite and mass polarization would actually be spurious, with both types of polarization being caused by media fragmentation instead.

Threats to inference such as reverse-causation and spuriousness must first be identified before they can be systematically addressed and (hopefully) ruled out as alternative explanations for the relationships we observe. Once again, theory is a crucial step in identifying possible reverse-causation and spurious relationships. Without a strong sense of what political scientists have learned about how the world may operate, it is less likely to occur to us that the relationship between elite polarization and mass polarization might be spurious. Once these alternative explanations have been identified, it may be possible for us to design our research in a way that systematically addresses these alternative explanations. For example, to address the possibility of reverse-causation, we may decide to measure polarization every year since 1970 rather than just at two points in time. With such an approach, we would be better able to determine whether the public's attitudes started to become more polarized before politicians or vice versa. We could also attempt to control for variables that may be causing spurious relationships; for example, perhaps we could track polarization among people who do not have access to cable television, thereby reducing the possible spurious relationship between media fragmentation and polarization.

Our approach to addressing the challenges of potential spurious variables or reverse-causation generally depends on the approach we are taking in our study. We discuss these approaches more specifically in Chapters 4–7. But one of the most important steps is simply being aware of these challenges in the first place.

THE IMPORTANCE OF THEORY

The ability to make robust causal inferences depends on a scholar's development of strong theoretical explanations that can support the causal processes she is asserting. Human beings are very good at recognizing patterns in the world, and, if we look at enough data, we are likely to see relationships simply due to happenstance. For many years, journalists noted an interesting pattern between World Series victories and presidential election outcomes. Specifically, from 1952 to 1976, whenever a team from the American League won the World Series in October, the Republican candidate won the presidential election that November. Whenever the National League won the World Series, the Democrat was the winner. Thus, there appeared to be a strong association between World Series outcomes and presidential election outcomes. Yet, one could hardly make the causal inference that the World Series determined the election results, largely because there is no good theory, or explanation, for why this would be so. Indeed, since 1976 there has been no strong relationship between the results of the World Series and the presidential election; the break in the pattern is hardly surprising given that we had no theoretical justification for expecting the two things to be related in the first place.

Post-Hoc Theory

The example of baseball results and election outcomes is an extreme one, but the issue of unidentified or under-identified causal theories is real for many research projects. One well-debated example comes from international relations in the form of the "Democratic Peace Theory."[18] The Democratic Peace Theory is not really a single theory, but rather a collection of post-hoc, or

18 For a review of the research in this area see James Lee Ray, "Does democracy cause peace?" *Annual Review of Political Science* 1 (1998): 27–46.

after-the-fact, theories developed to explain the persistent empirical finding that nations with democratic governments rarely engage in military conflict against each other. The two most prominent theories given for this empirical regularity is that (1) democracies share common democratic norms, which prevent them from coming into conflict with each other, and that (2) democratic institutions constrain leaders from engaging in such conflicts. However, these explanations have come under some criticism in the past several years. For example, Sebastian Rosato argues that "the causal logics that underpin the democratic peace theory cannot explain why democracies remain at peace with one another because the mechanisms that make up these logics do not operate as stipulated by the theory's proponents."[19] With regard to the first theory, Rosato points out that democracies frequently violate democratic norms when they carry out their foreign policy. One of the most consistent examples of this pattern is the extent to which European democracies were willing to engage in wars to maintain their autocratic rule over their colonies.

Rosato also calls into question the second theory for why democracies do not go to war—the fact that democratic leaders may be held more accountable for engaging in such conflicts. Rosato examines how frequently democratic leaders are removed from office following a costly war compared with the frequency with which dictators lose their positions under similar circumstances. Rosato shows that dictators actually lose their office at least as frequently as democratic leaders following a "costly war." Thus, the notion that democratic leaders will feel more constrained when deciding whether to engage in a conflict appears to be very questionable. As a result, Rosato finds that the democratic peace theory is not particularly convincing because the causal mechanisms specified by the theory do not appear to operate in the manner expected. Rosato's findings illustrate the importance of having a strong theory, or explanation, for why an independent variable causes a dependent variable.[20]

Deductive vs. Inductive Approaches

We do not mean to suggest that a relationship cannot be causal if scholars did not theorize a causal process in advance. As we will stress throughout this book, the research process is not an orderly one; often we must revisit our research

---

19 Sebastian Rosato, "The flawed logic of democratic peace theory," *American Political Science Review* 97 (2003): 585–602, p. 599.

20 Other research has suggested that the relationship between democracies and peace may be spurious. Democracies tend to join alliances and they also tend to have stronger economic ties. Nations that have alliances or are reliant on each other economically rarely fight each other. See Henry S. Farber and Joanne Gowa, "Polities and peace," *International Security* 20 (1995): 123–146; Henry S. Farber and Joanne Gowa, "Common interests or common polities? Reinterpreting the democratic peace," *Journal of Politics* 59 (1997): 393–417; Erik Gartzke, "The capitalist peace," *American Journal of Political Science* 51 (2007): 166–191.

question and our theories and hypotheses once we analyze the data. Indeed, it is often the case that we discover relationships through the analysis of collected data, and then we must rethink why those relationships may exist. It may be that there is a very good reason to expect a causal relationship but that we had simply not recognized that reasoning in advance of conducting our research.

In fact, one of the most robust debates in the social sciences has focused on this issue. **Deductive research** follows the approach outlined above: scholars begin with a research question, develop theory to provide an answer to that question, derive hypotheses from that theory to be tested, and develop and implement a research design to test these hypotheses. **Inductive research**, however, reverses this order. Rather than presume to know how the world works and test hypotheses, inductive research starts by observing the natural world and then derives hypotheses and theories from these observations.

Inferences based on an inductive approach are more likely to suffer from the challenges to causal inference discussed above. Continuing the example, an observed relationship between elite polarization and public polarization could be spurious if media fragmentation isn't taken into account. A deductive study, however, could be designed in such a way so as to control for variation in the type of media. Here again lies the benefit of building on pre-existing scholarship. Rather than just observe a topic for the first time, deductive research approaches can build on the findings of previous scholarship. Nonetheless, inductive approaches are particularly helpful for exploratory research on questions that have not been previously addressed or have not been well addressed by existing scholarship. Then the hypotheses generated through such an inductive approach can be more systematically tested through a well-designed deductive study.

SUMMARIZING COMMON THREATS TO INFERENCE

So far in this chapter, we have elaborated on many challenges to descriptive and causal inferences. We will continue to return to these and other inferential challenges throughout the text, as these challenges are what motivate our lessons regarding research design. However, we summarize the main threats to inference here as well as provide a road map to where solutions to these challenges are addressed in this book:

Operationalization of concepts

- Problem: If we measure our concepts in a way that is not consistent with how we defined those concepts in the first place, then the inferences we draw from the variables may not truly apply to our theoretical concepts.
- Solution: Make careful connections between our theory and how we measure our concepts (Chapter 3).

■ Case selection

- Problem: If the cases we choose to study are not representative of the world we wish to make inferences about, then our descriptive inferences may not be valid.
- Solution: Select cases systematically to ensure inferences are as valid as possible (Chapters 4 and 7).

■ Measurement error

- Problem: If there is a lot of error in how we measure our concepts, then we can be less certain about our descriptive and causal inferences. In addition, if our measurement error is systematic, then we run the risk of making biased inferences, inferences that are systematically wrong.
- Solution: Measure concepts in a way that minimizes systematic and random measurement error (Chapter 4).

■ Reverse-causation

- Problem: In many cases, it is possible that the dependent variable may actually be causing the independent variable, rather than the other way around.
- Solution: Attempt to rule out the possibility of reverse-causation, possibly by leveraging information about how the variables change over time (Chapter 6) or by using an experimental design (Chapter 5).

■ Spurious relationships

- Problem: The relationship we detect between an independent variable and the dependent variable may be caused by some third variable that causes changes in both variables at the same time.
- Solution: In an observational design, control for the variable that may be causing the spurious results (Chapter 6). Alternatively, use an experimental design to reduce the likelihood of spuriousness (Chapter 5).

EVALUATING INFERENCES

We noted above that people make inferences about the world every day, but it is critical to note that not all inferences are equally valid—that is, they are not all equally likely to be correct. This is where science comes in. Science is the process of making inferences in a systematic way. This process requires a disciplined and self-conscious approach. Making inferences scientifically entails a focused research question, theory that builds on previous research, testable hypotheses, and a detailed and systematic plan for collecting and analyzing data that can be used to test these hypotheses. Good social science goes a step further and ensures that the methods followed are made public so that others can judge the quality of those inferences.

The last point is perhaps as important as any: using a scientific approach to make inferences does not ensure that those inferences will be correct, but the fact that the procedures are public does allow other scholars to evaluate how likely it is that those inferences are valid. To ensure that the procedures taken in any study are public, every study should include a section that details as precisely as possible how the data were collected, how the variables were measured, and how the data were analyzed. In fact, any research paper should include enough information so that the reader could reproduce the study based solely on the information provided in the paper.

Box 1.2: Transparency, Replication, and Ethical Social Science

Social scientists are not often the focus of a flurry of news stories (even if their findings occasionally are), but in 2011 a media storm erupted around one prominent psychologist. The psychologist in question was a giant in his field—his research had been frequently published in the top academic journals and often received coverage in prominent news outlets such as the *New York Times*. Unfortunately, in 2011, it was discovered that most of these research studies were fraudulent. According to reports, the psychologist had rarely actually carried out the experiments that his articles were based on; rather, he simply made up data that would support his hypotheses and then published results from that manufactured data.[a]

When the professor's behavior was finally uncovered, there was outrage from social scientists across all disciplines. After all, to build knowledge in any field requires that we be able to trust that published studies are based on a scientific approach that is both valid and replicable. While nearly all social scientists are interested first and foremost in making valid inferences, there are a rare few who appear tempted to fabricate results in the pursuit of bolstering their own stature within the discipline. This is just one of many reasons why the social sciences have increasingly emphasized the importance of the replicability of published research. In political science, many of the top journals now require that when an article is published the authors of the article must make the data available to the scholarly community along with instructions on how the researchers analyzed the data. Such transparency and openness will not only allow scholars to be more confident in the results presented in a particular study, but it may also dissuade scholars from engaging in improper behavior.

a. See, for example, Ewen Callaway, "Report finds massive fraud at Dutch universities," *Nature* 479, November 3, 2011.

KEY TERMS

bias   22

case selection   21

causal inference   18

counterfactual   24

deductive research   29

dependent variable   16

descriptive inference   18

experimental studies   17

hypotheses   16

independent variable   16

inductive research   29

inference   18

measurement error   21

observational study   17

operationalization   16

random measurement error   22

reciprocal   25

research question   15

reverse-causation   25

sampling   21

spuriousness   25

systematic measurement error   23

theory   16

variable   16

APPENDIX

A PERSONAL EXAMPLE OF THE CHALLENGES OF INFERENCE

By Brian Schaffner

In my senior year as an undergraduate at the University of Georgia, I took a class on political science research methods. Early in the semester, I noticed a story in the local paper explaining that the city council was discussing the possibility of shifting to nonpartisan elections. Nonpartisan elections are elections where candidates do not run under a party label; specifically, candidates do not run in party primaries and they are not identified on the ballot as representing one party or the other. After some research, it became clear to me that very few studies had been conducted on this type of election format. Ultimately, the topic of nonpartisan elections motivated much of the research I undertook as a doctoral candidate. In fact, my first publication as a political scientist emanated from my interest in nonpartisan elections in the form of an article titled "Teams without uniforms: The nonpartisan ballot in state and local elections."[21] The article was the first major study to be conducted on nonpartisan elections in several decades and remains one of my most cited publications to date. But the process of conducting the research for the article was also a lesson in thinking carefully about inference and the many challenges we face when attempting to make inferences.

In developing the theory for the article, we drew on two different approaches to thinking about parties. One approach was that of the Progressives, the group that pushed for nonpartisan elections in the United States during the early twentieth century. Progressives believed that parties hampered citizens from making good decisions in the voting booth and that removing party labels from the ballot would help generate more desirable democratic outcomes. The other approach was that of political scientists, who generally view political parties as central for well-functioning democracies. Parties organize interests and make it easier for voters to participate in the political process.

Our theory led us to two clear hypotheses. Our first hypothesis was that people would be less likely to vote in nonpartisan elections compared with elections where party labels were on the ballot. We expected this to be the case because some individuals may not be informed about the specific candidates in an election and without the party label they may be unable or unwilling to make a choice between candidates. Our second hypothesis was that in the absence of party labels, other factors (such as incumbency) would become more significant. After all, if individuals cannot use party labels as a guide in the voting booth, they may rely on other clues such as which candidate's name is most familiar.

The inferential challenges in this project were many. First, we had to locate cities and states that had nonpartisan elections and, once we found such locales, we had to consider the counterfactual, that is,

---

21 Brian F. Schaffner, Matthew Streb, and Gerald Wright, "Teams without uniforms: The nonpartisan ballot in state and local elections," *Political Research Quarterly* 54 (2001): 7–30. There is no reason the paper you might be writing for your own research methods course couldn't end up being published one day. See the concluding chapter for more on publishing your work.

how would voters in these areas have behaved if they had voted in partisan elections instead? Given that we could not reproduce the counterfactual condition, we attempted to come as close as possible to creating a counterfactual-like baseline condition as a point of comparison. For example, Nebraska holds nonpartisan elections for its state legislature and as a point of comparison we used Kansas's partisan elections for its state senate. Nebraska and Kansas border each other and share many similarities (which are described on pp. 14–16 of the article), except that they use different electoral methods for selecting state senators. Thus, we used Kansas as our baseline for establishing what elections in Nebraska might be like if they were partisan.

When we compared Nebraska's nonpartisan elections to the partisan contests held in Kansas, we found that nonpartisan elections seemed to create lower turnout and that incumbents fared better in these contests than they did in Kansas. Of course, as similar as Nebraska and Kansas may be, they also differ in many ways as well. Thus, we cannot be fully confident that the differences we found are attributable to the use of nonpartisan elections in Nebraska and partisan elections in Kansas. To bolster our findings, we also looked for cases where the same jurisdictions changed from nonpartisan to partisan elections (or vice versa). Such a change (called an interrupted time series design) would allow us to overcome the problems associated with comparing different jurisdictions.

We found two examples where such a change occurred, the most notable being in Minnesota. Minnesota used nonpartisan elections for its state legislature through the 1972 election, but then switched to partisan elections beginning in 1976. Thus, we compared elections held in Minnesota in 1972 to those in 1976 to attempt to determine whether switching to partisan elections caused a change in behavior among the same electorate. As with the Nebraska/Kansas comparison, we found that incumbency was somewhat less important after the state switched to partisan elections and turnout was higher after the switch as well.

Based on our analysis of the cases, we make the inference that removing party labels from the ballot leads to decreased turnout and increased voting for incumbents. However, we must also acknowledge that our inferences are far from certain. Indeed, there are several challenges we faced when making these inferences. First, our study is not based on a random sample of elections across the United States. As a result, the nonpartisan elections we study may not be representative of all nonpartisan elections. Second, our design does not allow us to rule out the possibility of reverse-causation. This is a significant issue when it comes to studying electoral rules since it is usually the politicians who choose those rules and they are likely to do so strategically. In this case, it may be that politicians seek to institute nonpartisan elections when they think they might benefit from removing parties from the ballot. If that is the case, then we would only observe nonpartisan elections in places where incumbents thought they would benefit from them, which means we cannot be confident that nonpartisan elections will always lead to an increased incumbency advantage.

Third, the comparisons we make (whether across jurisdictions or within a jurisdiction over time) are not perfectly controlled. That is, as similar as they are, Nebraska still differs from Kansas in a variety of ways, including different voters and different candidates. Likewise, the 1972 elections in Minnesota featured different campaigns, different candidates, and different conditions than the elections held in 1976. If any of these differences affect the dependent variables we were interested in (such as turnout or the incumbency advantage), then we might wrongly infer that differences in those variables were caused by the type of election when it was actually caused by something else entirely.

In fact, for just this reason, subsequent research on the Minnesota case has cast doubt on the inference we originally drew from our analysis of that state. A study conducted by Stephen Ansolabehere and his colleagues examined Minnesota legislative elections from 1958 to 1990. After analyzing this much longer time period, they found that "the incumbency advantage in 1972 is much larger than any election in the pre-1973 era, and the incumbency advantage in 1976 is much smaller than in any other post-1973 election."[22] Because these elections were atypical of other elections held before and after the change to a partisan ballot, our results from the Minnesota case were misleading and the inference we drew with regard the effect of the nonpartisan ballot on the incumbency advantage in Minnesota appears to be invalid.

As a researcher, it is sobering when new research casts doubt on inferences you previously considered to be valid; however, as a social scientist, it can also be gratifying to feel as though a new study has generated a more valid inference. After all, as political scientists, our primary interest is in attempting to draw valid conclusions, regardless of whether those conclusions comport with how we thought the world worked. In this case, the contrary findings from the updated Minnesota analysis suggest that the evidence from Minnesota does not support our hypothesis regarding the increased importance of incumbency in the absence of party labels. While we still find evidence to support this contention in other parts of our analysis, it does temper our confidence in that particular inference.

22 Stephen Ansolabehere, Shigeo Hirano, James M. Snyder, *et al.*, "Party and incumbency cues in voting: Are they substitutes?" *Quarterly Journal of Political Science* 1 (2006): 119–137, p. 18.

CONTENTS

The Research Question

How do you develop a sound research question? Even when one is very familiar with the subject matter at hand, designing a good research question can be daunting. The time and effort it typically requires for a research *idea* to evolve into a *bona fide* research *question* may seem surprising, particularly for those new to the standards of academic scholarship in the social sciences. Unusual or puzzling events in politics and public policymaking are ubiquitous, after all—and, to the intellectually curious student, ripe for analysis.

The scholarly research question you settle on may very well be inspired by contemporary or historical events that you would like to understand, outcomes you would like to explain, or simply by a subject area that is of particular interest to you. However, the political science research question is likely to be arrived at through a different process and is typically structured quite differently from the questions that drive most other writing assignments undergraduates undertake. In this chapter, we clarify what those differences are and describe the key elements of a sound research question in political science.

Students seldom spend as much time as necessary on the matter of crafting their research question. The question may seem to be the most straightforward part of writing a paper. Gathering and reading prior research, collecting and analyzing data, and writing may appear far more urgent, especially when one has a "topic." It is true that you need to know something about a subject in order to construct a good question for further study, and we say more about this below. Yet, experienced researchers do not simply find a topic and dive in. Instead, political scientists take considerable time and care investigating the

scholarly literature[1] and other material pertaining to their specific research interest to ensure that the research question they settle on is both important and feasible.

As you settle on a timetable for completing a new project, then, bear in mind that you must build in enough time to hone your research question.[2] Poor questions (regardless of how much effort one expends to answer them) are unlikely to yield results that will prove useful to other scholars and may stymie a research project altogether. The justification for your study, the works you cite in your **literature review**, and the logic behind your research design are all set in motion by and intimately connected to your research question. The question affects all other components of your study. At the same time, since the research process is non-linear, these other components of your study will also very likely impact how you ultimately frame your particular question. Nevertheless, the "better" the question you begin with, the easier it will be to conduct your study, and the better the question, the more useful your results will prove to other scholars.

WHAT MAKES FOR A GOOD RESEARCH QUESTION?

Most research questions are ignited by an individual's passion or interest. Perhaps you once visited Mexico and became fascinated by their political system. Or, as a young woman interested in entering politics, you were puzzled by the fact that women are significantly under-represented at all levels of elective office in the United States. Or perhaps while interning for a campaign you wondered whether your candidate's strategies were likely to be successful in winning over voters. A personal interest in the subject matter is an excellent place to start your search for a question. While the research process can be challenging and, at times, tedious, beginning with an inherent enthusiasm or curiosity about the topic will ease your way through.

1 Throughout this book when we are talking about books, journals, articles, or other sources, we almost always mean *scholarly* works. When we use the term "scholarly" or "academic" literature, or simply "the literature" for short, we are referring to peer-reviewed social science journal articles and books written by doctoral candidates or those holding doctorates. Peer-reviewed research is subject to a vetting process in which multiple anonymous reviewers are asked to critique the work and recommend publication or rejection; the process includes additional editorial scrutiny (see Chapter 8). Peer-reviewed books are often easy to distinguish because they tend to be published by university presses, but a number of well-respected commercial presses are also known for publishing high-quality peer-reviewed academic research and should not be overlooked. Online listings of academic journals that publish peer-reviewed research in the different subfields in political science are available, as are lists of excellent non-university presses publishing scholarly research.

2 Even when you've settled on a question, it's important to keep an open mind. As one gets deeper into research, it is not uncommon to reframe the question somewhat to reflect new information.

Moving from an interest in a topic to a sound research question requires understanding what a good research question looks like. There are several key traits of a good research question, which we introduce here.

A good research question is non-normative and answerable.

Research questions should not ask about what ought to be, but rather seek to understand what is. It is natural for students to be drawn to questions that seek a definitive answer regarding how some problem in the political or economic world should be addressed. Questions that begin with the word "should," for instance, often intend to make a case about how a matter would be handled in an ideal world. Should the United States invade Iraq? Should there be more women in Congress? Should America have a single-payer health care system? These may all be interesting and important questions—and ones that could certainly spark the beginning of a research topic. The danger is that normative questions—such as one in which a student hopes to determine, say, *the* ideal outcome for an entire community or in which he is keen to discover *the* proper approach to addressing a social, economic, or political problem— all too often lead to position papers, rather than scholarly analyses.

Aside from their tendency to lead to what many students may recognize as the "Argumentative Essay," as opposed to a social scientific analysis, the trouble with "ought" and "should" questions (unless they are very carefully constructed) is that they share several troubling underlying global assumptions including the notion that: (1) ideal solutions exist and can be universally applied; and (2) politics don't matter.

Purely normative questions ask us to make a judgment call or offer an opinion about how we *believe* politicians and other policymakers *should* act. What kind of health care system the United States should have or whether we should invade a nation are questions that ask the writer to determine one "right" course of action. The burden of determining the "right" course of action, however, depends not solely on evidence, but on one's beliefs, point of view on a subject, and which values one prioritizes—not to mention one's personal social, economic, and political background.[3]

Furthermore, the "right" course of action depends on who is doing the asking. The "right" course of action for French leaders in terms of whether or

3 Our point here is *not* to suggest that, by eschewing more normative questions, social scientists can be confident that their life experiences will not impinge on the questions they choose to ask, the theories they privilege, the hypotheses they choose to test, and how they interpret their findings. By following the guidelines in this book, however, students reduce the chances that such biases will undermine the integrity of their study. For example, we point out that researchers (regardless of the methodology they employ) must make many judgment calls throughout the research process. We emphasize how essential it is that those judgments are made transparent to readers and that authors explicitly justify their choices through well-articulated logic and/or appropriate literature.

not to cut back on public sector expenditures, for instance, depends on many factors, including the stability of the government, the credibility of civilian threats to strike, the particular time period, and the nation's social, political, and economic institutions. Even within the same nation, what different French political parties believe is the "right" course of action is likely to differ, as are the opinions of various segments of the French citizenry. In other words, these are *political questions*, and as such they require substantial reframing before they can be deemed good research questions.[4]

Rather than focusing on how the world should be, most empirically oriented political scientists (in contrast with philosophers and political theorists) hope to contribute to our understanding of how the world works by asking questions that test alternative explanations for phenomena. Political scientists aspire to uncover mechanisms and factors that allow us to answer questions such as: "What caused that nation to follow a particular course of action?" (rather than "Did that nation follow the correct course of action?"), or "What factors explain the success or failure of a social movement?" (not "Was government suppression of a particular social movement fair?"), or "Why do some states rank higher than others on important social, economic, and political measures?" (not "Should all students have access to equal educational opportunities?"). Thus, instead of asking, "Should there be more women in Congress?" the empirical political scientist might ask, "To what extent does the presence of women legislators influence agenda setting and policy outcomes in the U.S. Congress?"

A good research question generates some implications for understanding real world problems.

Although a research question should not be normatively constructed, it should certainly in some way be connected to significant matters that affect us all, like representation and justice. Whether there should be more women in Congress is, in this construction, a normative matter and does not, without further refinement, constitute a viable research question. Yet, an awareness of gender disparities in elective office at the federal and other levels of government can certainly motivate the development of excellent research questions that clearly possess underlying **normative implications**. For instance, we may

4 These caveats notwithstanding, one can certainly ask questions within the social sciences that seek to determine better or worse courses of action or to compare policies based on criteria such as cost-effectiveness, efficiency, and effectiveness. One might ask, for example, whether, *given certain types of goals* (say, the diminution of global terrorist threats) that have been articulated by the president and the State Department and by some scholars, pre-emptively invading countries suspected of harboring or supporting terrorists is an effective strategy. The difference is that, in this case, the researcher is not assuming that there is one "ideal" answer: instead, she will explicitly compare alternative policies, keeping in mind that the answers *depend* on the goals of policymakers.

feel that gender imbalances in legislatures across the United States are bla-tantly unfair and unrepresentative. Fairness (or justice) and representation are normative concerns. As social scientists, we can frame questions that allow us to both document and better understand the implications of this apparent injustice and under-representation. One way to discern the effect of gender disparities is to ask whether legislatures with more women representatives pro-duce different types of policies than those with fewer women legislators. This question can be answered empirically; furthermore, the empirical answer to this question will also help support the researcher's capacity to discuss the nor-mative implications of the study, such as why it does—or does not—matter that male legislators are significantly over-represented in politics and policy-making in the United States.[5]

There are many questions that you might be curious about but which tell us very little about the political world at large. Why your preferred candidate in a particular election lost her race, for example, might matter to you quite a bit, but is it compelling beyond this particular context? We cannot overstate how crucial it is that a research question has some relevance in the broader scheme of things. This requirement is often referred to among academics as the "so what?" question. While one's ultimate research question and the an-swers to it will be quite specific, you should nonetheless be able to articulate why we should care about your question in your introduction and in your paper's concluding discussion. Lines of inquiry that matter in a larger sense are not difficult to find. Questions about international relations are often impor-tant, for instance, because how nations relate with one another can influence whether wars or humanitarian crises are averted or whether financial systems are stable. Questions about elections are significant because which party wins an election can influence which policies a government enacts, and so on.

As we discuss in more detail below, political scientists are obliged not only to *think* carefully about whether and how their own research relates to the social, political, or economic landscape, but they must also explicitly justify the broader significance of their question *in their study*. Indeed, good research papers almost always begin with an introduction of the research question and an immediate justification for why the question is an interesting and impor-tant one to study.

A good research question addresses a debate or puzzle in the literature.

A sound political science research question emerges from and relates to rel-evant prior scholarship on the topic. Note that this principle does not preclude your question and research from drawing upon other sources for inspiration,

5 While you may begin a project with very strong feelings on a subject, it is critical to ac-tively consider and test alternative theories and possibilities, as we discuss in more detail in Chapter 3.

background information, justification, and even data—including newspaper or magazine articles, for example. But your question should clearly explain its potential to shed new light on a puzzle, problem, or debate that has not yet been fully resolved in other scholarly research on the subject.

A good research question is not overly broad.

Research questions can be formulated in a way that makes them too big to answer. Indeed, many research ideas start with big questions that must be pared down to something more manageable. One might begin by wondering why countries go to war, but this does not make for a manageable research question. Indeed, volumes have been written on the subject, with most scholars focusing on more discrete questions that address that broader question. For example, some scholars ask whether authoritarian governments are more likely to start wars than democracies. Other scholars ask how effective treaties are in preventing wars. These questions all speak to the broader question about why countries go to war, but they do so in smaller, more feasible pieces.

A good research question is not too narrow.

A good research question is not so broad as to be unmanageable, but not so narrow that it loses its real-world importance. Indeed, a good way to think about whether your question has become too narrow is to think about how many people would care about the answer to your question. Following your internship working for a campaign for a candidate for the state legislature, you might be motivated to understand which campaign strategies were most effective in helping your candidate win more votes. However, if you ask, "Which campaign strategies were most effective in helping Candidate Smith win more votes?" only those who are interested in that candidate will find your question to be of interest. You can easily avoid this narrowness by asking, "Which campaign strategies are most effective in helping state legislative candidates win more votes?" This does not necessarily commit you to studying all state legislative campaigns, but it does indicate that you are interested in answering a broader question that more scholars will have an interest in.

In the discussion that follows, we discuss how a student researcher can formulate a good research question that meets these basic principles and other important ones as well.

BEGINNING THE RESEARCH PROCESS: WHAT DO *YOU* WANT TO KNOW?

How do you begin the process of developing your research question? First, there are some practical considerations. Adopt a suitable frame of mind for the project. Abandon any impulses you may have to come up with an argument you want to "prove." Instead, your goal is to formulate a question that you authentically want to know the answer to. In other words, ideally you do not actually know what the answer will be. Perhaps you have a strong hunch, but you cannot be sure.

This is an excellent time to obtain a research notebook or create a word-processing file that will help you collect your ideas, leads, and possible questions (See Box 2.1). Here is where you begin to research news sources online; check out a few political science journal articles; and consult with one or more professors in your department who work in an area close to the one you might want to focus on.

As you embark on the process, do take into account how much time you have for the project. If it is one semester, consider exploring a subject that you already have some background knowledge in and perhaps try to find a faculty mentor who is able to work closely with you. If you have an entire year, you can afford to be somewhat more ambitious.

Box 2.1: The Role of Record Keeping in Question Development and Research Progress

From the very beginning of your project, develop the habit of recording what you've read or learned, the source of the information, and the current date in a dedicated notebook or word-processing document. There are two main reasons to make recording your process and progress—whether it constitutes one sentence or source, a summary of a meeting with a faculty member, several pages' worth of potentially useful material, or that day's stab at refining your research question—a priority. The first rationale for the practice hinges on the matter of progress. Collecting your thoughts, possible sources, data, research notes, iterations of your question, and the like in one document or notebook promotes the development of a research question and one's overall project in several ways. For one thing, your collection of notes will stimulate your thinking and suggest fruitful avenues for further inquiry (and help you remember what lines of inquiry seem less interesting or worthwhile).

Your record keeping will also help you maintain your momentum over the course of the research. Frankly, the best way to stay on course is to do a little work on your project every day. In reality, however, it's more likely that at one point or another, for whatever reason, you will have to put your work aside for several days or more at a time. It's extraordinarily easy to lose your train of thought even over the span of a few days, particularly on a complex project. By referring to your notebook, you can jog your memory and avoid getting "stuck" in this fashion, which is a very common setback our students experience.

To make your notebook even more useful to you in terms of avoiding paralysis over "what to do next" we urge you to actively undertake to make a note about precisely what your next one or two concrete steps will be before you finish recording your work for the day. As the prolific and renowned writer, Ernest Hemingway, said:

> The best way is always to stop when you are going good and when you know what will happen next. If you do that every day . . . you will never be stuck. Always stop while you are going good and don't think about it or worry about it until you start to write the next day. That way your subconscious will work on it all the time.[a]

Author Cory Doctorow offers his own version of this technique, suggesting you always "leave yourself a rough edge":

> Stop even if you're in the middle of a sentence. Especially if you're in the middle of a sentence. That way, when you sit down at the keyboard the next day, your first five or ten words are already ordained, so that you get a little push before you begin your work. Knitters leave a bit of yarn sticking out of the day's knitting so they know where to pick up the next day—they call it the "hint." Potters leave a rough edge on the wet clay before they wrap it in plastic for the night—it's hard to build on a smooth edge.[b]

A second key reason to carefully track your efforts is a matter of housekeeping. Religiously kept records help ensure the integrity of your final work product. Always put quotation marks around anything you cut and paste into your working project document (or type in verbatim to the document) and cite the entire source and page number as well as the date you accessed it. You could also substantially summarize and paraphrase the information that interests you (while still, of course, making careful note of the original source), but keep in mind that mixing paraphrased with verbatim information can lead to significant errors if you are not well versed in the difference between paraphrasing and plagiarizing, and/or in using quotation marks every single time it is necessary. Taking care at the beginning of the project will save you much time, aggravation, and trouble in the end.

a. Larry W. Phillips, ed., *Ernest Hemingway on writing* (New York: Scribner, 1999).
b. Cory Doctorow, "Writing in the age of distraction," *Locus Magazine*, 2009. Accessed August 22, 2013. www.locusmag.com/Features/2009/01/cory-doctorow-writing-in-age-of.html.

On a related note, think carefully about the feasibility of your study. As you whittle down your area of interest and begin to draft possible questions, take into account the time you estimate that the project will require. The time needed will depend in part on the extent of your familiarity with the topic and the availability of faculty mentors. Even at this early stage you should begin considering what methodologies you might employ and how likely it is that you will be able to find the data you need, gain access to it, collect it, and analyze it appropriately given your skill set and time constraints. Seek out the advice of one or more faculty members to help you create a reasonable timeline. It is important, however, not to let issues of data collection or concerns about methods discourage you from pursuing a question you are interested in; almost all questions can be framed such that they can be studied using a variety of data sources and methodological tools.

To generate a preliminary research question (which, depending on your familiarity with the extant research on the particular subject, could take a day or several weeks), reflect on the issues or topics that interest or puzzle you. Consider what is going on in the news; think about other research papers you have worked on that might be worth expanding upon; find out what other faculty members and graduate students in your department are working on. You may, for example, be interested in the Occupy Wall Street protestors on or near your campus. This interest may then point you to the existing scholarship on protest movements or even to your school's faculty expert on such matters.[6] With further investigation and discussion, you may find yourself with a solid lead on a research question, perhaps one aimed at understanding what types of appeals are most effective at motivating college students to protest.

A shortcut to figuring out what kinds of questions scholars in different subfields of political science (which include comparative politics, American politics, international relations, political theory, and public policy) are grappling with is to read **review essays**. Review essays can be found in journals specifically devoted to such essays, such as the *Annual Review of Political Science*, but they also periodically appear in political science journals such as *Perspectives on Politics* and *Politics & Gender*.

A related strategy is to consult one or more of the several book series devoted to essays that summarize the state of the subfields in a variety of essays, including the Oxford Handbook series and the Cambridge Handbook series. Highly respected scholars in a particular area author these essays not only to review the research that has been conducted in an area but also to identify potential directions for new research. Another resource to consider are well respected edited volumes that regularly publish cutting-edge scholarship such as the New Directions in American Politics series from Routledge. Even upper-level textbooks devoted to a particular topic can prove to be valuable resources for question hunting.

In general, in the early stages of a project, the quickest way "into" a subject and the history of research on it is to skim the above sources as well as

---

6 If you can't find a mentor in your government or political science department, consider casting your net more widely. As we discuss in Chapter 3, your theories may very well be drawn from a wide range of subfields in political science or even from other disciplines. Political scientists regularly draw on work from the fields of economics, sociology, political science, political theory, communications, gender studies, and psychology, among others. Search your college or university's website to learn about faculty research specializations in different departments.

Box 2.2: Understanding the Organization of the Discipline

The discipline of political science is large and complex, with scholars asking research questions on a variety of phenomena both local and global. One way to get a sense of the many areas in which scholars conduct their research is to browse through the forty different sections of the American Political Science Association that are currently in operation. These sections are essentially subgroups of political scientists asking questions on similar phenomena.

Federalism and Intergovernmental Relations
Law and Courts
Legislative Studies
Public Policy
Political Organizations and Parties
Public Administration
Conflict Processes
Representation and Electoral Systems
Presidents and Executive Politics
Political Methodology
Religion and Politics
Urban Politics
Science, Technology, and Environmental Politics
Women and Politics Research
Foundations of Political Thought
Information Technology and Politics
International Security and Arms Control
Comparative Politics
European Politics and Society
State Politics and Policy
Political Communication
Politics and History
Political Economy
New Political Science
Political Psychology
Political Science Education
Politics, Literature, and Film
Foreign Policy
Elections, Public Opinion, and Voting Behavior
Race, Ethnicity, and Politics
International History and Politics
Comparative Democratization

Human Rights
Qualitative Methods
Sexuality and Politics
Health Politics and Policy
Canadian Politics
Political Networks
Experimental Research
Migration and Citizenship

political science journal articles, rather than to read entire books (though this may depend on the particular topic you choose). As you skim numerous **peer-reviewed** political science journal articles on your general subject, if you find a few that interest you, read the conclusions of those pieces carefully. This is where authors will often suggest a direction for future studies.

Academic books are obviously excellent resources, but, in the early days, consider reading just the introduction and conclusion to one or more academic books that interest you.[7] Introductions are wonderful resources as they discuss the book's motivating question or questions and previous research on the question, which essentially justifies why the book is a valuable contribution to the academic conversation. You will gain insight into where the debates lie among scholars on a particular subject. Again, conclusions can be equally valuable, as they often suggest questions that remain unresolved.

WHAT DO SCHOLARS *ALREADY* KNOW? THE CORE OF A RESEARCH QUESTION: WHAT IS THE CONTROVERSY, DEBATE, OR PUZZLE?

Once you have narrowed down your research interests substantially and have several ideas about potentially fruitful areas of inquiry, the next critical step is to begin carving out a sound, researchable question. Again, keep in mind that formulating a question is a process and not an event, especially (but not exclusively) for researchers newer to a topic. It is common to refine your question as you engage the scholarship in a particular area (and, indeed, throughout your project).

7 Again, by the term "academic books," we are distinguishing those that are written by scholars and published by presses that cater to a scholarly audience from those written by pundits or journalists. This is not to say that important insights or leads cannot be gleaned from the latter, but that ultimately their methods are different and less transparent than those of social scientists. They are also not bound by the imperative to systematically consider previous theories or findings within the academic conversation on a topic.

A good question aims to address a controversy, debate, or puzzle. It may be that the question is one you find, after some research, has been overlooked or under-studied within the academic literature. The question may arise from a current debate in the academic literature on your topic. Your question might also originate from a puzzle you have identified from your reading and experience outside of the literature; you believe you may be able to understand it better by examining the scholarship on the subject. It is worthwhile repeating that another appropriate strategy that too few students pursue is to discuss possible questions with a faculty member who has a research interest in the area you are considering working on.

What might a first attempt at a research question look like? In the preliminary stages, one might formulate them this way:

- Why aren't there more women in political office in the United States?
- How has social media transformed contemporary social movements?
- Has money in politics corrupted the political system in the United States?

All three are interesting and potentially important questions; they are a place to begin. Nevertheless, they are all far too broad. It is important that your question speak to broadly significant problems (more on that below) in some way. But the research question you end up pursuing will likely be a considerably distilled and more specific version compared with the examples above. The first question is an excellent one in the sense that this is one of the central puzzles that scholars of women and politics have been working on, and are likely to continue to be concerned with, for quite some time. As written here, however, the question, like the others, needs to be honed in light of the research already done on the matter.

Remember that a good question can be quite straightforward. In Chapter 1, you may recall, we provided an example of a question scholars have asked about the topic of partisan polarization—"Is polarization occurring or not?" While a seemingly simple query, the question nevertheless requires that the researcher make inferences from data and it addresses an ongoing debate in the literature on the topic.

Question Development: Intermediate Stages

One excellent way to grasp what a research question in political science looks like is to pay attention to how these scholars articulate their own questions. Carefully study several journal articles to see how the authors move the reader from a grand opening observation or a telling anecdote to a concise, answerable, and focused question. Examine, for instance, the abstracts of and the first page or two of some journal articles in a political science journal. You will see that while scholars signal to the reader the larger issues their study speaks to, their actual line of inquiry takes only a "bite" out of the problem. As a result, the following formulations, or variations of them, crop up frequently: "To what extent does . . ."; "Under what conditions do . . ."; "Given X, what accounts for Y?" Try to practice formulating your questions beginning with these phrases (again, your research journal will prove handy here).

Once you have begun to explore a particular subject more seriously, move from skimming to fully reading more journal articles that interest you. Once you've hit on a few that appear to be relevant to what you might like to work on, scan their works cited or bibliography section for leads to other articles that are relevant to your developing topic. As you move through this stage of the research process, take note of those authors that are continually cited in the research you read—such patterns reveal an ongoing scholarly conversation. Recognizing this pattern will ultimately help you anchor your own work in one or more scholarly conversations.

As you read these journal articles, continually ask yourself how (and document in your research journal the possible ways in which) you, like the authors of the journal articles you read, might also begin to narrow your focus. Again, choose more recent political science journal articles to skim or read first—you will more quickly grasp the debates and puzzles that are presently capturing scholars' attention (and will thereby avoid concentrating on an area that is already well traveled). The second benefit is that, as we mentioned above and discuss more fully in Chapter 3, journal articles review the state of the literature on their topic (as do academic books, though less succinctly). More recent journal articles will help you "catch up" relatively quickly by exposing you to the most recent lines of inquiry and findings (they will also include more recent work in their literature reviews). You will also begin to identify inconsistencies, puzzles, and arguments among scholars within the broader topic: these are common signs that a specific topic needs further study. In fact, if you come across clearly opposing "sides" of a particular debate, consider this an opportunity: evaluate whether and how you might be able to formulate a question and marshal data that will allow you to weigh in on one side of the debate or the other—you may even find that both "sides" are omitting crucial factors!

In addition to the efficiency of using recent journal articles to hone your question, much of the advice we suggested in the earlier stages of your project still apply here. Reviewing essays that evaluate the literature and point out discontinuities and suggestions for further analysis can be invaluable to your efforts at the intermediate stage as well. Concluding chapters of books and journal article conclusions are another source to revisit. For instance, Mona Lena Krook's final chapter in her book *Quotas for Women in Politics* is entitled "Conclusions and directions for further research."[8]

8 Mona Lena Krook, *Quotas for women in politics: Gender and candidate selection reform worldwide* (Oxford: Oxford University Press, 2009).

If you were interested in the first question above pertaining to women and elective office ("Why aren't there more women in political office in the United States?"), you would soon notice after strategically reading through some of the most recent journal articles that scholars attempt to gain traction on this question along many dimensions. Researchers choose a dimension, and then narrow their focus. When a field of researchers set about understanding big problems by tackling many smaller aspects of the issue, they are more likely to gain valuable information that will move the field forward.

Some scholars try to understand the low numbers of women in office in the United States by asking whether, how, or to what extent the political campaign process itself might be hindering women's progress. Others try to get a handle on the factors that affect women's political representation by comparing countries with different rates of females in political office because they have a hunch, from their informal observation perhaps, and a result of their exploration of the literature, that institutional or state-level characteristics play a role in explaining cross-national differences in women's political representation.

To give you a sense of question development and refinement, a student's intermediate attempts at developing a question on women's political representation might take the following forms:

- "To what extent does the role of money in politics affect women's ability to attain political office as compared with men?
- "Under what conditions are women in Western industrialized nations likely to constitute a higher proportion of nationally elected officials?"
- "Given that women have, over the previous five decades, substantially increased their educational attainment and entry into careers previously dominated by men, why have these changes failed to translate into more women holding elective office?"

Each of the above questions constitutes a solid intermediate step toward framing a research question. They all still need considerable work, however, since none meet all the conditions necessary for a fully developed research question. The questions remain either too broad or they have been studied quite a bit already.

For example, several studies have shown that money does not appear to be a deciding factor in terms of whether or not women win elective office. In the second possible question, notice that not all "Western industrialized nations" have similar political systems, so any comparisons that include the United States will prove difficult to make. One solution is to exclude the United States, instead focusing on other nations with comparable political systems. Note that limitations regarding your research design (i.e. what is actually possible) will also influence the type of question you can ask and hope to answer. You may be very interested in the relationship between human rights and policing practices in Turkey, for example, but what kind of data is readily available to you on these subjects? Will you be able to develop a question that both addresses your interests in the topic and, at the same time, is answerable, given the resources you are able to gather to answer it? As we continually stress throughout this text, the research process is a non-linear, or *iterative* one: scholars frequently revise their research questions to match what they can reasonably answer.

The third question, like the first, seeks to understand the factors that appear to be undermining women's progress in attaining elective office in the United States. The question sets up a puzzle: women have progressed socially and economically in key ways that should theoretically increase their political representation accordingly, but this has not occurred. A perplexing observation, to be sure, and a good "way into" the problem, but it is not entirely suitable as a research question yet because it is still too broad.

Why Do We Care? Or the "So What" Question

Social scientists make numerous judgment calls as they conceptualize and carry out academic studies. To ensure that their work generates some implications for understanding real-world outcomes, that it builds on prior knowledge, that it is carried out with integrity, and to assist other researchers' ability to replicate their work, scholars aim for as much transparency as possible by explaining the reasoning behind the choices they have made. You should follow this example by documenting the rationale for your choices as well as you can from the very beginning of your project.

One of the first choices you will have to justify is your choice of research question. You must be able to explain not only why answering this question could prove important to scholars but also how it relates to some "real world" political phenomena. For example, does your question have some bearing on citizens' political behavior, issues of democracy or representation, or the prospects for nonviolent democratization in autocratic regimes? As we noted earlier, political scientists often refer to this as the **"so what" question**. The reason for this is that nobody wants to finish a research project and have their audience wondering why they should care about the findings. Any good research question should demonstrate the potential to generate findings that will have some practical implications for the social and political world.

In the final research paper, a reader should know immediately what your question is and why he or she should care about it. Do not be shy about starting a paper with your research question and immediately stating after that question that "This question is important because. . . ." While we discuss the literature review at greater length in the next chapter, we signal here that another way in which you will have to defend or justify your research question is by demonstrating how it arises from and relates to an ongoing academic conversation.

Question Development: Advanced Stages

Further refinement of your research question, unsurprisingly, involves more research on your part. Moving from an intermediate to a more advanced stage of question refinement occurs when the following conditions have been met:

- You have gathered enough information to craft a clear question with a high level of specificity.
- Your question has a variety of possible answers.
- It addresses a debate or puzzle in the literature.
- It is manageable given your skill set, your knowledge base, and the time you have to conduct your research.
- It is guided by prior scholarship on the subject and has the potential to contribute to it.

What is the subset (community) of scholars who are asking questions that interest you?

As you venture toward a more advanced stage of question refinement, you will be engaging in many of the same activities and using some of the same tactics described in earlier stages, but now you will be sifting through journal articles and books that comprise a narrower area of inquiry and reading them more closely. Rather than reading any recent journal article on women and politics that seems interesting, you will increasingly focus your attention on the much smaller community of scholars who are studying, for example, the question of whether, and the extent to which, family responsibilities might play a role in gender differences in political representation. Alternatively, you might be drawn to the work of the community of scholars who explore gender disparities in politics by comparing the quality of women's representation in nations that employ quota systems. Still other scholarly circles are trying to determine what role, if any, different party systems play in enhancing or suppressing women's interest in running for office or for higher office.

Luckily, discerning the various scholarly circles within even a broad subject such as "women and politics" is not terribly complex, and you certainly do not have to be familiar with every individual who has published within your topic's community of researchers. As we mention above, in the process of reading journal articles whose authors' questions relate to one another, you will notice that certain scholars' findings are cited repeatedly. These authors are likely to belong to the community of scholars whose work you want to know more about and to speak to in some way. Look for such patterns as you carefully examine books' bibliographies and the works cited pages of journal articles (again, the questions these books and articles address should be closely connected). Record the authors' names and the articles that seem pertinent to your increasingly narrowed focus, then track those articles down, read them, and examine their works cited pages for more articles, and so on.

Using this technique, within a short time you will have developed a keen awareness of the researchers who are active and influential in the scholarly circle that interests you. Furthermore, having done this legwork you will find yourself in an excellent position to gauge where the debate and disagreements are among those in "your" community; what techniques, methods, and data these individuals are employing; what scholarly literature, findings, and theories are central to the community; and the different ways in which these scholars articulate their questions. Now you are truly in a position to refine your own question.

At the same time, you will have set yourself up for success well beyond the question stage (especially if you diligently maintained your research notebook). Your investment in the groundwork required to develop a solid research question will pay off in spades. You will have a head start on developing your theory and hypotheses, for one thing. Your close reading of books and articles whose authors are in conversation together will guide you as you make key decisions, such as how to go about choosing cases to compare, what data sources to employ, and what methods to use. Having read the relevant scholarship for your particular question, you will also be able to defend those choices. Justifying the grounds for your study should pose little trouble for you, and you will have a much clearer sense of how to structure your literature review.

Here is one example of a question relating to women and politics that has been refined; notice how the authors justify the grounds for their question's wider importance as well as its significance with respect to conversations relating to a particular scholarly circle (see Box 2.3 for another example as well).

Question: "How does the sex of political candidates affect voting perceptions and behavior in Turkey?"

Broader significance: "Patriarchal practices and understandings, especially those based on religious teachings, are seen as serious hindrances to women's access to political power."

How this question relates to problem/conversation in literature: "This obstacle is often seen as greatest in countries where Islam is the dominant religion. . . . [Turkey is] one of the few democratic countries with a Muslim majority population. . . . Yet virtually no work has studied systematically how citizens in Muslim majority countries view female political figures."[9]

Even as you finalize your working question, as you learn more about your specific topic, the limits of your data, and many other factors, your question can, and probably will, be refined further. With this in mind, we introduce

9 Richard E. Matland and Gunes Murat Tezcur, "Women as candidates: An experimental study in Turkey," *Politics & Gender* 7 (2011): 365–390.

Box 2.3: Another Example of a Refined Research Question

Question: State political parties differ with respect to the levels of women's representation within them. Is this because they have "distinctive cultures" that affect their "abilities to produce, recruit, and support women elected officials"?

  Broader significance: "Even a decade into the twenty-first century, women remain severely under-represented in state legislatures."

  How this question relates to problem/conversation in literature: "The representation of Democratic women in state legislatures has continued to increase, while the number of Republican women has actually decreased."[a]

a. Laurel Elder, "The partisan gap among women state legislators," *Journal of Women, Politics & Policy*, 33 (2012), p. 1.

---

several other pivotal matters to think about as you work, many of which relate to the list of the conditions a well-crafted research question should meet.

KEEPING THE BIG PICTURE IN MIND: OTHER FACTORS TO CONSIDER AS YOU REFINE YOUR QUESTION. HOW WILL YOU EXECUTE THE STUDY?

It is never too early to think about how you might carry out a research project and the data you might use, but as you begin fine-tuning your question it becomes essential to consider the various means by which you might answer it. In fact, particularly at this stage, you should be drafting possible questions, then diving back into the research to see what kind of data and methods others have employed. The benefits of habitually moving between thinking about how to frame your question and considering how you might carry it out are several. First, you will gain a better sense of what scope of project is doable given your own constraints, while still contributing something of value to the scholarly conversation. Considering the question and how you might go about answering it gives you an advantage as you head into the next stages of your project as well.

  As you read with an eye to your particular question, if you have followed our exhortations, you will have recorded the author's name and the article citation, along with other notes. Make a habit of briefly noting the data sources the author used, as well, and his or her method. One reason to pay attention to the author's data is that it is not uncommon for authors to share their data with others, upon request, via their own website, or through other data portals. Did the author use small-n techniques, such as interviews? How could you make this work for your project? Did the scholar conduct a survey or an experiment? How might you use this method in your study? Did the author make use of an existing large-n dataset (a dataset with a large number of observations), employing sophisticated statistical techniques? If you have limited time and lack the skill set to conduct large-n analyses, you need not necessarily abandon a question you are considering just because several key articles you've read employ large datasets. Think about how you might be able to gain purchase on your question in other ways. You may also find data suited to your question in one of the resources we list at the end of the book or through other internet-based sources. You can also consider creating your own dataset.

We repeat our advice to speak with your faculty members as you develop your question about how to construct the study. The fundamental message here is two-fold: as you draft your research question, reflect on how you might undertake the study. Second, remember that there are numerous creative ways to study political phenomena. Do not feel as though certain questions are necessarily off-limits because you believe you currently lack the skill set to answer them properly. For example, some basic statistical analyses can be learned over the course of a semester, as can interviewing techniques, survey and experimental methods, and case-study analysis.

Alternative Theories

Although we discuss this in more depth in the following chapter on theory, we do want to remind you as you work through the question development process to take note of various scholars and competing theories they put forth. Recall that your question will be one that is unresolved in the literature. The more you read and think not only about your question but also about the study as a whole, the more likely it is that you will develop strong hunches as to the answer to your question. This is natural and your observations will be useful as you proceed with your study. As you interact with the scholarship related to your question, avoid narrowing your focus so much that you become particularly attached to one explanation or set of hypotheses over others. To advance our repository of knowledge, social scientists seek to explicitly and fairly test rival theories rather than to "prove" the one they believe "fits" best. We discuss this dynamic in more detail in Chapter 3.

Definitions

As you read the literature in the pursuit of your research question, scholars will employ what you will eventually recognize as common terminology for particular phenomena or concepts. Whenever possible, make note of these definitions (and their sources) and use them when and if appropriate in your own work in lieu of creating your own definitions from scratch or prematurely revising one that is used in the literature. Reinventing the wheel, particularly for minor definitional tweaks, is not only a waste of your time, but it also signals that you are not participating in an ongoing conversation with other scholars, and it makes it harder for you or for them to build on common understandings. When scholars redefine concepts too frequently or without adequate justification for doing so, future researchers struggle to understand how to make sense of how they might contribute to the scholarly discussion. New researchers in particular should take great care before revamping important concepts. At the same time, don't ignore inconsistencies in the wording of the central concept definitions you encounter. Note them—they may suggest a possible disagreement among scholars that you can leverage into a viable research question.

SUMMING UP: THE RESEARCH QUESTION

In this chapter, we clarified the role of the research question in political science research. The research question will take time to develop, in large part because it should relate to, as well as seek to contribute to, one or more scholarly conversations. As you learn more about your subject and about the data available to you (or that you can reasonably collect on your own), you will likely adjust or reframe your question several times. Seek out the advice of faculty mentors, within and outside of your department. Use your time strategically. In this chapter we offer strategies for the beginning, intermediate, and final stages of the question development process.

If you've followed our advice, you will find yourself well prepared to situate your question within the scholarly conversations—conversations that ultimately constitute competing theories. In other words, you will not only have formulated a sound working question (or set of questions) but whether you realize it or not, you will also already have been considering the role of theory in your research. Thus, as we move on to Chapter 3, you will have already learned a bit about how scholars employ theory (embodied in "the literature") to support their work. In short, theory (derived from prior literature and logic) is used by scholars to justify their research questions, to derive their hypotheses, to explain the choices made in the conduct of their studies, to explain their findings, and to discuss the implications of their research.

KEY TERMS

literature review 37	review essays 44
normative implications 39	scholarly literature 37
peer-reviewed 46	"so what" question 50

Linking Theory and Inference

As you proceed with formulating and justifying your research question, you will begin to encounter and evaluate theories[1] that may help you to answer it. As we noted in Chapter 1, **theory** is quite possibly the most crucial part of the research enterprise because of its centrality to making inferences. Theory also informs every part of the research process, including the formulation of your research question, the design of your research study, and how you interpret the results. Our goal as political scientists is to test an existing theory or to modify or construct and test a new theory in an attempt to explain some phenomenon better than current theories do.

Fortunately, we do not develop our answers to a research question or our theories about how the world works in isolation. Instead, as we have emphasized, we build upon the thinking and research of the many scholars that came before us. In the process, however, if a researcher believes that the way previous analysts have thought about a problem is incomplete or incorrect, she can propose new ideas and argue against existing ones.

You should not feel pressured to develop a grand theory. Indeed, in our discipline, it is exceedingly rare for scholars to construct an entirely new theory or wholly invalidate a well-established one. However, it is quite common for researchers to make relatively modest but nonetheless significant theoretical

---

1 Some introductory research methods texts use the word "thesis" interchangeably with "theory." Because the word thesis is so commonly used in the undergraduate setting to refer to any kind of argument (and not one dependent on prior scholarship etc.) we avoid its use in this text.

contributions, perhaps demonstrating how extant theories are incomplete or fail to explain some class of phenomena. Proposing modest modifications to existing models, demonstrating the necessity of including previously omitted variables, theorizing that a debate or set of inconsistent findings can be resolved by modeling the problem in a different way—all of these can constitute perfectly valid and significant "middle range" theoretical contributions in the social sciences.

In this chapter, we demystify the concept of "theory," beginning our discussion by demonstrating the role theory plays in our daily lives and why theories are essential not only to scholars but also to everyone. We describe the characteristics of a good theory and how theory is incorporated into empirical political science research. In addition to clarifying the link between theory and **hypotheses**, we also explain the role theory plays in helping us make stronger inferences from our findings.

In the latter part of this chapter, we turn to the practical problem of the literature review, suggesting that you think of it as a means of demonstrating how you used theory and prior scholarship that is closely related to your question to support every aspect of your research design, from your question selection to your choice of the particular factors you will describe or include in a causal model. Finally, we provide several examples of theory building.

WHAT IS THEORY? WHY ARE THEORIES SO IMPORTANT AND SO VALUABLE?

Many excellent definitions of the constituent elements of a theory have been offered by scholars in the social sciences. Here is one iteration: "A general explanation is called a theory. It is a set of principles that tells why people do what they do in a variety of contexts."[2] In fact, perhaps the broadest definition of a theory is that it is a statement about how one thinks the world works. A theory is fundamentally a generalization. The purpose of scientific studies is typically not to describe or explain one event. Rather, researchers hope that their theories, when supported by the evidence, can be applied to other related phenomena. Theories, or **generalizations**, provide us with a foundation of general knowledge that we can then apply to past, current, or future problems.

Generalizations allow us to make sense of the world. Thousands of significant events occur each and every day; theory plays an essential role in helping us understand our social, political, and economic environment because theories reduce mountains of observations to a set of regular patterns or relationships. Theories can be applied to contexts beyond the specific occurrence that initiated its development. Well-developed theories that have stood the test of

---

2 Paul S. Gray, John B. Williamson, David A. Karp, *et al. The research imagination: An introduction to qualitative and quantitative methods* (New York: Cambridge University Press, 2007), p. 4.

time serve as critical short cuts, or heuristics, for scholars, policymakers, and the public as they make decisions large and small.

In fact, individuals rely upon, construct, and apply theories in their everyday lives to make decisions, often subconsciously. We develop many theories on our own, often as a result of having noticed a pattern. A student might suspect, for example, that his new habit of studying for examinations in his international relations course while chatting online with friends appears to correspond to a recent succession of low marks he has received in that course. He might develop a theory, inductively, based on his own experiences and, deductively, based on some background literature about how the brain works, that his academic performance is related to distractions in his study environment.

Our student has begun to develop a theory, or a generalization about the relationship between an outcome of some importance to him—his academic performance—and a factor that he believes influences that outcome—distractions. Based on his experiences, he infers, or makes an educated guess, that distractions undermine his ability to learn because they interrupt his flow, or immersion in the task at hand.[3] He can't be sure, however, how sound his theory is without testing it. He is likely to begin questioning some aspects of his original theory after studying alone in a library cubicle in complete silence for a while. What qualifies as a "distraction" exactly? Does his theory suggest that he must eliminate *all* distractions in his study environment, or might some types of distractions hamper his studies more than others?

Our student could refine his theory by defining the notion of "distraction" more clearly. Perhaps he could examine some academic literature on the matter. Ultimately this student could use the theory to formulate a hypothesis: the more students look away from their work, the less they will be able to remember about what they were studying. Notice that he has "operationalized" or refined his definition of the concept of "distraction" in a measurable way.

Of course, many, if not the vast majority, of theories that we use to navigate our daily lives are not entirely self-generated but are relayed to us from professionals we trust, like doctors and educators, from friendship networks, family, and from a wide range of media sources. Our hypothetical student might have heard about the problems associated with multitasking or about the importance of a state of flow through one or more of these routes as well.

Without theories, or the ability to generalize, we would have to investigate all situations, at all points in time, individually, and repeatedly. Having a toolkit of theories, in contrast, allows us to apply knowledge from one situation to another. For example, over the years, political scientists have empirically tested and refined their theories about how Congress operates such that we can now explain with some confidence why many bills never make it out

---

3 For an explanation of this term, see Mihaly Csikszentmihalyi and Jeanne Nakamura, "The concept of flow," in *The Handbook of Positive Psychology* (Oxford: Oxford University Press, 2002), pp. 89–92.

of a committee or why the president often declines to exercise the veto. As a result, we do not have to undertake new studies every time a new Congress has been installed, a new bill has been proposed, or a new president has been elected, saving not only scholars but also all those interested in or affected by politics and policymaking an incalculable amount of time and resources.

Beyond Generalizability

Theory plays a special role in scholarly research for reasons beyond the notion of generalizability. We outline below the ways in which theory promotes sound research design.

Theory is critical in terms of guiding researchers as we determine which alternative theories to consider; in setting the stage for our ability to develop interesting hypotheses to test; in helping us discern which factors, or independent variables, to include and control for in our studies; and in terms of ascertaining "which way the causal arrow goes." *No method you choose can substitute for the work theory does in your research.* In the absence of strong theory guiding you through the many judgments you will be called upon to make during the research process, it is highly unlikely your findings or the inferences you make based on them will be sound. For example, how does one figure out which are your independent variables and which are your dependent variables? The answer is—theory. You must be familiar with the theoretical literature to make this judgment call for your research question. How do you know the relationship that your results appear to show are robust, and not an artifact or a spurious correlation? Again, theory.

Even when you see the finish line to your research project—you've obtained results from your research—you are *still* not finished with theory. Data can't tell you *why* you see the patterns you see or *why* your results differ from your expectations. Because we cannot ever be entirely certain that our models perfectly reflect how the world works, the best we can do is to design our research as mindfully as possible, guided by strong theory in an effort to make robust inferences about our findings. Again, no method can explain what your results mean—you must make inferences about your findings, informed by theory, to help interpret and explain your results.

WHAT CHARACTERIZES A GOOD THEORY?

We now turn from explaining what a theory is, generally speaking, and why it is so valuable, to understanding the components of a good theory. We offer the following definitions that will shape our discussion:

A social science theory is a reasoned and precise speculation about the answer to a research question, including a statement about why the proposed answer is correct. Theories usually imply several more specific descriptive or causal hypotheses. A theory must be consistent with prior evidence about a research question.[4]

> A theory is an interrelated set of constructs (or variables) formed into propositions or hypotheses that specify the relationship among variables (typically in terms of magnitude or direction). The systematic view might be an argument, a discussion, or a rationale that helps explain (or predict) phenomena that occur in the world.[5]

These definitions align with our preceding point that theory makes claims about how the world works, but they also begin to identify some essential qualities of good theory that we have not yet discussed.

Good Theory Builds on Existing Theory

The conceptual and theoretical understandings that predominate in political science—or "what we know"—are continually subjected to a winnowing process in which old theories are questioned and new theories (which bring with them fresh hypotheses to test) arise to refine or even replace prior formulations. The process of advancing our knowledge of a subject takes place most efficiently, as we discuss in the Introduction and in Chapter 2, when scholars develop studies that are driven not only by their personal interests or hunches but when they also self-consciously understand that they must build on the work of scholars before them.

Theories that are "well grounded" in prior literature are valuable because they speak to the common interests and mutual understandings of others who are interested in the subject that the theory addresses. Well-grounded theories are therefore *accessible* to others. By drawing on prior theories and addressing ongoing conversations, a researcher is more likely to influence others' thinking on the topic they are studying.

For example, in their article "Protest and democracy in Latin America's market era," Paul T. Bellinger, Jr. and Moises Arce want to know "whether and how political democracy has influenced societal responses to economic liberalization."[6] In their introduction, the authors clearly note the contradictory implications of two important theoretical streams of literature: one that

---

4 Gary King, Robert O. Keohane, and Sidney Verba, *Designing social inquiry: Scientific inference in qualitative research* (Princeton: Princeton University Press, 1994), p. 19.

5 John W. Creswell, *Research design: Qualitative, quantitative, and mixed methods approaches* (Thousand Oaks, CA: Sage, 2013), p. 82.

6 Paul T. Bellinger, Jr. and Moises Arce, "Protest and democracy in Latin America's market era," *Political Research Quarterly* 64 (2011): 688–704, p. 689.

emphasizes the "depoliticizing" effects of economic reforms in democracies—in other words how economic reforms in democracies can suppress protest—and another, the "repoliticization" literature, which suggests that political democracies promote protest activity.[7]

Not only do the authors use these two theoretically contrasting literatures to shape their own thinking about the relationship between democracy, economic reforms, and political protest, but Bellinger and Arce also bring in a third theoretical literature to help them mediate between the contrasting perspectives. The authors note that to

> advance the current debate . . . the article expands the theoretical scope of the repoliticization perspective by drawing on an established literature on contentious politics. This literature informs us that grievances increase the willingness of collective actors to mobilize, while democracy creates a favorable environment (or opportunity) for societal responses.

Capitalizing on the theories advanced in these three streams of literature to inform their study, Bellinger and Arce were able to formulate their own theory to test: "Seen in [the light of the contentious politics perspective] democratic politics—however imperfect—ought to encourage collective political activity, not render it obsolete."

As the example above demonstrates, well-grounded theories are valuable because they can be "leveraged" or applied to other topics and situations by different scholars and policymakers (a concept we discuss below in greater detail in Box 3.1); they can be employed and tested in a variety of contexts to understand multiple phenomena.

Good Theory Concretely Specifies the Concepts and/or Variables It Invokes

Concepts are words that represent some idea and must be clearly defined in any research project. If a scholar is trying to explain variation in corruption across countries, for example, she must specify what she means by "corruption." Does she intend to analyze petty administrative corruption (paying bribes to bureaucrats) or grand corruption by high-level officials (embezzlement, kickbacks from contracts)? The researcher's precise explanation of what she means by "corruption" in her study is key because the causes of the former type of corruption (recruitment, selection, training, promotion criteria, accountability mechanisms) might be very different than the causes of the

---

7 Bellinger, Jr. and Arce, "Protest and democracy in Latin America's market era," p. 688.

Box 3.1: Avoid Substantially Revising Existing Definitions of Concepts

Scholars often consider ways to increase how "leverageable," or applicable, their work is to others in their discipline and beyond. What they want is to ensure that their study is useful to other scholars or to a broader range of scholars. By relying to the extent possible on the concepts and the definitions of concepts that previous scholars have already employed in the development of your theory, you increase the ability of researchers to leverage your work. Our knowledge base is, in part, constituted by a common vocabulary, which extends to how we define concepts. Drawing on that common vocabulary as we employ central concepts facilitates our ability to contribute to the advancement of knowledge—the goal of the scientist—rather than simply the production of information.[a]

We therefore advise students to avoid, whenever possible, redefining terms and concepts that are widely used in the literature. The first rule of specifying your concepts, then, is to comb the literature to discover how others have done so. Your new theory of representation will be more likely to contribute to scholarly conversations if you define the concept of representation in a way that reflects the understandings of others who have developed theories relating to the subject.

The caveat here is that when you find scholars divided over definitions, you may be able to take advantage of these differences as you develop and refine your approach to the topic. In fact, some concepts, like the concept of representation, are so central to so many scholars that entire articles or books may be devoted to clarifying them. Hannah F. Pitkin's 1967 book entitled *The Concept of Representation* continues to shape the theoretical foundations of countless studies in political science and beyond.[b] More recent examples of scholars seeking to elucidate the notion of representation, but whose views differ in important ways, can be found in a series of scholarly conversations between two political scientists, Jane Mansbridge and Andrew Rehfeld. To date, their discussion on the concept of representation comprises four articles (their most recent engagement appears in the August 2011 issue of the *American Political Science Review*).[c]

a. Note that the cautions in this section about revising commonly accepted definitions can be broadened to include a warning about making other changes to conventions in your research area. For example, those conducting surveys are advised to carefully consider the costs and benefits of revising survey questions that have been widely used and tested before doing so.

b. Hannah F. Pitkin, *The concept of representation* (Berkeley: University of California Press, 1967/1972).

c. See: Jane Mansbridge, "Rethinking representation," *American Political Science Review* 97 (2003): 515–528; Andrew Rehfeld, "Representation rethought: On trustees, delegates, and gyroscopes in the study of political representation and democracy," *American Political Science Review* 103 (2005): 214–230; Jane Mansbridge, "Clarifying the concept of representation," *American Political Science Review* 105 (2011): 621–630; Andrew Rehfeld, "The concepts of representation," *American Political Science Review* 105 (2011): 631–641.

latter (insufficient checks and balances, lack of public information, perverse electoral incentives).[8]

Many, if not the majority, of the most commonly invoked concepts in political science research have already been defined in multiple literatures as well as in other disciplines including sociology, psychology, economics, public administration, public policy, and history. It is not uncommon to find disagreements regarding the definitions of concepts within a particular discipline's literature or across disciplines. Students are advised to research existing definitions, consider the implications of the differences among them, and be clear about the definition they decide to employ (including its provenance).

Some concepts are quite broad and obviously demand careful specification, such as: power, democracy, representation, equality, political efficacy, or political ambition. But even terms one might imagine to be self-evident must be carefully defined for the reader. The case of voter turnout provides a useful example of how even seemingly self-explanatory concepts must be clearly specified. Voter turnout is an example of a concept that can be conceived of in a variety of ways, and how it is defined can affect what we conclude about turnout. For instance, one way of defining voter turnout is by taking the percentage of the voting-age public who vote in a particular election. If we define turnout in this way, only about half of American adults vote in presidential elections, a fraction that has declined since the middle of the twentieth century. Yet, political scientists Michael McDonald and Samuel Popkin (2001) pointed out that, because a non-trivial share of adults (such as non-citizens and felons) are not eligible to vote, it makes more sense to conceptualize turnout as a percentage of adults who are eligible to vote.[9] When defined this way, turnout in the United States is about 5 percentage points higher, suggesting that voter turnout has not declined nearly as much as earlier studies suggest. The example of voter turnout demonstrates that how one defines a concept can have important consequences, including influencing scholars' findings. This is a point we discuss in more detail in Chapter 4.

Good Theory Clarifies the Relationship between Concepts and What Is to Be Explained or Described

Both definitions of "theory" presented at the beginning of this chapter highlight the point that sound political science requires the scholar to specify as precisely as possible what he is positing. Whether one is conducting research leading to descriptive or causal inferences, theories must clearly describe one's

---

8 We return to the discussion of conceptualizing corruption in Chapter 4.
9 Michael P. McDonald and Samuel L. Popkin, "The myth of the vanishing voter," *American Political Science Review* 95 (2001): 963–974.

conclusion about the relationship between phenomena and the factors that explain, shape, influence, or cause it. Theories must state how you think the world works, but they must also state *why you believe it works that way*. If your research question tests causal relationships, your theory should explain why you expect the independent variable(s) (the factors you believe are influencing what you are trying to explain) to cause the dependent variable (what you are trying to explain). Your theory must elucidate the causal mechanisms you argue are "doing the work" or affecting the outcome of interest to your study.

For example, if you are trying to understand why some people are more likely to vote than others, it would not be sufficient to merely state that you expect that people with more education are more likely to vote. A good theory would also explain why you expect that the number of years of education an individual completed would be related to turnout. In this case, we might "unpack" the causal mechanism by describing how individuals with more education tend to know more about politics, thereby making it easier for them to decide who to vote for. Indeed, this is just one of many reasons that having more education makes one more likely to vote. Keep in mind, of course, that your explanation of the relationship between your concepts and what you are trying to explain will again be rooted in and guided by prior scholarship relating to your analysis.

If your research question involves making descriptive inferences, your analysis should describe the implications of your examination of prior theories in light of any new observations you have collected or obtained with respect to your research question. How might your analysis of prior studies and collection of new data influence the course of a debate or problem in the literature? Barakso, for example, joined an ongoing discussion regarding the decline of civic engagement in the United States by demonstrating weaknesses in the literature and by offering evidence from her own research.[10] She argued that, while recent studies provided important clues as to the nation's civic health, contemporary theories about the causes of the decline in civic engagement failed to take into account the way organizations operate. Barakso theorized, based on earlier research and her own study of the National Organization for Women and other organisations, that in order to evaluate changes in levels of civic engagement, it was not enough to consider whether the numbers of groups or the numbers of group members have changed over time. Groups can be organized in ways that promote citizens' civic participation or in ways that discourage it. As a result, Barakso argued that scholars should examine whether and the extent to which changes in the levels of internal democracy within citizens' groups have played a role in the decline in civic engagement in the United States. This study posited a clear theoretical relationship between

10 See, for example, Maryann Barakso, *Governing NOW: Grassroots activism in the National Organization for Women* (Ithaca: Cornell University Press, 2004), and "Civic engagement and voluntary associations: Reconsidering the role of the governance structures of advocacy groups." 2005. Polity. Vol. 9, No. 1.

levels of civic engagement and interest group governance; it also laid out the implications of her argument for future researchers.

Good Theory Is Falsifiable

Another important criterion for a good theory is **falsifiability**—whether it can be proven wrong. We cannot ever "prove" our theories are correct, but by using a variety of techniques, we can estimate how confident we are in them. A theory that cannot be falsified prevents us from testing it in meaningful ways, which in turn means that we are unable to evaluate the extent to which the theory explains anything. For example, a theory that states that "the Wars in Iraq and Afghanistan prevented another terrorist attack in the United States" is not refutable because we can never observe what would have happened had the United States *not* engaged in those conflicts.

A falsifiable theory, on the other hand, allows one to test, preferably in more than one way, its soundness. The theory above could be refined to say, "military invasions of terrorist states reduce future terrorist attacks." This theory is potentially refutable because we can generate a variety of testable hypotheses, such as "worldwide terrorist incidents will diminish in the wake of an external military intervention to counter terrorism"; or "larger and more extended military interventions in a country will cause a more substantial decrease in terrorist incidents launched from that country." We can't know whether invading Afghanistan reduced terrorism in the United States, because we cannot observe what would have happened if the United States had not invaded Afghanistan, but we can compare it to another state the United States did not invade.

Sometimes robust scholarly conversations emerge around theories that are, in essence, non-falsifiable but which nevertheless attract scores of researchers, often because the theories engage highly salient political concepts. The literature on deliberative democracy, for example, links key concepts of representation, democracy, and the citizenry (members of the polity) to posit that democratic processes that encourage and facilitate open deliberation lead to better outcomes. Diana Mutz argues that "deliberative democracy theory" is not falsifiable and that this is one key reason why scholarship in the area falls short of advancing our collective understanding about the nature and role of deliberation in democracies.[11]

Critics argue that because deliberative theory is often conceived as a normative theory and is "value laden" (in other words, scholars assume that deliberation is a good thing), the theory itself is not often exposed to empirical tests. Too little emphasis is placed on studies that, for example, examine the

---

11 Diana C. Mutz, "Is deliberative democracy a falsifiable theory?" *Annual Review of Political Science* 11 (2008): 521–538.

conditions under which deliberative democracy is more or less effective or that test alternative theories in which deliberation might actually lead to suboptimal outcomes. Furthermore, Mutz points out that definitions of deliberative democracy theory are far too broad as well as quite variable from one study to the next, thereby "insulating" the theory from tests that could undermine its soundness.

In her article "Is deliberative democracy a falsifiable theory?" Mutz makes the case that rather than focusing on deliberative democracy as a grand overarching theory, scholars would better serve the advancement of scholarship in the subject by aiming to develop and test middle-range theories relating to particular aspects of deliberative democracy. Middle-range theories are quite common in the social sciences and consist of "intermediate to general theories of social systems which are too remote from particular classes of social behavior, organization and change to account for what is observed."[12] Underscoring many points we make in this chapter as well as more generally in this book, Mutz urges scholars to focus on generating intermediate theories

> that are each important, specifiable, and falsifiable parts of deliberative democratic theory. By replacing vaguely defined entities with more concrete, circumscribed concepts, and by requiring empirically and theoretically grounded hypotheses about specific relationships between those concepts, researchers may come to understand which elements of the deliberative experience are crucial to particular valued outcomes.[13]

Good Theory Leads to Testable Hypotheses

Good theory specifies what we would expect to observe if the theory constitutes an accurate generalization about how the world works. Whether the focus of your study is descriptive or causal, your theories must lend themselves to the generation of specific, testable hypotheses—or implications. In Chapter 1 we noted that a "hypothesis is a specific statement based on our theory that we can test in the real world." Testable hypotheses enable you and other scholars to establish the soundness of your theory, as we discuss later in the chapter.

But the ability to validate a theory is only one (albeit a very important) reason to carefully consider how you formulate it. Recall that our overarching goal is to contribute to an ongoing conversation. A theory constructed in a way that allows for the generation of multiple testable hypotheses, especially hypotheses that stretch beyond the issue your particular study addresses, benefits the broader academic community by providing more avenues to explore and ultimately improve our knowledge on a wide range of topics.

---

12 Robert K. Merton, *Social theory and social structure* (New York: Free Press, 1968), p. 39.
13 Mutz, "Is deliberative democracy a falsifiable theory?" p. 521.

Compare the observable implications of the following theories:

- Incumbents win re-election more often because they tend to have more money.
- Incumbents win re-election more often because they tend to have more resources.

The first theory can generate only a relatively small set of **observable implications**, which includes the amount of money incumbents accumulate compared with challengers. Yet the second theory lends itself to many more observable implications because it theorizes the relationship between incumbency and re-election slightly more broadly, using the concept of resources rather than money. If the latter theory is correct, one would expect to see that incumbency re-election is bolstered by factors including not only financial donations but also their name recognition among constituents, the number of campaign workers they can employ, the goodwill they have generated by doing casework for constituents, and the favorable coverage they tend to win in the news media. Note that a theory with more observable implications tends to be broader, and therefore more useful, than one with fewer observable implications.

INCORPORATING THEORY INTO YOUR STUDY: THE LITERATURE REVIEW

In Chapter 2 we explain that the development of your research question is intimately tied to the prior literature on your topic. In this chapter we have explained what a theory is, the basics of building a sound theory, and why theory is so important in the advancement of knowledge. Now we turn to the practical matter of how to incorporate others' theories into your study, often described as "the **literature review**."

By this point, bear in mind that you have already gained many of the tools necessary to grasp and begin to outline your literature review.[14] You developed your question based on your reading of the literature and on other relevant information. In fact, the development of your question likely grew out of the competing theories that you encountered as you read the literature about your

---

14 Drafting an outline of a literature review at this stage can help you make links between and among literatures, help highlight main points of contestation, clarify various theories that may be in play, and promote the development of hypotheses. Nevertheless, we suggest you defer drafting a full literature review until after you have made substantial progress on your project. As we've discussed, the research process is a fluid one. You may end up feeling boxed in to a certain theoretical logic prematurely, having invested time in writing a literature review.

issue (or your realization that the latest theories were lacking in some important way). Through that process you also undoubtedly began formulating your own views with respect to the debates on your topic.

You will need to decide whether you will test or otherwise explore an existing theory, or whether you intend to propose your own explanation—in other words build your own theory—for the phenomenon you are studying and that you will test as clearly as you can. You will likely decide which of these paths to take as you progress in your reading of the literature and as you continue to ponder and refine your research question in the context of that literature (along with other background material and data related to your question).[15]

Thinking about the Literature Review

How do you justify the theory or theories you are examining or proposing, and how do you discuss theory in your study? In academic journal articles, the discussion of the theories driving a study may appear in a section formally titled "literature review," though this is by no means always the case. Essentially, the purpose of a literature review is to explain the logic driving your study. This logic, as we have emphasized, should be grounded in prior research (theory). The literature review reveals to the reader the main theories that make your research question worthy of study. The review also specifies the key theories that led you to determine that a particular theory was an especially fruitful one to explore further or to test—or, if you are proposing your own theory, the shortcomings of prior theories in an area that prompted you to generate a new theory or to modify a prior one. The literature review contains the theoretical justification of any hypotheses you will test and how you will test them, that is, which variables you consider to be important and why, and how you define your central concepts. Finally, theory informs your interpretation of your findings.[16]

Although the section of a research paper that discusses theory is not infrequently called a literature review, the terminology sometimes leads students astray because it suggests that the goal of this portion of the paper is to list

15 The "back and forth" we describe here underscores a fundamental point about the research process, and that is its inherently iterative nature. Your research question needs to be refined as we explain in Chapter 2, and yet in truth this is a "working question," which means you should remain open to developing it further as you progress through your project. Similarly, while the theory you propose to examine or test must also be as refined as possible and contain the elements we outline above, consider it, too, your "working theory"—subject to tweaking as you grow more knowledgeable about your topic.

16 It is worthwhile to note that in your study, as in all scholarly research, literature citation is not confined to one section of a journal article, paper, or book. You will cite scholarly literature substantiating your statements and the decisions you have made in your study as you discuss your question and its justification, as you present and justify your theory, in the description of your research design, in the discussion of your results, and in your conclusion.

every author, study, and finding a student has read that is remotely related to his or her research question. The point of the literature review section is not to catalog all you have read and learned in the process of developing your study (although it may feel painful to omit the many articles and other material that one has pored over!). Thinking about this part of your paper as the *theory section* may prove a better way to maintain your focus on its purpose.

Three Goals of the Literature Review

The goals of the literature review are three-fold. First, the review must include an expanded discussion of the research question that you presented at the beginning of your paper by systematically and selectively discussing the key problems, theories, and data that justify the salience, importance, and the particular formulation of your research question.

The second goal of the literature review is to delineate the key discussions, debates (or lack thereof), and data in the literature that relate specifically to your question and to the theory you intend to examine or test. Where does your own theory, if you are proposing one, emerge from? Writing this portion of the theory section should follow a tight, logical progression that moves from the more general "big picture" concepts and theories that establish the wider significance of your study to the debates or issues that lead you to the construction of your own theory. Of course, it is not enough to describe your own theory. Explicitly state (or succinctly restate) what, in your view and the view of other scholars, are the most plausible alternative or rival theories that you will examine alongside your own. To grapple with the challenge of inference, we must give full attention to these rival theories.

The third goal of the literature review is the narrowest in scope. Here you present your own working answer to the research question you posed, or the theory you will test. Researchers test theories by formulating (typically multiple) hypotheses. Hypotheses are explicit statements that express what we would expect to find if our theory is correct. It can be helpful to word these as "if–then" or "when–then" statements. What are some hypotheses that one could formulate to test a theory that gender imbalances in electoral office can be explained by the fact that men have better and/or more information than women regarding the process of attaining political office? One might hypothesize that "Women's estimation of the costs of running a political campaign are significantly less accurate than men's." Another hypothesis might be that "When men and women are exposed to the same information about the process of attaining elective office in our survey experiment, [then] we expect to find no gender differences in terms of interest in pursuing political office."

Keep in mind that this final component of the theory section is intimately linked to and sets the stage for the next critical section of your paper in which you describe your data and methods. You explain the choices you made in terms of defining the concepts you are employing (if you have not done so earlier). You will also note the factors that you have decided to incorporate in your analysis. Perhaps your theory posits that individuals are less likely to vote in state-level elections when state officials have been accused of misconduct or implicated in a major scandal in the previous year. You may decide that factors you will have to take into account in your analysis include (1) whether the pool of potential voters includes all voting-age citizens or just those who are eligible to vote; (2) what constitutes a "major scandal"; and (3) other factors that may explain turnout differences across states (such as differences in election laws). These should be factors that, in your reading of the literature and analysis of other material, may be influencing the outcome your research question is trying to answer. You will also briefly explain any other potentially significant factors that scholars have suggested may be related to your question, but that you have concluded are tangential to your particular question and can thus be omitted from consideration as you test your theory.

Writing the Literature Review

Many students consider the literature review a highly mysterious, confusing, and onerous exercise. We don't dispute the fact that students would do well to budget a healthy chunk of time to write a literature review. This advice is not based on our sense that it is an especially difficult task. Nevertheless, it is one that calls for the thoughtful integration of all of the central elements of your project. In this way, putting together your literature review can be seen as a puzzle; each piece should tightly interlock. The trick to the literature review is that there are multiple ways to "solve" the puzzle. In short, you will need to include, discuss, and support or justify with the literature:

- The broader problem or puzzle motivating your inquiry.
- The broader implications or importance of the problem or puzzle driving your inquiry.
- Your research question.
- Its broader implications or importance.
- The theories, concepts, empirical evidence, and hypotheses your study draws upon.
- Your own theory.
- Any rival theories that may also explain the phenomenon you are studying.
- Your own hypotheses.
- The particular variables that you intend to include or exclude in your study.

Perhaps part of the mystery of the literature review stems from the fact that there is no formula for writing one. As you read through political science journal articles, you will undoubtedly detect patterns in terms of how authors use the literature in their papers, but they will all differ slightly nonetheless. Some authors clearly designate a section in their papers that announce "literature review," whereas others discuss the relationship between the literature and their particular study under a descriptive subheading. Other scholars don't include a singular literature review section at all. Instead, the appropriate theories and findings necessary to support the aims and claims of the paper are cited throughout the work.

While there is a variety of ways of organizing the literature review, in all cases writing the review requires that you see yourself as a leader communicating with an audience to whom you must provide a clear and thorough outline of your study. Remember that the literature review has nothing to do with summarizing the findings of a stack of journal articles and books. It is not a dumping ground for everything you've ever read with respect to your study.

A related misconception among students is the idea that the literature is in the driver's seat. We often see this confusion manifest itself when students begin each paragraph of their literature review by referring to a new author, rather than a new idea or key set of findings. In contrast, we want to emphasize that while the literature should be cited to support you as you build your theory; it should not be the focal point of the review. One way to consider the role that the literature should play is to write the review in a way that minimizes how frequently you make a research study the subject of your sentence. For example, instead of writing, "A research study by Campbell *et al.* (1960) showed that party identification is a strong predictor of vote choice," you can simply write, "Party identification is a strong predictor of vote choice (Campbell *et al.* 1960)." The difference may seem subtle, but the act of making the empirical finding or theoretical insight the focal point of the sentence, rather than the author, will help you stay true to the central goal of this section—theory building.

While the literature review contains multiple components, its fundamental purpose is to guide the reader through the author's logic in designing her study. The literature review, then, serves as a vital roadmap for your audience; it is a tightly focused discussion and justification of your research design.

The literature review is sometimes described as taking the shape of a funnel, with the broadest section at the top. Begin by discussing the problem, puzzle, or debate you intend to weigh in on, citing central scholarly works that help you establish the foundation for the study. You may then turn to discussing the broader implications of the problem, puzzle, or debate, citing select literature as appropriate to bolster your arguments. These two elements of the review might comprise a page or so. Bear in mind that your analysis of the literature to this point must be configured so that by the time you reveal your particular research question it will appear to have emerged quite logically from your earlier analysis of the literature on your topic.

Box 3.2: The Increasing Prevalence of Co-authorship in Political Science

You have probably become accustomed to writing papers on your own, but increasingly political scientists are conducting their research collaboratively. In 2006, the American Political Science Association (APSA) released a report showing that 40 percent of the articles published in the discipline's top journals included more than one author; this is four times the amount of co-authorship present in those same journals in the 1950s and 1960s.[a] According to the report, co-authoring is more common when the subject is American politics, but even about one-third of studies in comparative politics and international relations were co-authored.

Co-authorship has a variety of benefits for scholars. The exchange of ideas among a group often leads to new insights that a single scholar would not have discovered on his own. Furthermore, different scholars often have unique areas of expertise that complement each other. For example, a study about how the news media cover Congress might benefit from a collaboration including an expert on Congress and an expert on political communication. A comparative study analyzing ethnic conflict in Africa and Latin America might benefit from having not only an expert on ethnic conflict, but also experts on Africa and Latin America. And, increasingly, scholars from entirely different disciplines are forming research teams. Such collaborations might help bring insights from psychology or economics to a study of voting behavior.

One issue raised by the APSA report is how to accurately acknowledge the contributions of each co-author in the final study. In the field of economics, the norm is for co-authors to always be listed alphabetically, regardless of how much (or little) they contributed to a study. In psychology, on the other hand, authors are typically listed in order of how much they contributed to the research. These norms are important because the order in which authors are listed appears to influence the amount of success scholars have during their careers. In fact, even though economists are aware of the norm regarding the alphabetical listing of co-authors, economists whose last names come earlier in the alphabet are still more likely to hold tenured positions at highly ranked schools.[b]

a. Report of APSA Working Group on Collaboration, August 9, 2006, American Political Science Association.
b. Liran Einav and Leeat Yariv, "What's in a surname? The effects of surname initials on academic success," *Journal of Economic Perspectives* 20 (2006): 175–187.

Now that you have shown the reader the "big picture," you should articulate your specific research question. In this section you should present theories and findings of studies that don't simply *relate* to your question but that are directly *relevant* to your study. In other words, every work you cite in this section must plainly signal to the reader precisely how it influenced (1) the framing of your research question; (2) the definition of important concepts; (3) the key

Box 3.3: What is Plagiarism?

As noted throughout this chapter, academic knowledge builds on existing scholarship. But it is important to recognize the distinction between building on existing studies and plagiarizing from them. Unfortunately, the pressure to "publish or perish" in academia occasionally drives some scholars to do just that. The act of plagiarism is serious, as it involves the theft of another's intellectual work. Virtually every college and university has a multitude of resources, often housed on the library's website, to help you recognize the difference between what is acceptable and what is not. There are even online tutorials and self-tests you can use to determine whether you need more help.

Another important way to avoid plagiarism is to take scrupulous notes as you read the literature. Never copy and paste anything from someone else's work into your own working document. If you use this method to take notes, copy and paste into an entirely separate document that is reserved specifically for the collection of potentially helpful information from other texts. Immediately add the complete source and citation information.

In a footnote in an essay on plagiarism, law professor Stuart Green cites a contemporary rabbi, Joseph Telushkin:

'If a person presents as her own an intelligent observation that she learned from another, then it would seem that she did so only to impress everyone with how "bright" she is. But if she cites the source from whom she learned this information, then it would seem that her motive was to deepen everyone's understanding. And a world in which people share information and insights to advance understanding, and not just to advance themselves, is one well on its way to redemption.[a]

a. http://chronicle.com, Special Report 51(17), p. A9.

variables you have chosen to focus on;[17] and (4) your methodology more generally speaking, including the theories from which you derived your hypotheses, the hypotheses themselves, etc. Note that there are many ways to arrange this section. The general rule is to move from the broad to the most specific. In short, your goal is to clearly account for how and why the prior literature led you to *ask* the question the way you did and to *study* it the way you did.

17 The discussion should include those factors, or variables, that you believe, based on the literature and logic, might influence your dependent variable, or an outcome. If there are factors that appear in the literature but you have chosen not to include them in your analysis, you should justify this, possibly in a footnote. You should also review which factors you believe you expect will have more or less of an effect on what you are trying to explain. Finally, with respect to a discussion of variables, you should include a brief treatment of control variables, or common factors that must be taken into account (due to their inherent relevance or prevalence in the literature, like demographic information or partisan affiliation), but are not the factors of most interest to you.

TWO EXAMPLES OF THEORY BUILDING

In this section, we discuss how one might approach the development of a theory around two of the key examples in this text—the role of racial prejudice in voting for Barack Obama and whether women's groups are governed more democratically than other organizations.

Racial Prejudice and Voting for Obama

Following the 2008 presidential election, there was much debate about whether some whites chose not to vote for Obama solely because of his race. As is typically the case, scholars approaching this question had a significant body of research they could draw from in developing their own theories related to the 2008 election. A search for "racial prejudice and vote choice" in Google Scholar or JStor quickly returns an existing body of research on the topic, including studies with titles like "When white voters evaluate black candidates" and "Prejudice and politics." By downloading and reading a handful of these studies, a researcher would quickly be introduced to most of the relevant literature on the topic; after all, these scholars had to build on (and cite) the research that came before them.

A scan of the existing research on this topic would reveal that most studies have found that some whites fail to support minority candidates who they may have otherwise voted for. Of course, this collection of findings on their own do not constitute a theory; indeed, not only is it important for a theory to generate an expectation about whether the independent variable (the race of the candidate) affects the dependent variable (white support for the candidate), but it is also crucial for a theory to describe why this relationship exists. Schaffner's study of white support for Obama summarizes the potential causal mechanisms at play:

> Overt racism may depress support for African American candidates if some portion of white voters refuse to support a black candidate based on skin color alone. However, white opposition to African American candidates may also arise from the stereotypes that are associated with race. For example, whites perceive black candidates as less competent and more liberal than their white counterparts (Sigelman et al. 1995; McDermott 1998; Citrin et al. 1990). Some white voters may be willing to vote for an African American candidate in theory, but their propensity to attribute negative stereotypes to that candidate on the basis of his or her race makes it unlikely that the candidate will win their votes in reality (Sears et al. 1997).[18]

18 Brian F. Schaffner, "Racial salience and the Obama vote," *Political Psychology* 32 (2011): 963–988.

Thus, there are several reasons why we might expect whites to be less likely to support minority candidates.

Schaffner's particular study on white support for Obama then builds on this existing theory by suggesting that not all prejudiced whites would necessarily be led to vote against Obama in 2008. Schaffner incorporates the research on priming into his theory. Priming is a concept that refers to the ability of campaigns and events to make some considerations more or less important to an individual's vote decision. Obama's race is one consideration that could be primed in the minds of some voters but not in the minds of others. Schaffner notes, "Thus, in 2008, a white voter may have expressed racially conservative attitudes, but if that voter gave little weight to Obama's race when determining who to vote for, those conservative racial views would be less likely to lead the voter away from supporting Obama."[19] On the other hand, if the same racially conservative voter had been primed to think about race when considering their vote choice, that would have made him less likely to support Obama. This is Schaffner's contribution to the existing theory on racial prejudice and white support for minority candidates. The existing theory treated all prejudiced voters as equally likely to oppose a minority candidate, but Schaffner notes that prejudiced voters who are primed to think about the candidate's race will be much less likely to support the minority candidate.

Schaffner's theory ultimately leads to the hypothesis that whites will be least likely to support minority candidates when they have high levels or racial prejudice *and* they are placing more weight on the race of the candidates. His study finds support for this hypothesis, and, by extension, his theory. Ultimately, this example illustrates the progress that can be made when scholars combine previously unrelated concepts—in this case priming—to add nuance to existing theory.

Are Women's Organizations More Democratic?

Political scientists have generally paid little attention to how interest groups govern themselves. Yet, the research that has been conducted on this topic reveals that there is much variance in the extent to which groups allow their members to influence the decisions they make (such as which policies or candidates to support). One question of interest to scholars of women and politics is whether women govern the groups that represent them differently than mixed-gender groups are governed.

An article by Barakso asks, "Is there a 'woman's way' of governing?"[20] Unlike the previous example, there was essentially no existing research on how women's interest groups govern themselves before Barakso's study. However, this did not preclude her from building a theory about how she expected

19 Schaffner, "Racial salience and the Obama vote," p. 966.
20 Maryann Barakso, "Is there a 'woman's way' of governing? Assessing the organizational structures of women's membership associations," *Politics & Gender* 3 (2007): 201–227.

Box 3.4: How Political Science Draws from (and Contributes to) Research in Other Disciplines

When a political science researcher embarks on a research study, it is likely the case that she will first turn to other political science research relevant to the research question being posed. But it is important to remember that many of the social science disciplines focus on phenomena that are either directly or indirectly related to politics. Scholars have recently mapped just how interconnected political science research is with other social science disciplines by examining how frequently journal articles in each discipline cite articles for another discipline.

Figure 3.1 maps the social sciences according to these criteria. The larger disciplines are those that have more journals and the thicker the arrow between two disciplines, the more those disciplines cite work from the other. Political science is located in the mid-center of the map. Note that political scientists appear to be most connected first to economics and then to sociology. Economics is a discipline that attracts significant attention from most of the other disciplines, in part because it is one of the most developed of the social sciences. Sociology and political science have often been relatively closely linked as well, in part because both disciplines involve understanding how humans cooperate and organize to effect change in society. The next discipline that political science draws from is psychology. Psychology is an increasingly relevant field for political scientists who study how individuals think about politics and make political decisions, as they draw from more general psychological research on attitude formation and decision-making.

Overall, the figure demonstrates that scholars in each discipline do not conduct their research in isolation from other fields. Rather, the best research often makes abundant use of theories and findings from economics, sociology, psychology, and other social sciences.

women's organizations would be governed. Barakso notes in her theoretical section that

> a substantial literature in a variety of fields, including psychology, business administration, sociology, and political science, finds that women are more likely than men to encourage cooperative behavior, are more concerned with achieving consensus, and are more likely to seek out others' opinions than men.[21]

The research that Barakso incorporates includes studies showing that female corporate managers are more likely to delegate authority to others and that female committee chairs take a more integrative approach to managing proceedings.

21 Barakso, "Is there a 'woman's way' of governing?" p. 203.

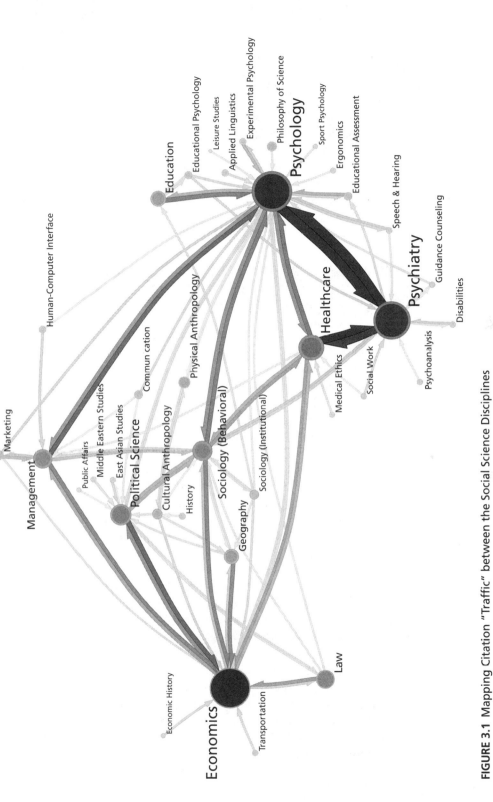

FIGURE 3.1 Mapping Citation "Traffic" between the Social Science Disciplines

Source: Martin Rosvall and Carl T. Bergstrom, "Maps of random walks cn complex networks reveal community structure," *Proceedings of the National Academy of Sciences* 105(4) (2008): 1118–1123.

Ultimately, Barakso notes that the abundance of research from a variety of disciplines points to a consistent expectation—because women tend to favor more consensus-oriented approaches to decision making, women's organizations should be more democratic than other groups. Despite a paucity of literature on the precise question that Barakso was asking, she was able to consult literatures from a variety of disciplines to formulate a clear hypothesis. Notably, Barakso did not find support for her expectation—women's organizations were no more likely to be structured democratically than other groups. This finding is difficult to reconcile with the existing research Barakso drew from, but that merely creates another puzzle for future scholars to address.

TAKING ALTERNATIVE THEORIES SERIOUSLY: WHAT DO YOU DO WHEN YOUR THEORIES AND HYPOTHESES DON'T MATCH YOUR FINDINGS?

Despite your efforts to draw carefully from theories developed in the scholarly literature and to develop well-supported hypotheses based on prior research, in the end, your findings may contradict your expectations in one or more ways. Unexpected results—particularly those in the "wrong" direction—can be particularly unsettling to beginning researchers harboring strong personal feelings about or political commitments to their topic.

Unexpected results should cause the researcher, first, to re-examine his assumptions and his model, as well as prompting a close look at the data that were employed in the analysis to check for coding or other errors. Once the scholar has ruled out such problems, however, it is extremely important that the study is not abandoned simply because its results do not "fit" with the current scholarly conversation on the topic or because they demonstrate "null" findings.

Unexpected results that can't be readily explained by the above suggest several possibilities. One is that the researcher failed to draw widely enough on extant theory to allow him to consider a range of alternatives to his favored theory. He may also have failed to use prior literature to derive well-supported hypotheses. As a result, the researcher's paradoxical results may reflect omitted information. A key means by which we reduce the risk of omitting relevant information (or key variables) is by actively considering and testing alternative theories and explanations (see the section above, "Incorporating Theory into Your Study"). Remember: fundamentally, empirical political scientists aim to (carefully) reduce information to make sense of a vast world. We must choose which information to include in our studies and what information to exclude in our efforts to be able to explain, as parsimoniously as possible, how, why, when, where, and under what conditions political phenomena occur. Reducing information is both absolutely necessary and yet inherently risky because we may inadvertently be omitting relevant information from our analysis, thus tainting our findings.

For example, in Chapter 2, we suggested that one might evaluate the extent to which gender disparities in legislative bodies make a substantive policy difference by comparing policy outcomes in legislatures with more women with those with fewer women. A researcher taking on a question about "whether women matter" must consider the possibility that she may find little difference in the kinds of policies adopted by legislatures with more women as compared with those with fewer—even if she strongly suspects that this is not the case based on prior literature, public opinion surveys, and other sources.

But what if the researcher ultimately finds no relationship between the number of women in state legislature and policy outcomes?[22] Would such results suggest that women's under-representation in legislative bodies does not matter, at least insofar as policy is concerned? In her discussion of her results, the researcher should certainly weigh this possibility, alongside others. Yet, if her theoretical framework and data analysis are sound, the scholar may argue that, although her findings do not appear to support the theory that women's equal representation is problematic, in part, because female legislators prefer different policies than men, the results don't necessarily undermine the notion that the under-representation of women legislators affects policymaking.

Faced with a scenario like this, the author could discuss why she thinks her findings contradict extant literature and her expectations; whether and how her methodology may have skewed her results; and the various reasons why women might not behave differently than men in the legislative settings studied despite theory that suggests they should. One reason the study may not have found an effect is that men and women do in fact hold very similar policy preferences in a number of areas. Another possibility is that women, even in the most gender-balanced legislatures, feel some conscious or subconscious pressure to conform to male colleagues' policy preferences, say, in order to reach higher-status positions. The author's methodology may not have allowed her to account for this problem. Yet another key alternative explanation to consider is that both men and women face the same fundamental electoral pressure—to remain in office, legislators must carefully weigh the preferences of their particular constituencies. Numerous other, far more nuanced explanations for the paradoxical results could be considered, but the point we are trying to make here is that unexpected results, or those that upend the conventional wisdom on a subject, can be highly illuminating and, when carefully parsed, make a valuable contribution to the literature.

22 Note that this is a purely hypothetical example: substantial evidence suggests women's presence in legislatures does in fact influence policy outcomes.

SUMMING UP: THEORY AND INFERENCE

Serious attention to theory building is essential for making strong causal inferences. Existing theories help us consider our expectations and hypotheses to maximize the chance that we will be able to contribute to the body of knowledge in a particular area. Additionally, theory is essential for informing the choices we will ultimately make when it comes to designing our study. Theory helps us to identify not just the variables we are most interested in studying, but also the variables that we should be sure to pay attention to in order to make strong inferences. Theory also helps us to elucidate the causal mechanisms underlying the results our study ultimately produces. Finally, theory provides us with a way of demonstrating how our research can contribute to more general knowledge about how the political world operates. Theory is therefore a fundamental building block, perhaps *the* fundamental building block, for political science research.

KEY TERMS

concepts   62

falsifiability   65

generalizations   57

hypotheses   57

literature review   67

observable implications   67

theory   56

A Menu of Approaches

CONTENTS

The Challenge of Descriptive Inference

In Chapter 1, we introduced the idea of descriptive inference. We noted that inference is "the process of using the facts we know to learn about facts we do not know," and we divided inferences into two types: descriptive and causal.[1] As the term suggests, in making descriptive inferences, our goal is to describe. This might mean determining what something is, establishing how prevalent or common a phenomenon is, or resolving if it is increasing or decreasing over time. For example, we might want to know: What are the voter turnout rates across different U.S. states? What percent of Afghanis supported the NATO-led military intervention in their country in 2001? Is corruption in African countries increasing or decreasing? Descriptive inference can be contrasted with causal inference, which goes a step further and asks *why* something occurs. Why is voter turnout higher in Midwestern states than in Southern states? Why did some Afghanis support the NATO-led intervention and others did not? Why is corruption increasing in some countries and decreasing in others? As we noted, however, we cannot make causal inferences until we are confident in our descriptive inferences. For example, it would not make much sense to ask why corruption is increasing in Africa, if it is actually stable or even decreasing. As we can see, making descriptive inferences is an important research goal in its own right, and it is also an essential first step to making causal inferences. In this chapter, therefore, we will focus on description.

---

1 Gary King, Robert O. Keohane, and Sidney Verba, *Designing social inquiry: Scientific inference in qualitative research* (Princeton: Princeton University Press, 1994), p. 46.

In Chapter 1 we introduced three broad challenges to making descriptive inferences: (1) conceptualization, (2) measurement, or operationalization, and (3) case selection, or sampling. In this chapter we pick up these threads and explore these themes in greater detail. The chapter first explores the challenges to defining the concepts that we are interested in measuring and studying. Before moving directly into a discussion on measurement, the chapter explores how the difficulties that we face vary based on the type of data that we are studying. For example, a comparative study of countries produces very different challenges and opportunities than a survey of the U.S. public. Then we explore the challenges of measurement and sampling using different types of data. Having examined the major challenges, the chapter turns towards some of the basic, practical tools available to students and researchers to draw descriptive inferences. These range from basic bar charts and measures of central tendency, used with quantitative data, to narratives and quotes, used with qualitative data.

CONCEPTUALIZATION

The first step in drawing a valid inference is to be clear about just what it is we are making inferences about. Defining our variables of interest is known as **conceptualization**. Perhaps not surprisingly, most of the variables that we are concerned with in political science are difficult to define. Consider for example the difficult task of defining democracy, human rights, globalization, corruption, and even war. We use these terms commonly in political science courses, and yet they mean very different things to different people. Many other variables are not just difficult, but controversial to define. Virtually any hot topic in U.S. politics involves a conflict over definition. Consider for example defining gun rights, religious freedom, or free speech. Individuals on one side of these issues typically favor very broad definitions while their opponents prefer narrow conceptualizations.

Let's explore a concrete example: in the last few decades scholars have had an interest in trying to measure corruption. Understandably, people want to know just how pervasive corruption is in a given country, how that country compares with other countries, and whether the problem is increasing or decreasing over time. These are all great questions, but, before being able to answer them, scholars first have to define what is meant by "corruption." The non-governmental organization Transparency International, one of the pioneers in the study of corruption, uses the simple definition of "the abuse of entrusted authority for private gain."[2] On the one hand, this definition seems perfect because it is straightforward and because it appears to capture what most of us have in our head when we hear the term "corruption." However, if

2 Transparency International, "The Corruption Perceptions Index" (Berlin: Transparency International, 2010).

we dig a little deeper, we can identify several problems with this definition. For example, who defines abuse? Is it defined by the specific laws of a country, by the culture of a country, or are there conceptions of abuse that can be applied universally across legal systems and across different cultural groups? Likewise, who defines authority? Should corruption be limited to public officials or should abuses of "authority" in a business, a non-profit organization, or even in a family be calculated into a country's measure of corruption? What is private gain? Does private gain require a monetary exchange? If an elected official abuses her office for the benefit of her family, is that private gain? What if she commits abuses to benefit her friends or her political party?

In short, corruption *could* be defined as a universal concept or as something very specific to country and culture. It could be defined very narrowly, as specific behaviors that involve public officials and entail a monetary benefit, or it could be defined very broadly, as any abuses of authority for a wide variety of benefits. Our point is that the term "corruption," a term that students of politics use extensively in daily life, is much more complicated than it first appears.

Here is one of the key points in research where we can clearly see the non-linearity of the process. Ask yourself which definition will be easier to operationalize, or to measure: (1) a broad concept that varies based on the cultural context and involves a wide array of behaviors and actors or (2) a narrow set of specific behaviors involving specific actors that can be observed in any cultural context? From a measurement perspective, the latter is clearly preferable. With this in mind, when trying to arrive at a definition of their concept of study, many scholars have to already be thinking ahead to what they will actually be able to measure in the real world.

This is a major challenge for many students engaging in empirical research for the first time. In much university course work, students are asked to embrace complexity and nuance rather than to simplify and reduce. In fact, if your class had a group activity and tried to define corruption, we are fairly confident that you would arrive at a very broad definition rather than a narrow one. Making our definition of a concept dependent on our measurements can at times be frustrating. Consider for example the idea of "democracy." If democracy is defined literally as "rule by the people," then few countries would actually qualify as democracies. As a result, most political scientists have defined "democracy" as a form of representative democracy involving free and fair elections. Even this narrowing of the concept begs the question: What is meant by free and fair? Narrow definitions of free and fair elections would likely have to tolerate some abuses of civil liberties, press restrictions, abuses of power, nepotism, and clientelism, all of which do not necessarily match with the idea of "democracy" that we have in our heads. Some scholars attempt to recognize this tension by using the term **operational definition**, meaning a definition that can be measured, or operationalized.[3]

3 Operationalization is the process of moving from a theoretical concept to a measurable variable.

Another approach is to move up and down what Giovanni Sartori referred to as a "ladder of generality."[4] Rather than study "democracy," we could move up the ladder of generality and study "regimes," or we could move down the ladder of generality and study a subtype of democracy, such as "parliamentary democracy."[5] In like fashion, we could study a type of corruption, such as "petty corruption," or relatively small bribes paid to public officials to perform or fail to perform their duties. Once we have arrived at an operational definition, we are now ready to think more specifically about measurement. The first step in this process is considering the enormous amount of variation in the type of measurements that we could develop.

DIFFERENT TYPES OF DATA

It stands to reason that conceptualization and measurement challenges will vary considerably based on the type of information that we are interested in. A natural scientist interested in arsenic contamination in water is going to use a very different set of tools and face a very different set of challenges than a political scientist interested in corruption, the effect of negative campaign advertising, or governing common pool resources. Data can be divided into a number of different categories based on the answers to the following questions:

- What is the unit of analysis?
- What is the level of analysis?
- Do the data cover the entire population or are they based on a sample drawn from a larger population?
- Are the data cross-sectional or longitudinal?
- Are the data qualitative or quantitative?

These terms might not have much meaning to you yet, but we will explore each in turn. The **unit of analysis** is simply what is being studied or compared; in political science research, the units of analysis are typically political actors, political acts, or geographic areas. For example, one might study citizens, households, countries, U.S. states, U.S. or foreign cities, legislation introduced in a legislative body, roll call votes of legislators, laws, newspaper articles, court decisions, or words used in speeches of prominent politicians, to name just a few. Different units of analysis present different challenges. For example, even if a researcher compares all the countries in the world, he or she would still have a limited number of observations—just under 200 depending

---

4 Giovanni Sartori, "Concept misformation in comparative politics," *American Political Science Review* 64 (1970): 1033–1053.
5 David Collier and Steven Levitsky, "Democracy with adjectives," *World Politics* 49 (1997): 430–451.

on how one defines a country. (Yes, just about everything in political science confronts a definitional problem.)[6] Survey data from a survey of U.S. households, on the other hand, often entail far more observations (typically over 1,000 households) but confronts challenges in ensuring that those households studied are representative of the larger U.S. population.

Comparing a study of countries and a study of households illustrates two more distinctions in the types of data political scientists study. The first of these is the level of analysis. The **level of analysis** refers to the scale of the data, or whether or not they have been aggregated. For example a country is made up of millions of households and households are made up of several individuals. At the micro-level, an individual earns an income. At a slightly higher level of analysis, all the individual incomes in a household can be added to yield the household income. Scaling up yet another level, household income can be combined from throughout a country (along with the income from firms and a few other sources) to derive the Gross National Income.

Moving from the micro-level (e.g. individual) to the macro-level (e.g. country) is known as **aggregation**, and moving in the opposition direction is known as **disaggregation**. Often times we are more interested in aggregated data, particularly for making descriptive inferences. For example, if we conduct a survey of 1,000 Americans about whom they plan to vote for in an upcoming presidential election, it doesn't really tell us much to know that respondent number 342 favors the Republican candidate. Instead, we would rather "aggregate" all the individuals' responses to learn that 51 percent of surveyed Americans favor the Republican candidate. As we will see below, however, aggregated data generate their own challenges.

There is another important difference in a study of countries and a study of households. In a study of countries, it is possible (although often difficult) to collect data for all countries. In a study of households, doing so is extremely rare. Once every ten years the U.S. Census Bureau does attempt to conduct a **census**, or a survey of all U.S. households; however, political scientists do not have this luxury. Instead, political scientists interested in public opinion typically study a **sample**, or subset, of the larger **population**, or universe of subjects. How that sample is selected is an essential challenge to making descriptive inference. If inference is using the facts we know to generalize about the facts that we do not know, then it is essential that our sample be representative of the population that we wish to generalize about.

Data can vary in other ways as well. While some data capture a snapshot at one point in time, what we call **cross-sectional data**, other data include

---

6 Who defines a state? If we use membership in the United Nations as our definition of a state, then there are 193 member nations and two observer states. If we use external recognition as our criteria but not consensual recognition, then non-member states such as Kosovo and Northern Cyprus could be considered states. If statehood is determined irrespective of external recognition, then Somaliland could be considered a state.

changes over time, known as **longitudinal** or **time series data**. For example, a cross-sectional study might measure the level of corruption across all countries for a given year and then compare across countries. A longitudinal study, however, might compare levels of corruption in one country over time. A third approach, called **panel data**, merges these two types of data and compares all countries over time. Obviously, panel data requires collecting a great deal of data, but several ambitious studies have used the approach to answer a variety of research questions.[7] Survey data can also be cross-sectional or longitudinal. Survey firms often include the same question wording in multiple iterations of a survey, allowing us to observe, for example, presidential approval ratings over time. In some special cases, researchers are actually able to survey the same individuals over time. This type of panel study would allow researchers to not just describe the movements of a president's aggregate approval rating over time, but explain why an individual's evaluation of the president improves or worsens over time.

Many of the examples that have been given thus far have been examples of **quantitative** data, or data that can be given a numerical value. However, an enormous amount of data generated in political science are **qualitative**, or non-numerical. For example, given the difficulties in measuring an often illegal act such as corruption, many researchers have favored a more qualitative approach. For example, researchers studying police corruption might conduct in-depth interviews with high- and low-level police officers, journalists, and heads of civil society organizations involved in policing issues. These interviews typically produce reams of interview transcripts that are often not quantified.

In short, there is a great deal of variation in the types of data used by scholars. As summed up in Table 4.1, data vary based on (1) the unit of analysis—ranging from survey respondents to bills introduced in the legislature to countries, (2) the level of analysis—including micro-, meta-, and macro-level data, (3) whether the data covers an entire population or a sample of that population, (4) whether the data entail multiple observations at one point in time, one observation at several points in time, or multiple observations over multiple time periods, and (5) whether or not the data are qualitative or quantitative.

Consider for a moment all the different combinations of these five categories that exist in the political world. For example, a cross-sectional study of the population of countries, using aggregated quantitative data, would be different from a longitudinal study of a sample of countries using aggregated quantitative data. This would, in turn, be distinct from a panel study of a

---

7 See for example Michael Alvarez, José Antonio Cheibub, Fernando Limongi, *et al.*, "Classifying political regimes," *Studies in Comparative International Development* 31 (1996): 3–36; and José Antonio Cheibub, Jennifer Gandhi, and James Raymond Vreeland, "Democracy and dictatorship revisited," *Public Choice* 143 (2010): 67–101.

TABLE 4.1 Different Types of Data

Type of data	Examples
Unit of analysis	Individuals, households, countries, U.S. states, U.S. or foreign cities, roll call votes of legislators, laws, newspaper articles, etc. . . .
Level of analysis	Micro-, meta-, macro-
Temporality	Cross-sectional, longitudinal, panel
Coverage	Representative sample, non-representative sample, population
Category	Quantitative, qualitative

sample of households using micro-level quantitative data and yet even more different than a cross-sectional study of political elites using micro-level qualitative data. A given combination of these elements is not necessarily preferable to another; however, each combination does produce its own unique set of opportunities and challenges for measurement and research.

OPERATIONALIZATION AND MEASUREMENT ERROR

Returning to our topic of "corruption," let's explore some of the measurements that have been developed, what operational definitions they use, how they vary along the above-mentioned categories, and what measurement challenges they confront. Despite many challenges, corruption researchers have developed several methods to measure slightly different conceptualizations and/or aspects of corruption.

One popular measure used is Transparency International's Global Corruption Barometer, which simply asks citizens if they have had to pay a bribe in their interactions with government officials, such as police officers or personnel from the water or electrical utility company. This certainly seems like a reasonable means to measure corruption, but what "concept" does such an operationalization actually measure? First, such a survey question would only measure "bribery." Second, it is focused only on public officials. And third, it measures what scholars refer to as petty corruption rather than grand corruption. For example, it would not capture an organized crime leader buying off a high-level police official, a construction contractor bribing an administrator for a contract, or a firm bribing a member of parliament for beneficial legislation. The Barometer can therefore be considered a measurement of a subcategory of corruption further down Sartori's ladder of generality, what is sometimes referred to as "administrative corruption," or "petty corruption."

What type of data is a source like the Global Corruption Barometer?

- The unit of analysis is the individual being surveyed.
- As we are dealing with individuals, the level of analysis is micro-; however, if we wanted to know what percentage of respondents in a given country had paid a bribe, then the data could be aggregated to the macro-level.
- If the survey is only conducted one time, then it would be considered cross-sectional; however, because this survey has been conducted almost every year since 2003, it can also be analyzed as longitudinal data.
- The data are based on a sample of a larger population of interest.
- Because respondents are asked to answer "yes" or "no" to questions about bribery, the data can be quantified.

Knowing this basic information about our data allows us to better assess what types of challenges we are likely to face in making descriptive inferences. Let's first consider measurement error. Imagine that our survey asks respondents: "In the last twelve months, have you or anyone living in your household paid a bribe in any form to a government official?" This is a variation of what appears in the Global Corruption Barometer. What potential measurement errors might result from such a survey question?

First, this question is likely to engender **social desirability bias**—that is, the tendency of survey respondents to give a socially desirable response rather than an honest one when asked sensitive questions. In this example, some people might not be comfortable admitting to having paid a bribe, so the survey runs the risk of under-reporting the true amount of bribe payments occurring in a society—introducing **systematic measurement error**, or **bias**. The error is *systematic* because it will consistently underestimate the amount of bribe payments. Scholars often refer to systematic errors as producing **validity** concerns, as the bias might invalidate the measure. Social desirability bias can also produce over-reporting of some behaviors. For example, when asked in surveys if they voted in a presidential election, a large percentage of non-voters will report that they actually voted.[8] This is clearly evidenced by comparing survey data from the National Election Survey with actual voter turnout, the former of which shows considerably higher turnout than the latter.

As you can probably imagine, social desirability bias creates an obstacle to measuring any number of subjects, and, therefore, pollsters have to carefully consider the way questions are worded. In the case of bribery, a researcher might instead ask: "In the last twelve months, has a public official *solicited* a bribe from you?" In this case, a survey respondent answering in the affirmative would be admitting no wrong-doing, reducing the risk of bias.

Beyond social desirability bias, there are other ways that systematic error can find its way into survey data. Suppose you were interested in determining

---

8 Allyson L. Holbrook and Jon A. Krosnick, "Measuring voter turnout by using the randomized response technique: Evidence calling into question the method's validity," *Public Opinion Quarterly* 74 (2010): 328–343.

how a corruption scandal had impacted a political office holder's approval rating, you would not want to ask, "Following the recent corruption scandal, do you approve or disapprove of the way political officer holder X is handling his job?" By priming the respondents to think of the corruption scandal, this question wording would likely bias the responses. Poor question ordering can create the same problem. For example, consider a survey that primes respondents with a series of questions about governmental corruption, waste, and mismanagement, and then asks respondents if they approve of how the government is performing.

While asking respondents if a public official has *solicited* a bribe might reduce systematic measurement error, the question still risks some **random measurement error**. Random error also causes a measurement to deviate from the concept being studied; however, it does not do so in a predictable way. To illustrate, one could imagine that a given survey respondent had a bribe solicited from him over a year and a half ago, but at the time of the survey he remembered incorrectly and stated that, yes, he had a bribe solicited from him in the last twelve months. One could also imagine a different respondent that had a bribe solicited eight months prior, but he remembered it as having been from a long time ago. Requesting that respondents think back into the past introduces error into the data because recollections are often unreliable. In other words, some people may mistakenly report more bribe payments while others may report less; the measurement would be **unreliable**, but there is no reason to expect the error to be consistent in one direction or the other.

There are several additional ways that a survey question could invite unpredictable error. Questions that are too long, too hard to understand, or too ambiguous might invite multiple interpretations. A common mistake in surveys is a **double-barreled question**, or a question that really ask about two things. For example, a survey of citizens using government services might ask: "In your interactions with local government officials, did you have your problem addressed and were you treated well?" In this case the question is asking about both how a citizen was treated and about the outcome of the interaction. It is of course possible to be treated well but without a positive outcome, or to receive a positive outcome but be treated poorly. Such questions are usually easy to identify because they contain the word "and." While question wording can minimize random error, some random measurement error will always exist. Respondents might misunderstand the question, not give it adequate thought, or be in a bad mood that day—all of which might impact their response and introduce error.

In summary, a survey question asking about bribe payments produces a measure of petty corruption with some risk of understating the true level of corruption because of a social desirability bias. The question also invites random error as it asks respondents to recall a year into the past. Both biases and random error can be reduced through question wording; however, some random error is inevitable. Now let's see how the challenges of conceptualization and systematic and random measurement error manifest themselves with another example.

A very different measurement is produced by another non-governmental organization Global Integrity. Arguing that corruption cannot be effectively measured, "Global Integrity quantitatively assesses the opposite of corruption, that is, the access that citizens and businesses have to a country's government, their ability to monitor its behavior, and their ability to seek redress and advocate for improved governance."[9] Rather than survey citizens about these issues, Global Integrity, based in Washington D.C., hires researchers in each country of study to conduct research and provide responses to over 300 questions, both about the laws on the books and their enforcement. Such a methodology has several advantages. Rather than simply focus on petty corruption, this methodology allows Global Integrity to address a much broader concept. Furthermore, by relying on experts with specialized knowledge, Global Integrity's measure attempts to achieve both breadth and depth.

There is, however, one major problem with this methodology that should be evident. Because different researchers conduct the scoring for different countries, it is almost impossible to ensure that all the researchers are using the same criteria in their evaluations, a problem known as **inter-coder reliability**. Global Integrity offers several examples of this in their methodology white paper. For example, its score card asks experts to determine if "In practice, civil service asset disclosures are audited," but researchers might respond to this question differently if only senior civil servants are audited or if audits are not conducted regularly.[10] The organization attempts to overcome these problems by providing researchers with a great deal of guidance in filling out the scorecards and through a peer review process, whereby experts review the researchers' findings. In 2011, they added the extra step of convening regional peer reviewers to compare several country scores with a regional perspective. These are good steps that reduce the inter-coder reliability problem, but they cannot remove it entirely.

Perhaps the most commonly referenced cross-national measures of corruption come from Transparency International's Corruption Perception Index (CPI) and a similar index of corruption from the World Bank's governance indicators. The term **index** tells us that the final measurement is produced by combining different pieces of data. In this case, these indices are based on surveys of elites, businesspeople, and analysts conducted by risk assessment firms, development banks, and other groups. These sources ask questions about the respondents' perceptions of corruption in a particular country using questions such as, "How widespread do you think bribe taking and corruption are in this country?"

---

9 Global Integrity, "Global Integrity Report: 2011 Methodology White Paper," Washington, D.C.: Global Integrity. Accessed January 2013. www.globalintegrity.org/report/methodology/white-paper.
10 Global Integrity, "Global Integrity Report: 2011 Methodology White Paper."

As you can see, the CPI uses a very different conceptualization than in the previous examples. It uses a broad conceptualization of corruption and measures "perceptions" rather than actual corruption. In this case, the data are aggregated to the country level and countries are quantitatively ranked on a 1–10 scale. One can identify several measurement concerns with such indices. For example, the data used to calculate these indices come from a variety of different sources, meaning that the questions used or the type of respondents asked might be somewhat different from country to country. In addition, as the index attempts to measure a broader conceptualization of corruption than petty bribery, different respondents might understand corruption differently. Furthermore, because the data are aggregated from individual respondents, it might mask disagreements among respondents regarding their perception of corruption in a given country. To be sure, the end product is attractive: a scale of corruption along which each country in the world can be placed. However, the easy availability of such scales risks blinding the reader to the limitations of the measurement. Consumers of such indices often fail to recognize that there is considerable uncertainty in the data.

The existence of different measurements, using divergent conceptualizations of corruption, and confronting different types of error, has major implications for research findings. This is evident when one compares indices like the CPI with surveys of self-reported bribe payment like Transparency International's Global Corruption Barometer. Figure 4.1 does exactly this. Specifically, the figure, called a scatterplot, places forty-five nations (represented by open circles) on the graph according to its value on the CPI (the x-axis) and the Global Corruption Barometer (the y-axis). As Figure 4.1 clearly shows, corruption perceptions by elites are very different than self-reported bribe payments by ordinary citizens. While countries that score well on the CPI also generally have fewer self-reported bribe payments, countries that score poorly on the CPI have both high and low levels of bribe payments.

Aggregating data, as done in the Global Corruption Barometer or the CPI, is attractive as it allows us to compare countries; however, as alluded to above, doing so risks masking differences among the individual respondents. In his famous 2006 Technology, Entertainment, Design (TED) Talk, Hans Rosling lays out the problem with aggregation. He notes that, in 2003, Sub-Saharan Africa had an average GDP per capita of only $1,750, clearly the poorest region in the world. Nonetheless, Rosling argues that it is misleading to think about Sub-Saharan Africa as a whole. He notes that, at that time, Sierra Leone only had a GDP per capita of $518 while Mauritius's GDP per capita was an impressive $10,700. Still, country-level data are also an aggregation, so Rosling moves one more step down the ladder of aggregation and divides the data by income quintiles. He notes that after a terrible famine in Niger, the lowest-income quintile (the income for the poorest one-fifth of the country) only had a GDP per capita of $102. During the same time, the highest income

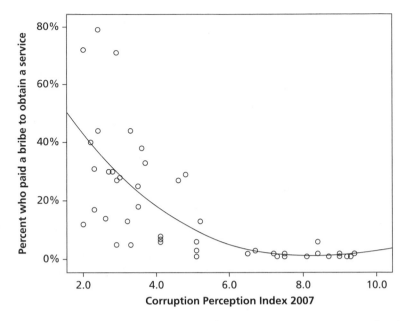

FIGURE 4.1 Scatterplot of the Relationship between Transparency International's CPI and Its Global Corruption Barometer

Source: Author's calculations based on data provided by Transparency International for 2007.

Note: n = 45 as the Global Corruption Barometer is only conducted in some countries.

quintile in South Africa had a GDP per capita of $30,400. In response to this dramatic difference he states:

> And yet we tend to discuss on what solutions there should be in Africa. Everything in this world exists in Africa! You can't discuss universal access to HIV [medication] for that quintile up here [South Africa] with the same strategy as down here [Niger]. Improvement of the world must be highly contextualized. And it is not relevant to have it on a regional level. We must be much more detailed.[11]

As you can see, clarity about the level of analysis is particularly important for making descriptive inferences. To offer another example, consider employment rates in the United States. As of December 2012, the unemployment rate in the United States was 7.8 percent. While this is an important piece of information, it is potentially very misleading because it is an aggregation. Among individuals with a bachelor's degree or higher, unemployment was only 3.9 percent compared with 11.6 percent among those with less than a

11 Hans Rosling, "Debunking myths about the third world," *TED Talks.* 2010. Accessed February 8, 2013. www.youtube.com/watch?v = RUwS1uAdUcI.

high school diploma.[12] In short, aggregation is often desirable, but it masks important variation in the data. Having now considered the challenges of conceptualization, measurement error, and aggregation, one last major challenge to descriptive inference remains to be explored: sampling error.

OPERATIONALIZATION AND SAMPLING ERROR

In many cases, particularly when we are dealing with large populations (like all American voters, for example), it is not feasible to collect data on everybody we are interested in. In these situations, we take a subset of the total population, which we refer to as a sample. As alluded to above, research that does not include the entire population to be studied but rather uses a sample to represent the population faces an additional challenge to inference: sampling error. For example, in calculating the percentage of the adult population that supports the 2010 health care law signed by President Obama, pollsters calculate a sample statistic. A December 2012 survey of 1,000 likely voters by Rasmussen Reports, for example, finds that 46 percent view the law favorably while 49 percent have an unfavorable impression.[13] What social scientists really care about, however, is not the percentage of the *sample* that approves of the health care law, the **sample statistic**, but the percentage of the *population,* which is known as the **population parameter.** In order to draw inferences from a sample about the larger population, the sample must be drawn in such a way that it is *representative* of the population. Every sample runs the risk of **sampling error.** This is to say that any sample might vary either systematically or randomly from the true population.

In drawing representative samples, researchers must first and foremost be very clear about the population that they wish to make inferences about. While it is common for news reports to contend that the approval rating of a president represents the views of all Americans,[14] this is rarely the case. Most opinion polls exclude young people under the age of eighteen, homeless people, prisoners, and Americans living abroad. Furthermore, in predicting

---

12 "Employment status of the civilian population 25 years and over by educational attainment," Bureau of Labor Statistics. Accessed February 8, 2013. www.bls.gov/news.release/empsit. t04.htm.

13 "73% think health care law likely to cost more than projected," Rasmussen Reports. Accessed October 1, 2012. www.rasmussenreports.com/public_content/politics/current_events/health care/december_2012/73_think_health_care_law_likely_to_cost_more_than_projected.

14 For example, "A CNN/Opinion Research Corporation survey released Monday indicates that Obama's approval rating among Americans stands at 54 percent, with 45 percent saying they disapprove of the job he's doing as president." CNN Political Unit. 2011. "CNN Poll: Obama's approval rating edges up thanks to foreign policy." CNN. http://politicalticker. blogs.cnn.com/2011/05/30/cnn-poll-obamas-approval-rating-edges-up-thanks-to-foreign-policy/. May 30.

elections, pollsters are not so much concerned with the general population, but those who are likely to go to the polls and actually vote. This distinction can be an important one, as the voting population tends to be older, more affluent, and better informed about politics than the larger adult population. In addition, surveys measuring petty corruption often limit their population to those individuals who have had contact with government officials.

Once the population is clearly defined, we can then consider how to draw a representative sample from that population. As with measurement error, a sample can diverge either systematically or randomly from a population. **Systematic sampling error** typically results from coverage bias or non-response bias. **Coverage bias** occurs when the **sampling frame**, or the group from which the sample is actually drawn, is somehow different from the population.

Say that we are interested in conducting a survey of students' political attitudes on campus. How should we go about collecting a sample of students to represent the population? Perhaps the easiest means to select survey participants would be to post interviewers in frequently traveled locations on campus and conduct face-to-face interviews. Such a sampling method is known as a **convenience sample**, as it selects participants who are conveniently available. We could imagine several problems with such a method. Those students who are on campus more regularly would be more likely to be selected for the sample. Furthermore, if we surveyed during business hours, then many working students who take evening classes would be excluded altogether. In this case, the sampling frame, or the pool from which our sample is drawn (students on campus during business hours), would not be representative of the population we are interested in (all students).

The best means to avoid coverage bias is through random sampling. Instead of a convenience sample, researchers could obtain a list of names of all the students at the university and then develop a means to randomly select names from that list. This could be done by assigning each student a number and then having a computer develop a list of random numbers. Those students whose number was selected by the computer would enter the sample. Regardless of the exact method, the key element of a **random sample** is that each member of the population has an equal probability of being selected for the sample. (Box 4.1 goes into greater detail in how this is done in practice.) As we will see below, a random sample is not only important for avoiding coverage bias, but it is also essential to quantify how uncertain we are about the inferences we make from our samples.

Even if a researcher uses a random sampling technique, he still faces another potential source of systematic sampling error called non-response bias. **Non-response bias** occurs when we cannot collect data from every observation *selected* into our sample. In public opinion surveys, this happens because many individuals who have been selected choose not to participate. The Pew Research Center, a well-regarded polling organization, reported in 2010 that despite at least seven attempts to contact those selected to be in recent Pew

Box 4.1: Sampling in Practice

Developing a random sample of telephone numbers is a little more complicated than randomly selecting from a known list of students, but it follows a similar logic. Surveyors do not know all the available numbers in the U.S., but they do know all the available area codes. They also have estimates of the population living in each area code. If one area code has twice the number of people of another area, then a computer can be told to generate two random telephone numbers from the first area code for every random number from the second. This form of sampling is known as **probability proportionate to size** sampling.[a]

In the early days of polling, surveys in the United States had to be done door to door because many low-income people did not have a telephone. A telephone survey would have produced a biased sample of the American people. Today the sampling challenge is that more and more households have given up a landline telephone for a cell phone. The National Center for Health Statistics estimated that, as of late 2009, 25 percent of households were cell phone only, and this number is increasing dramatically each year.[b] If those households with and without landlines had the same political views, this sampling concern would not be a problem; however, this is clearly not the case. Christian *et al.* found that only 20 percent of a cell phone-only sample identified as Republican compared with 26 percent of a landline sample. Why the difference? Among other differences, Hispanics and young people are more likely than the rest of the population to live in cell phone-only households and less likely to identify as Republicans. For example, of those adults between the ages of twenty-five and twenty-nine, 49 percent lived in cell phone-only households. As a result, since the 2008 presidential election, most major polling companies have incorporated cell phones into their sampling; however, generating random samples of cell phone numbers is more complicated and costly because of legal protections and because cell phone area codes are not as meaningful as landline area codes.[c] Furthermore, individuals who own both a landline and a cell phone have a higher probability of being selected for a sample than someone who just has one.

Outside the United States, sampling concerns vary. While many developed countries use the same approach to sampling as the U.S., in most low-income countries telephone-based sampling would generate a coverage bias problem. As a result, face-to-face interviews remain the predominant means to collect survey data in the developing world. Because there is no list of every resident, however, a computer-generated random selection process cannot be used. Instead, surveyors most commonly employ a method called **cluster sampling**. Imagine a country divided into clusters, something along the lines of U.S. counties. One could develop a list of all the counties in the country and then randomly select counties to be included in the sampling frame. As with telephone survey area

a. Survey firms use slightly different methodologies to select their samples; however, most major firms offer a description of their methodology on their webpage.
b. Leah Christian, Scott Keeter, Kristen Purcell, *et al.*, "Assessing the cell phone challenge to survey research in 2010," Pew Research Center (2010).
c. Paul Lavrakas and Charles Shuttles, "Cell Phone Sampling Summit II statements on accounting for cell phones in telephone survey research in the US" (2005).

codes, the probability of selecting a given county could be proportional to its population. Once counties are randomly selected, surveyors could randomly select neighborhoods within those counties and randomly select homes within those neighborhoods.

In some ways, sampling in developing countries is more accurate than in the United States. ABC/BBC's polling in Afghanistan, for example, obtained a response rate of 95 percent, essentially eliminating the problem of non-response bias so salient in U.S. polling.[d] In other ways, however, challenges remain. In 2007, for example, the Joint United Nations Programme on HIV/AIDS (UNAIDS) estimated that there were 33.2 million people living with HIV. This represented a major decrease from the agency's previous estimate of 39.5 million.[e] The difference, however, was not due to a drop in actual HIV rates, but to a change in methodology to adjust for sampling bias. The data collection method employed in most countries used prenatal care clinics as the primary means of data collection; however, such clinics were more likely to operate in the urban areas where HIV was more prevalent. The result was sampling bias.

d. Gary Langer, "Afghanistan: Where things stand," ABC News (2009). Accessed February 1, 2013. http://abcnews.go.com/PollingUnit/story?id=6787686&page=1.
e. "AIDS epidemic update. Joint United Nations Programme on HIV," UNAIDS, Geneva (2007).

samples, only 5 to 20 percent typically agreed to participate, a statistic known as a **response rate**.[15] If those who are too busy for a survey, opposed to taking surveys, or are otherwise difficult to reach have different political views than those who end up participating in the survey, then the low response rate will create non-response bias. To illustrate this type of systematic error, one could imagine a survey firm calling randomly selected households and asking them if they want to participate in a poll on terrorism. Those who decide to participate would probably have stronger feelings on terrorism, and therefore different attitudes than those who decline, creating a non-response bias.

It is important to emphasize that issues of coverage and non-response bias are not limited to public opinion polling. For example, one might wish to understand how members of parliaments vote on legislation; but what if not all votes are recorded? Indeed, voice votes do occur with great frequency in many parliaments, and their exclusion from studies of roll call voting may affect the conclusions we reach. This is a form of coverage bias—the researcher is interested in understanding how legislators vote on all pieces of legislation, but the sample is limited to bills on which a recorded vote was held. Because voice votes are more likely to be used when there is less party cohesion, a study

15 Lee Rainie, "Internet, broadband, and cell phone statistics," *Pew Internet & American Life Project* 5 (2010).

of roll call votes would over-estimate the degree of party unity in the legislative body.[16]

Cross-national research is often subject to the equivalent of non-response bias due to missing data. While many indicators are available for all countries, data are often missing from low-income countries with inadequate data collection capacity. Since these omissions have a systematic rather than random cause, they may produce biases in the inferences we draw from cross-national comparisons.

Accounting for Error: Quantifying Uncertainty

The discussion above should make clear that most studies run the risk of error: both measurement and sampling, and both systematic and random. To be able to make inferences, therefore, we have to understand the nature of the error in our data and the amount of uncertainty that it introduces. Fortunately, at least in the case of quantitative data, researchers have developed tools to estimate error and to quantify the amount of uncertainty that it introduces. Not surprisingly, it is hard to "quantify" the error in qualitative data, but qualitative research can still benefit from understanding the logic used to do so with quantitative data.

The most straightforward type of error to account for is random sampling error. Leaving aside systematic sampling error for a moment, random sampling error is a function of two factors: the size of the sample and the amount of variation in the data. One could imagine conducting a study of household income in a large city with a wide range of income levels: low to high and everything in between. In this case, if a surveyor only examines a small random sample of say 300 households, it seems likely that his sample would fail to capture all the variation in the population. If, however, the surveyor increases the random sample to 1,000 households, then there is a higher probability that the sample will reflect the population. Alternatively, one could imagine another city where everyone has close to the same level of income. Now a random sample of 300 might be sufficient to adequately capture the population. By taking into account these two components, sample size and variation, researchers are able to estimate the amount of random error in the data: an estimate known as the **standard error**.[17]

---

16 Clifford J. Carrubba, Matthew Gabel, Lacey Murrah, *et al.*, "Off the record: Unrecorded legislative votes, selection bias and roll-call vote analysis," *British Journal of Political Science* 36 (2006): 691–704.

17 The standard error for interval-level data (such as income) equals the standard deviation (*s*) divided by the square root of the sample size.

$$std.error = \frac{s}{\sqrt{n}}$$

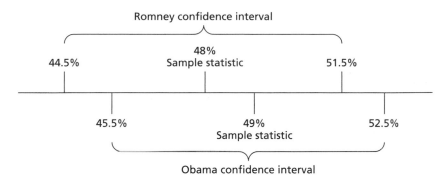

FIGURE 4.2 Confidence Intervals
Source: UPI-CVoter poll, 2012.

Most students first come into contact with the standard error through a term more commonly used in the media: the **margin of error**. For example, in their final poll before the 2012 presidential election, the UPI-CVoter poll of 1,000 likely voters found that 49 percent of likely voters reported an intention to vote for Barack Obama and 48 percent intended to vote for Mitt Romney. The margin of error for the study was reported at 3.5 percent. What that means is that UPI-CVoter was confident that the population parameter, the percentage of the "population" (in this case likely voters in the United States who intended to vote for Barack Obama), was 49 percent plus or minus 3.5 percent, or between 45.5 percent and 52.5 percent (see Figure 4.2). In other words the pollsters found that Obama supporters led Romney supporters in their *sample*, but, when they tried to generalize about the broader *population* of likely voters, they could not be sure of this lead. The one percentage difference observed in the sample statistics could have been due to random chance.

This range of the sample statistic plus and minus the margin of error is known as a **confidence interval** because pollsters are *confident* that the true population parameter, the actual percentage of likely U.S. voters intending to vote for Obama, lies within the range of 45.5 to 52.5 percent. But how confident? The first thing we must stress is that we can never be 100 percent confident; however, pollsters and social scientists want to get as close to 100 percent confidence as is possible. As we said above, the margin of error is related to the standard error. While a margin of error is generally a single measure of uncertainty applied to an entire survey, a standard error is a measure of uncertainty

For sample proportions (such as the percentage of survey respondents who approve of the job the president is doing), the standard error equals the square root of the proportion (p) times 1 minus p. Then this number is divided by the square root of the sample size.

$$std.error = \frac{\sqrt{[p(1-p)]}}{\sqrt{n}}$$

calculated for each statistic generated with a sample. In most cases, the margin of error is roughly twice the size of the standard error. Thanks to something called the Central Limit Theorem, we know that, 95 percent of the time, a value obtained from a random sample will fall within about two standard errors of the population value. Thus, in our example above based on the UPI-CVoter poll, there is only a 5 percent chance that support for Obama in the population is outside of the 45.5 percent and 52.5 percent range. Another way to think of this is if we conducted 100 surveys of 1,000 likely voters, 95 percent of the time, the sample statistic would be in the 44.5–51.5 percent range.

You might note that this is a pretty large margin of error, which would not be very useful in predicting the outcome of a close electoral race. Nonetheless, as discussed above, pollsters can reduce the uncertainty in the data (reduce the random sampling error) by increasing the sample size. For example, a *Washington Post*–ABC poll conducted right before the election surveyed 2,345 likely voters instead of just 1,000, which reduced the margin of error down to 2 percent.[18] It is important to note, however, that the reduction in the size of the standard error is not consistent. While one can achieve a significant reduction in error when moving from a sample of 500 to one of 1,500, the reduction in error is smaller when moving from 1,500 to 2,500 respondents.[19]

While it is tempting to just focus on the sample statistic and ignore random sampling error in the data, doing so can get us into trouble. Take for example the CPI. Figure 4.3 plots the score for each of the 178 countries rated by Transparency International. The bars on either side of each plot represent 90 percent confidence intervals around each statistic. For example, while Transparency International estimates that Romania scores a 3.7 on its 1–10 scale (where 10 is low corruption), we know that there is random error in this estimate. Taking this random error into account, we are 90 percent confident that the true corruption score falls between 3.3 and 4.2. This is actually a fairly wide range, and this confidence interval overlaps with the intervals for fifty-eight other countries—about one-third of the entire set of countries! Reporting such uncertainty is an extremely important responsibility of researchers,

18 Jon Cohen, Peyton M. Craighill, and Scott Clement, "Wa-Po-ABC tracking poll: Final weekend tally is Obama 50, Romney 47, still a 'margin of error' contest," *Washington Post* (2012). Accessed November 5, 2012. www.washingtonpost.com/blogs/the-fix/wp/2012/11/05/wapo-abc-tracking-poll-final-weekend-tally-is-obama-50-romney-47-still-a-margin-of-error-contest/.

19 Interestingly enough, because today there are so many polls conducted in the lead up to an election, electoral predictions need not rely on any one poll. Websites such as www.huffingtonpost.com/news/pollster/, www.realclearpolitics.com, and http://fivethirtyeight.blogs.nytimes.com/ aggregate the different polls and derive their own estimations based on the sum of all individual estimations! In the lead up to the 2012 election, Barack Obama rarely had a statistically significant lead over his Republican opponent Mitt Romney in any one poll. Nonetheless, because the vast majority of polls consistently showed Obama with a slight lead, pollsters were still confident that he would win the popular vote, which he did.

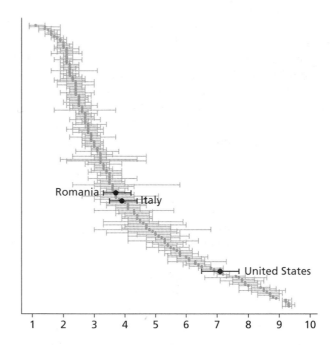

FIGURE 4.3 Plotting Estimates and Uncertainty for the Perception of Corruption Index in 178 Countries

Source: Created by the authors using data from Transparency International.

Note: Bars represent 90 percent confidence intervals.

and paying close attention to such error is an important responsibility of consumers of research.

Researchers and survey analysts use the term **statistically significant difference** to indicate when the differences observed are greater than the error in the data. For example, the confidence interval for the CPI score for the United States runs from 6.5 to 7.7 (See Figure 4.3). Since the lowest end of this range is greater than the high end of the confidence interval for Romania (4.2), we can be more than 90 percent confident that the United States has a higher CPI score than Romania.[20] Alternatively, we cannot be confident that Italy has a higher CPI score than Romania since the confidence interval for Italy overlaps with that for Romania. While it is important to take care to point out when differences we observe are statistically significant, the term needs to be used with caution. For many people the word "significant" implies "substantial," and they are tempted to interpret a "statistically significant difference" as a "large difference." This is incorrect. Statistical significance only suggests that we are

20 In this specific scenario, we would actually be far more confident than 90 percent because the probability is lower that we have underestimated the U.S. score at the extreme of the confidence interval and overestimated the Romanian score at the extreme of the confidence interval.

reasonably confident that there is a difference; however, that difference might actually be very small.[21]

It is also important to recognize that **standard errors and margins of error do not take into account systematic measurement error or systematic sampling error**. We have placed this in bold because it is a common mistake made by both scholars and readers alike. A "statistically significant difference" might be incorrect if there is systematic error in the data.

Taking systematic error into account is more complicated than estimating random error, but it can be done in some cases. To do so, the researcher needs to know certain parameters about the population. Say, for example, a hypothetical polling company measures the attitudes of American adults towards climate change. Having randomly selected its sample, the polling company calculates a sample statistic and the appropriate standard errors. Based on this information, the firm should be confident that a majority of Americans do not view climate change as a priority. However, before going to press with its findings, the company considers the possibility of systematic sampling error. Based on data from the Census Bureau, the firm knows that young people between eighteen and thirty make up about 30 percent of the U.S. adult population. Nonetheless, the pollsters notice that this demographic only makes up 15 percent of their sample. For some reason, perhaps because of their preference for cell phones or a lack of interest in surveys, young people are under-represented in their sample. This would be problematic because their findings also show that young people are more likely to be concerned with global warming.

Fortunately, the pollsters do not have to throw out the data. Instead they can address the systematic error by **weighting** the data. Because they know that young people make up around 30 percent of the population, they can mathematically adjust their sample, or "weight" their data, to look like the population. Researchers can do this by counting each young survey respondent as more than one observation and each person over thirty as less than one observation. Once they have rerun the numbers with the weighted data, the percentage concerned about climate change will increase and the pollster will likely have a more accurate estimation of American adult attitudes towards climate change. Data can be weighted along as many factors as pollsters have population parameters for. The Pew Research Center, for example, notes that it weights its data by household size, combined landline and cell phone users,

---

21 It should be mentioned that there is some debate about the nature of the error that the standard error actually accounts for. Traditionally, scholars have considered the standard error to be solely a measure of random *sampling* error. Nonetheless, others have noted that some random *measurement* error is also a function of variation and sample size. These researchers contend that the standard error is actually an estimate of all random error: sampling and measurement. Therefore, researchers will often use standard errors and margins of error even when they are studying an entire population. However, from a technical perspective, standard errors and margins of error are calculated in a way so that they are technically only a measure of random sampling error.

age, gender, education, race/ethnicity, and population density. In addition to random sampling, weighting is the reason that U.S. pollsters have been able to accurately capture U.S. public opinion and overcome the problems of non-response bias discussed above (recall the very low response rates cited by the Pew Research Center).

In theory, measurement error can be adjusted in a similar fashion, but again it requires information about the population. We say "in theory," because this practice is far less common in political science. An interesting example can be found in the case of drug consumption. Every year the U.S. Department of Health and Human Services (DHHS) conducts a massive 65,000-person National Survey on Drug Use and Health to measure drug consumption in the United States. Respondents are asked to report on the consumption of various illegal drugs in the past year; however, just as some survey respondents might be hesitant to confess to having paid bribes, some might lie about drug consumption. Recognizing this problem, Kilmer and Pacula compared self-reported drug consumption with more accurate drug tests and estimated that 20 percent of marijuana users fail to report their use of the drug.[22] In a sense, Kilmer and Pucula had developed an estimate of the systematic measurement error in survey data. As a result, when tasked with measuring marijuana consumption in California to predict the impact of a potential legalization initiative, rather than try to administer thousands of drug tests, Kilmer *et al.* adjusted existing survey estimates to account for the known tendency of respondents to under-report their drug use.[23]

In summary, there are means to deal with sampling and measurement error through improved measurements, random sampling, tests of statistical significance, and data weighting, but such tools might not always be readily employable. Moreover, such problems can only be minimized, not eliminated. As social scientists, it is our duty not only to minimize potential threats to inference, but also to report on these threats and to be as specific as possible about how certain or uncertain we are about our inferences. Typically, this involves reporting standard errors and confidence intervals for our estimates, but it may also include discussing how and why our estimates may be biased by sources of systematic error. The reader and the researcher should resist the urge to allow the perceived precision of numeric indicators to generate a false sense of confidence in the resultant numbers.

As mentioned above, there are less clear procedures for estimating and reporting measurement and sampling error in qualitative data; however, the same basic logic can be applied. Imagine that a researcher wanted to conduct a study of corruption in a corruption-prone government agency. It would certainly be important to interview officials from the agency in question, but the researcher

---

22 Beau Kilmer and Rosalie Liccardo Pacula, *Estimating the size of the global drug market: A demand-side approach, Report 2* (Santa Monica: RAND Corporation, 2009).

23 Beau Kilmer, Jonathan P. Caulkins, Rosalie Liccardo Pacula, *et al.*, *Altered state?* (Santa Monica: RAND Corporation, 2010).

would also have to recognize the potential bias in information provided by such officials. Nonetheless, qualitative researchers also have the luxury of asking more detailed follow-up questions and comparing official answers with those of journalists, members of civil society, and other key informants knowledgeable about the agency. In turn, this interview data can be complemented with other pieces of data—perhaps newspaper articles or citizen complaints filed with an oversight agency. In short, the qualitative researcher is able to use several pieces of information to arrive at an inference, a process often referred to as **triangulation**. By being transparent regarding the method used in arriving at such inferences, by considering what type of random and systematic and measurement and sampling error might be present in the data, and by using wording that recognizes the potential for error, the qualitative researcher can also take error into account.

MAKING DESCRIPTIVE INFERENCES AND PRESENTING DATA

Having discussed several challenges related to conceptualization, measurement, aggregation, and sampling, we are now ready to explore some basic tools used in making descriptive inferences. As the challenges to inference vary with the type of data being analyzed, so too do the tools for descriptive inference. Let's begin with quantitative data and use the concept of "democracy" as an example. Quantitative data can be divided into different levels of measurement, including nominal-, ordinal-, and interval-level data as well as a final level that is far less common in political science research and not addressed here: ratio data (see Figure 4.4).[24]

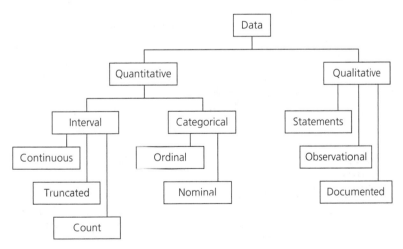

FIGURE 4.4 Different Types of Data

24 Ratio-level data are based on a comparison of two pieces of data to each other: for example the speed of one object compared with another.

TABLE 4.2 Regime Classification

Regime type	Frequency	Percentage	Valid percentage
Parliamentary democracy	56	29.3%	29.6%
Mixed democracy	21	11.0%	11.1%
Presidential democracy	37	19.4%	19.6%
Civilian dictatorship	38	19.9%	20.1%
Military dictatorship	24	12.6%	12.7%
Monarchic dictatorship	13	6.8%	6.9%
Missing data	2	1.0%	
Total	191	191 (100%)	189 (100%)

Source: Democracy Cross-National Data.[25]

Nominal-level data can be divided into different categories, but these categories cannot be placed in an order and the differences between them cannot be described with a precise number. For example, Alvarez *et al.* classify governing regimes into parliamentary democracy (United Kingdom), presidential democracy (Mexico), mixed democracy (France), civilian dictatorship (China), military dictatorship (Equatorial Guinea), and monarchical dictatorship (Saudi Arabia).[26] These are all distinct regime classifications, but it would be difficult to put them in a sequence. One could divide the democracies from the dictatorships, but is a monarchical dictatorship more authoritarian than a military dictatorship? Is a parliamentary system more democratic than a mixed system? Not necessarily. Examples of nominal data in a survey might include religious affiliation, ethnicity, and geographic region of residence.

With nominal-level data we have limited tools of descriptive inference. Useful descriptive statistics include **frequencies**, the number of countries that are classified into each of the six regime types; **percentages**, the percent of the total number of countries, the **valid percent**, the percent of the total number of countries minus any missing data, and the **mode**, or the most common category. This data can be presented visually using either a frequency table (see Table 4.2) or a bar chart (see Figure 4.5).

Ordinal-level data are also divided into set categories, but as its name suggests, these categories can be placed in a sequence. The Freedom House measure of democracy, for example, is often divided into three categories: free,

25 Democracy Cross-National Data, Release 3.0, spring 2009. Accessed August 22, 2013. https://sites.google.com/site/pippanorris3/research/data.
26 Alvarez *et al.*, "Classifying political regimes."

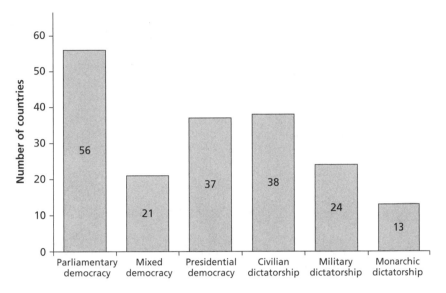

FIGURE 4.5 Nominal-Level Data: Regime Classification across Countries
Source: Democracy Cross-National Data.[27]
Note: *n* = 189 countries.

partly free, and not free. While these categories are clearly in an order, they
do not communicate precise differences. For example, according to the 2011
rankings, Mexico and Kuwait were rated as partly free and Argentina and the
United States as free.[28] Such broad categorizations fail to distinguish between
the rather small difference in the level of freedom between Argentina and
Mexico and the large difference between Kuwait and the United States. This
same issue can be seen in survey data. Surveys often ask respondents the extent
to which they strongly agree, agree, disagree, or strongly disagree with a given
statement. Although these categories can be ordered, the difference between
strongly agree and agree might not be the same as the difference between agree
and disagree.

Ordinal-level data can be presented with the same descriptive tools, including frequencies, percentages, and the mode. Because the categories can be
placed in an order, we are also able to calculate a **median**, or the category that
represents the halfway point in the data. In this case the mode is "free" and
the median value is "partly free." Figure 4.6 offers a bar chart of the Freedom
house rankings for 190 countries.

Bar charts offer a great way to explain data visually, but, if done poorly,
graphical representations can be not only confusing, but they also can be

27 Democracy Cross-National Data.
28 Freedom House data along with a white paper explaining the methodology behind their
  measures is available at www.freedomhouse.org.

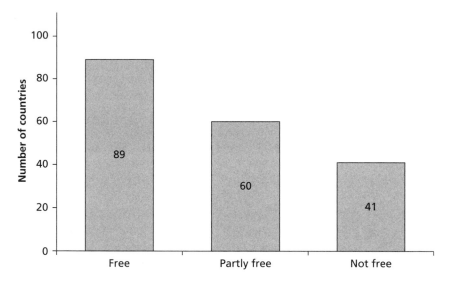

FIGURE 4.6 Ordinal-Level Data: Freedom across Countries
Source: Freedom House 2008.
Note: n = 190 countries.

misleading. Consider the differences between the two bar charts based on the same data presented in Figure 4.7 and Figure 4.8. Figure 4.7 is an example of what not to do.

▦ The first difference is the scale of the *y*-axis. The smaller scale in Figure 4.7 makes the difference between the two bars look bigger than it actually is, potentially misleading the reader.

▦ Figure 4.7 also presents the *number* of respondents in each category rather than the *percentage* of respondents. While we do want to know the total sample size, this information can be included in a note. Frequencies are generally more helpful when dealing with smaller sample sizes, and in this case and with most survey data, percentages are clearly more meaningful for the reader.

▦ Figure 4.8 has clear titles and text and correctly cites where the data came from. Rather than have the reader guess, Figure 4.8 also includes labels specifically stating the value of each bar.

▦ Figure 4.8 also takes advantage of the fact that many software packages are able to calculate and visually illustrate the confidence intervals around a sample statistic. These error bars clearly show the reader that once we take error into account, the proportions in the population might be a little higher or a little lower than 32 percent and 68 percent.

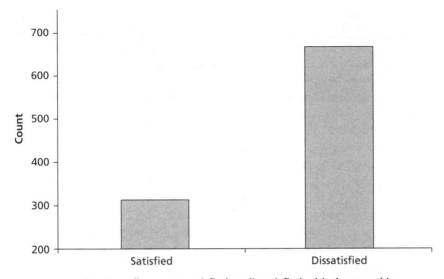

FIGURE 4.7 Example of Poor Data Presentation: Satisfaction with the Way Things Are Going in Egypt, 2010

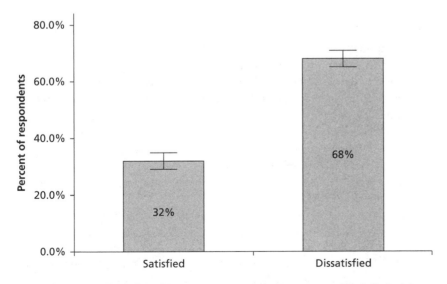

FIGURE 4.8 Example of Good Data Presentation: Percentage "Satisfied with the Way Things Are Going" in Egypt, 2010

Source: Produced by authors using data from the Pew Global Attitudes Project, 2010.

Note: Thin bars represent 95 percent confidence intervals.

The third level of measurement is interval level data, which is both ordered and communicates precise differences. To illustrate, Tatu Vanhanen created an index of democracy based on Robert Dahl's concept of polyarchy, defined by competition and participation.[29] Vanhanen's polyarchy index calculates the percent of seats held by the largest party, as a measure of competition, and electoral turnout, as a measure of participation. He calculates a polyarchy score of 20.78 for Mexico (higher numbers being more democratic) and a score of 26.14 for Argentina, yielding a precise difference of 5.35. Financial indicators are even more intuitive. According to the World Bank, Mexico's GDP per capita in 2011 was estimated at $10,047 and Argentina's was $10,942: a precise difference of $895 per capita.[30] Interval level data can take different forms, for example, some data is **continuous** with no set minimum or maximum. Other data, however, is **truncated**, with a set floor or ceiling. For example, the percent of a country's population that is literate cannot rise over 100 percent. Still other interval level data, such as the age of a survey respondent (if measured in years), is **count data** made up of whole numbers.

Interval level data presents us with a different set of descriptive tools. Frequencies and percentages are generally not particularly helpful with interval level data. For example, there is probably only one country with a GDP per capita of $10,942. Nonetheless scholars have at their disposal a number of other tools, including measures of central tendency and measures related to the distribution or dispersion of the data. We have already mentioned two measures of central tendency, the mode and the median, but for interval level data we can also calculate the mathematical average, or the **mean**. Other measures estimate the distribution of the data. Consider, for example, if we measured income among the inhabitants of two separate islands. On one island everyone earns roughly the same income and on another there are dramatic differences in income. The **standard deviation** allows us a precise measurement of the amount of variation in the data by comparing how far each observation is from the mean.[31] Data from the first island would yield a small standard deviation, with most values close to the mean, and data from the second island would yield a large standard deviation, with many values far away from the mean.

One might also measure the **skewness** in the data or the extent to which the data is lopsided. Income is a case in point. In most communities, there are

---

29 Vanhanen's democracy index and information about the measurement is available at www.prio.no/CSCW/Datasets/Governance/Vanhanens-index-of-democracy/

30 World Bank data can be easily accessed through its data portal http://data.worldbank.org/.

31 The standard deviation $= \sqrt{\dfrac{\sum(x_i - \bar{x})^2}{n}}$. The formula simply indicates that to find the standard deviation we must (1) square the difference between the value of x (our variable) for each observation and $\bar{x}$ (the mean for that variable), (2) take the sum of all those squared differences, and then (3) divide by the total number of observations (n), and then (4) take the square root.

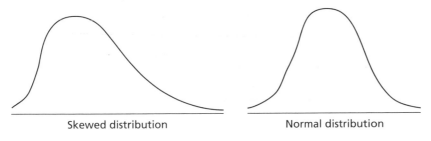

FIGURE 4.9 Skewed and Normal Distributions

large numbers of lower-income and even middle-income individuals but very few high-income individuals (see Figure 4.9). We call this distribution skewed. This distribution of income looks very different than say a distribution of height, where most people are around the mean height and there are a roughly equal number of very short people and very tall people (see Figure 4.9). Such a distribution is known as a **normal distribution**.

Figure 4.10 presents a graphical representation of the CPI across countries. This figure is known as a **histogram**. Because there are probably only one or two countries with a CPI score of say 5.8, a bar chart would not be particularly helpful. Instead a histogram groups values across a range into one bar, or what is sometimes called a bin, and then this bar represents the number

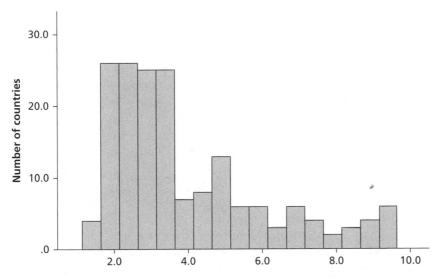

FIGURE 4.10 Example of Histogram: Corruption Perception Index, 2007

Source: Constructed by authors using data from Transparency International.

Note: x-axis represents values on the index of corruption, with low values representing higher levels of corruption; n = 174.

or percentage of countries in this range. In the histogram above, one bar represents a range of approximately .5 on a 1–10 scale. As we can see, the data are very clearly skewed. There are very many high-corruption countries, fewer medium-corruption countries, and only a small minority of low-corruption countries. As a result, while the median is 3.3, the mean is pulled upwards by the low-corruption countries to 4.0. Because the mean is affected by the high-corruption values, we prefer to focus on the median when describing skewed data.

In fact, reporting the mean when we should report the median is an extremely common mistake in describing data. Consider for example the 2012 discussions in the U.S. Congress to avert the so-called "fiscal cliff." One of the issues at hand was the expiration of tax cuts. As it was reported by countless news outlets, the expiration of the tax cuts would cause the average tax payer to pay an additional $3,400 in taxes. While this was mathematically correct, the benefits for the tax cut produced a very skewed distribution. The top 1 percent stood to lose $120,537 in tax cuts while the lowest fifth of households would only pay an additional $412 in taxes. The middle fifth, which contains the median taxpayer and should have been what the media was reporting, stood to lose under $2,000: still a large amount but considerably less than $3,400.[32]

Because interval level data communicates precise differences and includes many different values, there are a host of statistical techniques that we can use with such data. The distinctions between nominal, ordinal, and interval level data offer far more than an interesting classification; the level of measurement determines what statistical techniques we use to describe and present our data. So while we use one set of tools for interval data, we use a very different set of tools for nominal data.

It is a little less clear how to divide qualitative data, but many scholars divide qualitative data into three categories primarily based on the source of the data. These include (1) statements that might be made in a survey, interview, or focus group, (2) observations made by the researcher, or (3) documented information (see Figure 4.4). The presentation of qualitative data can vary considerably. To illustrate, consider for example that we are interested in U.S. citizens' attitudes towards gun control. One qualitative research approach might entail conducting observation and interviews at a protest calling for greater gun control. A researcher could present his data through a narration that describes the protest in depth. Such a narration might entail the use of both quotes from protesters and observations by the researcher to convey the emotions, frustrations, and sentiments of the protesters. Such an account would likely be illuminating, interesting to read, and help the reader understand the viewpoint of the protesters.

32 Rick Newman, "How much the 'fiscal cliff' will cost you," *U.S. News and World Report* (2012). Accessed February 1, 2013. www.usnews.com/news/blogs/rick-newman/2012/11/12/how-much-the-fiscal-cliff-will-cost-you.

Nonetheless, from a point of view of "inference," you should immediately spot the limitation of such a narrative. Individuals attending a gun control protest certainly would not be representative of the broader public or even people sympathetic towards gun control. So how is the qualitative researcher able to respond to this problem?

One option is to be clear about the "population" being studied. Rather than try to make broad generalizations, the goal of the researcher could simply be limited to describing one particular group of protesters. In this case, the researcher would infer from his observation and from interviews about the protesters and the protest itself, but not beyond. This approach has its advantages. The researcher's narrative could provide the reader with a depth of understanding that would be difficult with a survey of gun control attitudes or other quantitatively oriented methods.

The researcher could go a step further and conduct similar research activities at other protests and even at protests defending gun rights. This approach maximizes the strengths of qualitative research. While a survey could give us a sense of general attitudes towards gun control among the population as a whole, observing and interviewing protesters would allow for an analysis of two groups at either end of the political extreme that would otherwise be hard to identify and randomly survey.

Another option would be to use qualitative methods to help better describe quantitative findings. The researcher could use quantitative survey data to broadly describe an issue and then complement this with qualitative data to provide greater depth and understanding. For example, if a survey found that 69 percent of respondents favored a ban on assault weapons, interviews with experts and activists, focus groups, observations at protests, and a review of newspapers or other documents could help explain this 69 percent number in greater detail.

SUMMING UP

There are many cases where we will want to make descriptive inferences. In order to do so scientifically, we have to recognize the numerous challenges to inference that we confront and take steps to minimize these challenges. Based on the discussion above, we can offer the following advice for either conducting your own research or critically analyzing others' research:

- Be very clear about the concept that you want to measure, ensure that the concept can in fact be measured, and confirm that your measurement matches the concept.
- Carefully select the type of data to be collected (e.g. the unit of analysis, qualitative and/or quantitative) and recognize the specific challenges this particular combination of data attributes confronts. For example,

you would want to recognize that aggregating data might mask important differences.

▨ Select a measurement that minimizes measurement errors. This includes those that produce biases, such as social desirability bias in a survey, and those that produce random measurement error, such as a double-barreled question in a survey.

▨ If you are not studying the whole population, minimize sampling error through random sampling. Ensure that the sampling frame is constructed to minimize the potential of coverage bias. To the extent possible, reduce non-response bias and missing data.

▨ Use measurements of random error (e.g. the standard of error and the resultant margin of error) to operationalize uncertainty in the data. Regardless of whether the data are quantitative or qualitative, be transparent about uncertainty in the data.

▨ When possible, use information available about the population to develop weights and correct for any systematic sampling and (potentially) measurement errors. When not possible, be transparent about any potential systematic error.

Students might not have adequate training to complete these last two steps, but the most important thing is that students and scholars alike are thoughtful about the error that is in their data. They should try to minimize that error whenever possible, and, even when it is not possible, they should be clear about the limitations of the data. Most research papers include a methodology section, where authors should be very specific about any methodological limitations of their study. Valid and reliable descriptive inferences are the first step in ensuring valid and reliable causal inferences. In the following chapters, we will explore three broad approaches to making causal inferences: experiments, large-n observational studies, and small-n observational studies.

▨ KEY TERMS

Experiments

Chances are, an experiment was one of the first research designs you ever executed. Most primary school students in America are asked by their science teachers to conduct an experiment of some kind, with the results presented at science fairs across the country. These experiments may have involved exposing the same types of plants or seeds to different types of light, different temperatures, or different types of soil and then observing whether they grow at different rates. The point of the exercise was not to generate some new scientific finding, but rather to teach you how to use the scientific method to better understand how the world works.

Ironically, despite the fact that they were introduced to the method early in their lives, most college students do not even consider conducting an experiment to learn something about politics. In fact, over the years, few political scientists have considered this method either. Figure 5.1 tracks the percentage of articles published in the *American Political Science Review* (APSR, the discipline's top journal) that used an experiment of some kind. Note that prior to the 1990s, experimental work was quite rare. Prior to 1975, only five articles that appeared in the journal made use of an experiment. Between 1975 and 1990, another sixteen articles in the APSR produced findings from an experiment.

However, political scientists have increasingly begun to recognize the possibilities that experiments hold for answering political questions.[1] During the

---

1 An alternative interpretation of these figures would be that the top journals have simply become more willing to publish experimental work than they had been previously. But a comparison of papers presented at political science conferences suggests that this is not the case. More political scientists are doing experiments now than ever before.

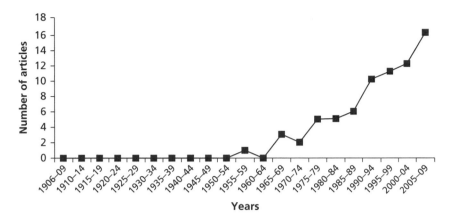

FIGURE 5.1 Articles in the *American Political Science Review* Using Experimental Methods

Source: Druckman, Green, Kuklinski, *et al.* (2011).[2]

1990s, twenty-one articles published in the APSR utilized experiments, about twice as many as during the 1980s. And during the first decade of this century, experimental research was used in twenty-eight articles published in the top journal. To put it simply, the experimental method has graduated from obscurity in the discipline and is now extolled as the "gold standard" of research methods by many methodologists.[3] As political scientist Rose McDermott notes, "No other methodology can offer the strong support for the causal inferences that experiments allow."[4]

Why has experimental research made this transition so quickly and emphatically? One reason is that experiments are now easier to conduct than they have been in the past. As we discuss below, the ability to carry out experiments on computers and over the internet has greatly increased access to the experimental method from a wide array of researchers, including student researchers. Another reason for the increasing use of experiments is that political scientists are increasingly collaborating with scholars in other disciplines, such as psychology and economics, which have used these techniques for years. Finally, after decades of advancements in statistical methods designed to draw stronger inferences from observational data, several political scientists have actively promoted the expansion of experimental methods in the discipline. This movement largely focuses on the notion that experiments (and natural experiments) hold enormous potential for allowing political scientists to draw stronger inferences about causal relationships in the political world.

2 James N. Druckman, Donald P. Green, James H. Kuklinski, *et al.*, eds, *Cambridge handbook of experimental political science* (Cambridge, UK: Cambridge University Press, 2011).

3 Donald P. Green and Alan S. Gerber, "The underprovision of experiments in political science," *Annals of the American Academy of Political and Social Science* 589 (2003): 94–112.

4 Rose McDermott, "Experimental methodology in political science," *Political Analysis* 10 (2002): 325–342, p. 38.

WHAT IS AN EXPERIMENT?

An experiment is generally defined by the researcher's control over what is called the **data-generating process**.[5] In observational research, as will be discussed in the next two chapters, the researcher does not affect the generation of the data; she simply observes whatever data is produced, however it is produced. In an experiment, the researcher manipulates some variable herself, thereby directly intervening in the production of the relevant data. To understand the distinction, let's take the example of research on the effects of campaign advertisements that appear on television. This topic is one that has generated significant debate both in political science and in other disciplines like communication. Some scholars argue that television advertisements have "minimal effects" on persuading the public, while others suggest that advertisements can be more influential. We will set aside, for now, the question of which side is right and instead discuss two different ways that one might study this question.

If a political scientist was going to take an observational approach to the study of advertising effects, such a study might look something like the following. First, the researcher could collect data on which candidates ran which advertisements in which television markets.[6] Then, the researcher might go about collecting election results for each of those television markets. Once the researcher had collected both sources of data, he could examine whether, for example, the Democratic candidate received a greater share of the vote in markets where she ran more advertisements than the Republican. By extension, the researcher would also look to see whether the Republican won more votes in areas where he ran more advertisements than the Democrat. Such a design would be deemed observational because the researcher had no hand in the process that generated the relevant data that is being analyzed. Specifically, candidates, parties, and interest groups made decisions about which advertisements would be aired and where those advertisements would be aired, not the researcher.

An experimental study of advertising effects would look quite different. Specifically, the researcher might take a variety of different approaches in order to exercise some control over how the data are generated. For example, a researcher might work with one or more of the candidates to determine which television markets to show advertisements in. This way, the researcher is helping to determine how the data are generated. Alternatively, the researcher may set up a living room with a television and invite people to watch different

5 Rebecca B. Morton and Kenneth C. Williams, *Experimental political science and the study of causality: From nature to the lab* (Cambridge, UK: Cambridge University Press, 2010).
6 Indeed, such a dataset exists for elections held in 1996, 2000, 2002, 2004, and 2008 through the Wisconsin Advertising Project (http://wiscadproject.wisc.edu/).

advertisements. Some participants might see only the Democratic candidate's advertising while others might only see the Republican's ads. The researcher could then ask participants which candidate they would be more likely to support. In either case, the researcher now has a hand in the process that is producing the data. She is determining which people will see which ads and then looking for the effects of the different conditions after the fact.

It is important to note that the key here is that the researcher has control over some important variable being studied, not just that the researcher is involved in some way. For example, it would not be sufficient for the researcher to help a candidate place orders for television advertisements. Rather, the key distinction would be whether the researcher was able to determine, to some extent, which advertisements would be aired and where they would be aired. This control is crucial for drawing strong inferences, as we shall see.

WHY CONTROL MEANS STRONGER INFERENCES

The political world (alas, the world in general) is a complicated place. There are innumerable variables that affect every outcome we observe, whether political or otherwise. For example, an individual's vote may have been influenced by seeing television advertisements, but it will also have been affected by his sense of loyalty to one party or the other, how he has fared economically in recent years, how his friends and relatives are voting, and countless other factors. This matters because to determine whether advertisements influenced his vote, we must isolate this factor and understand its effect separately from the other factors.

To explain this point more clearly, let's imagine a simpler world where the only two factors that affect vote choice are party identification and the advertisements that an individual sees. In such a world, we might be tempted to simply compare whether individuals exposed to more of a particular candidate's advertisements were more likely to vote for that candidate. Whatever difference we found between voters who saw more of the candidate's advertisements compared to those who saw less could then be attributed to the effect of the advertising. Or could it? The problem, even in this simple world, is that an individual's party identification is likely to affect how much advertising they see. We know, for example, that candidates attempt to show more advertisements to individuals who do not affiliate with either party in order to win over these "swing voters." It is also the case that Democratic candidates tend to show more advertisements to Democratic voters (as a way of encouraging them to turn out to vote), while largely ignoring Republicans. The opposite is true for Republican candidates.

Figure 5.2 presents a representation of how this could interfere significantly with the inferences we would draw in an observational study. This figure shows a hypothetical group of sixty voters—twenty Democrats, twenty

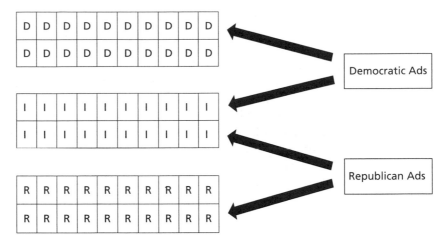

FIGURE 5.2 How Advertising Might Be Distributed in the Real World because of Strategic Targeting by Candidates

independents, and twenty Republicans. Because the Democratic and Republican candidates are acting strategically, both candidates target the same number of advertisements for independents, but only the Democratic candidate airs ads that are seen by the Democratic voters and only the Republican candidate shows ads to the Republican voters. Imagine that before the election began, every Democratic voter already had a .8 probability (or 80% chance) of voting for the Democratic candidate and every Republican voter had a .8 probability of voting for the Republican. Independent voters were equally likely to vote for either candidate (thus, they had a probability of .5 of voting for the Democrat and a probability of .5 of voting for the Republican).

You might see the problem that this will create for drawing a causal inference about the effect of advertising on vote choice. If we just look at the relationship between these two factors while ignoring partisan identification, we would erroneously observe a strong effect for advertising. Even if exposure to advertising had no effect at all, we would find that when a voter saw only Democratic advertisements, their probability of voting for the Democrat was .8; when they saw only Republican advertisements, their probability of voting for the Republican was .8, and when they saw advertisements from both parties, their probability of voting for either candidate was .5. Based on these data, we might conclude that when a voter sees only one candidate's advertisements, her probability of voting for that candidate increases by .3 (from .5 to .8). But we would be wrong: the advertising did not change anyone's vote preferences; the effect was merely **spurious**.

The problem with the observational study is that we had no control over which voters saw which advertisements. A voter's party identification, which influences that individual's vote choice, was also closely related to which candidate's advertisements she saw. Unless we accounted for voters' party affiliations in some way, we would be misled into thinking that advertising had an effect when it did not. Of course, there are ways to account for such confounding factors in observational studies, and those will be discussed in the following chapters. But the additional problem is that the world we observe is rarely so simple and it may often be the case that we are unable to account for all of the confounding explanations. Indeed, we often do not even know what all of those confounding factors are.

By providing researchers with control over the data-generating process, experiments offer a way to remove any confounding factors rather than attempting to account for all of them. To see why this is the case, let's return to the example above. Imagine that at the beginning of the campaign both candidates decided that they wanted to learn whether it was worthwhile to spend so much money on advertising. Thus, for this campaign they decided to give control over their advertising budgets to an enterprising researcher. With control over the data-generating process, the researcher now has to decide the best way to allocate the advertisements so that it is unlikely that there will be any confounding explanations for any vote differences he observes. If the researcher makes the allocations randomly, then, by definition, they will be uncorrelated with other factors. The researcher should now be free of any worry about alternative explanations if any differences are uncovered.

Figure 5.3 shows how this could work in practice. The same sixty individuals have been divided into the same three different advertising conditions: one group will receive the Democratic advertisements, another group will receive the Republican advertisements, and the last will receive both advertisements. Now, however, the three groups have been randomly assigned rather than selected by the candidates. Because of this, there will always be about the same percentage of Democrats, Republicans, and independents in each condition (as long as the sample size is sufficiently large).[7] As in the previous example, half of the sixty individuals will vote for the Democrat and half will favor the Republican, and because of randomization, each group should also be divided 50/50. If advertising has no effect at all on vote preferences, then we should observe relatively similar support across each condition, or across each of the three groups. However, if advertising is influential, then the group receiving the Republican advertisements should have a higher percentage of Republican voters and the group receiving the Democratic message, a higher percentage of Democratic voters. Thus, by allowing the researcher to control the distribution of advertising rather than the candidates, and by that researcher randomly assigning which individuals saw which advertisements, we can more clearly determine whether campaign ads are effective (or not).

7   The point about a large enough sample size (or subject pool) is an important one that we address below. For the time being, it is sufficient to say that, with a small sample size, one group might have a disproportionate amount of one party just by random chance.

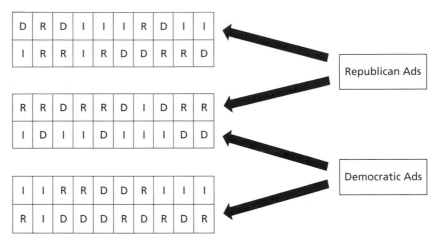

FIGURE 5.3 How a Researcher Might Distribute Advertising after Randomization

TYPES OF EXPERIMENTS

An experiment is defined by the ability of the researcher to exercise some control over the data-generating process. However, it is possible to execute an experiment in a variety of different ways. Generally speaking, political science research has been conducted via laboratory experiments, survey experiments, and field experiments. We discuss each in turn here.

Laboratory Experiments

The most commonly executed experimental design in political science has been the "**laboratory experiment**." Rest assured that this is not as ominous as it may sound. Political scientists rarely (if ever) get involved in poking or prodding individuals with needles and we are aware of few political science experiments that have required the use of petri dishes. Rather, a typical laboratory that political scientists operate with tends to look like nothing more than a sophisticated computer lab. On those computers, political scientists run programs that ask participants to engage in a wide variety of tasks designed to mimic political situations.

While political scientists were slower to adopt laboratory experiments compared with disciplines like economics and psychology, they have now been used to focus on a wide array of questions using a variety of approaches. A relatively simple form of a laboratory experiment might invite subjects to watch television advertisements for some fictional candidate(s). Subjects would be randomly assigned to view different commercials, and, typically, the researcher would assign one group (called the **control group**) to see no advertisements

Box 5.1: Genes Affect Your Political Attitudes: A Different Kind of Experimental Design

While experimental methods are relatively new to political scientists, an even newer strand of research is focused on linking our understanding of politics to biology and genetics. One of the first major studies in this vein was authored by John Alford, Carolyn Funk, and John Hibbing, and published in 2005.[a] The authors asked a simple question: "Are political orientations genetically transmitted?" Previously, political scientists had not seriously considered a role for genetics, instead focusing on understanding how childhood socialization played a role in attitudes taken by citizens later in life.

To examine whether genetics played any role in shaping future attitudes, the authors used what can best be described as a natural experiment. To do this, they compared monozygotic (or "identical") twins with dizygotic (or "fraternal") twins. The key to this comparison is that monozygotic twins share 100 percent of their genetic material while dizygotic twins share only 50 percent (on average). To determine how important genetics were in causing political attitudes, the authors examined the rate at which identical twins shared political views to the rate at which fraternal twins did so. They found that identical twins were much more likely to share opinions on a range of political issues, a finding they attributed to the fact that identical twins shared a much higher percentage of genetic material compared with fraternal twins. In fact, the authors found that genes play a substantial role in accounting for issue attitudes. They conclude, "We find that political attitudes are influenced much more heavily by genetics than by parental socialization . . . genetics accounts for approximately half of the variance in ideology, while shared environment, including parental influence only accounts for 11%."[b]

Of course, no methodological approach is perfect, and the twin design that this study was based on has received some criticism.[c] One basic critique with twin studies is that they rely on an assumption that fraternal and identical twins are raised in the same types of environments (the Equal Environment Assumption). But research has found that identical twins are treated by parents and others as if they are more alike compared with fraternal twins. Thus, it may be difficult to disentangle just how much of the increased similarity between the attitudes of identical twins is due to the fact that they are treated differently rather than the fact that they share more genetic material.

a. John R. Alford, Carolyn L. Funk, and John R. Hibbing, "Are political orientations genetically transmitted?" *American Political Science Review* 99 (2005): 153–167.
b. Alford, Funk, and Hibbing, "Are political orientations genetically transmitted," p. 164.
c. Evan Charney, "Genes and ideologies," *Perspectives on Politics* 6 (2008): 299–319.

at all. After watching the advertisements (or not watching them in the case of the control group), subjects would be asked, for example, to evaluate the candidate(s). Because the groups were randomly assigned and because they were identical in every way but the advertisement, if the researcher detected differences between the groups who saw advertisements (called the **treatment groups**) and those in the control group, then she could conclude that those differences had been caused by the advertising.

Stephen Ansolabehere and Shanto Iyengar used a series of laboratory experiments to examine the extent to which citizens were influenced by negative advertising.[8] Subjects were recruited to watch a local television news program for fifteen minutes. During a commercial break for that program, subjects would see an advertisement for a candidate who was currently running either for president or statewide office. Depending on which condition subjects were randomly assigned to, the advertisement they saw was either positive or negative in tone. This was the only aspect of the videos shown to subjects that differed across conditions. Ultimately, one of the key findings from this study had less to do with persuasion than it did with de-mobilization; specifically, the authors found that when subjects viewed negative advertising, they became less likely to want to vote at all.

The above example is a relatively simple experiment because individuals are examined as unitary actors. That is, a subject comes into the laboratory, is subjected to some treatment, asked some questions, and is then dismissed. More complicated laboratory experiments have studied decision-making processes by having multiple subjects interact with each other in the laboratory during the experiment. Often, these experiments are constructed to examine the extent to which individuals are able to reach collective decisions under different rules and circumstances. Consider for example, the research question posed by Nobel Laureate Elinor Ostrom and her colleagues: Under what conditions can members of a community overcome the obstacles to collective action and self-govern common pool resources? If you'll remember the discussion from Chapter 1, the tragedy of the commons posited that when individuals derive private gains from using the commons but only share the costs with all other users, they will overexploit the commons. This poses a problem of collective action, as the actions of one individual depend on the actions of another. If I live in a community where everyone is exploiting the resource as fast as possible, then I had better try to get my share before it is gone. If, however, I live in a community where other users sustainably use the resource and levy sanctions against those who over-exploit, then I might adapt a different strategy.

Using both small- and large-n studies, Ostrom and her colleagues found that self-governance can and does occur. (We will take a look at some of these studies in the next chapter.) The next question was under what conditions does self-governance occur? This was a harder research question to answer. The world is a messy place and determining *why* someone decided to limit his share of a resource is not an easy question to answer. The controlled environment of the laboratory was, therefore, particularly attractive. In their article "Covenants with and without a sword: Self-governance is possible," Ostrom

---

8 Stephen Ansolabehere and Shanto Iyengar, *Going negative* (New York: Free Press, 1995).

and her colleagues James Walker and Roy Gardner specifically wanted to test the impact of (1) communication and (2) sanctions, or *covenants* and *swords* in the terminology of Thomas Hobbes.[9] For Hobbes and many social scientists, covenants not backed by the credible threat of sanctions are meaningless. As he writes, "And Covenants, without the sword, are but words, and of no strength to secure a man at all."

To test these two factors, Ostrom and her colleagues developed an experimental game that simulated the commons. The rules of the game ensured that the research participants were interdependent on one another. Game participants, undergraduate economics students, could either invest in maintaining the commons or they could invest in some alternative activity. If they invested in the alternative activity, they were sure to get a return. If they invested in the commons, their return would depend on how much others invested in the commons. If other game participants also invested, they would do very well, but if other game participants did not invest, then they would be better off investing in the alternative activity. The game tried to simulate reality in that participants invested actual money and got to keep money won through the game. The experiments had one control group, where participants could not communicate and could not sanction, and three treatment groups: one that could only communicate, one that could only sanction, and one that could both communicate and sanction.[10] After repeated rounds of play, game participants in the control group only earned 32 percent of what they potentially could have. They performed on par with the group that could only sanction, which earned 38.8 percent of the potential total. The group that could only communicate did surprisingly well, even when the stakes were high, and earned 75 percent of the total. The group that could sanction and communicate earned 97 percent of the total. The authors were not surprised to find that the sanction and communication group did well, but their findings that communication was a more important factor than sanctions contradicted a good deal of political theory that had posited the opposite.

Ostrom and her colleagues were able to confidently identify the importance of communication because the laboratory is a relatively controlled venue. This control provides the experiment with a great deal of **internal validity**. In the laboratory, each subject tends to operate in the same environment with the only differences being those that the researcher controls. However, laboratory experiments tend to be criticized for their lack of **external validity**. This critique is largely based on the fact that, for a variety of reasons, subjects may respond quite differently to treatments in a controlled venue like the laboratory

---

9 Elinor Ostrom, James Walker, and Roy Gardner, "Covenants with and without a sword: Self-governance is possible," *American Political Science Review* 86 (1992): 404–417.

10 In the actual experiment, the authors varied additional factors, including the total amount of money at stake, how much the participants were able to communicate, the number of rounds of play, and the option to choose to have a sanctioning device for a small fee.

compared with out in the real world. Take the television advertising experiment for example. When subjects are invited to come to a laboratory to watch campaign advertisements, they likely will watch those ads much differently than they would in their own homes. In the laboratory, subjects know that they are being watched, so they may pay more attention to the advertisement than they would at home, where their attention would be divided by children, pets, etc. Indeed, how many people (who aren't political science majors) do you know who watch campaign ads intently?

In order to isolate a cause and effect, laboratory experiments are designed to simplify the world, but the real world is messy. Individuals in the real world are also bombarded with emails and phone calls from the candidates; they read newspaper articles about the candidates; and they have conversations with friends and family about the candidates. All of these things would likely have some effect on their vote choices and the competing sources of information would likely mute the effects of advertising in the "real world."

Political scientists who conduct laboratory experiments often address the external validity critique in several ways. First, experimental political scientists often note that, while their experiments may be somewhat lacking in external validity, the gains made on internal validity are worth it. Additionally, there is great value in approaching political questions with a variety of techniques that have different strengths and weaknesses. Laboratory experiments can help us uncover causal mechanisms and generate stronger causal inferences while observational studies can help us determine how generalizable those inferences might be in the "real world."

Second, it is often possible to design laboratory experiments so that they come closer to simulating reality and political scientists are becoming increasingly adept at doing this. For example, Richard Lau and David Redlawsk created a computer program that helped to better account for the variety of factors competing for a voter's attention during a campaign. As the authors explain:

> We have designed an interactive experimental paradigm to study voter decision making that captures the crucial features of modern political campaigns: They are media-based; they provide an overwhelming amount of relevant information, some of which voters choose to expose themselves to, some of which comes to voters without any conscious decision to learn it, and much of which is simply missed; and they are dynamic, in the sense that information available today may be gone tomorrow.[11]

Subjects in these experiments sit at a computer screen while links to items about the candidates scroll down the screen. Subjects can click on those links

11 Richard R. Lau and David P. Redlawsk, "Voting correctly," *American Political Science Review* 91 (1997): 585–598, p. 587.

to read more, but, while they are reading about that information, other information is scrolling by in the background. Furthermore, at certain points during the experiment, a political advertisement appears on the screen and the individual can do nothing else but watch the ad until it is over. The idea behind this elaborate set-up is that campaigns are full of information, and the better a researcher can approximate that environment in the laboratory, the more generalizable those conclusions will be for how voters behave in the real world.

Ansolabehere and Iyengar were also careful to design their experiments in order to maximize the external validity of their findings.[12] First, rather than show subjects advertisements from fictional candidates, they focused on real candidates and conducted their experiments during the actual campaign. Second, the researchers were careful to make the advertisements look realistic, often by making only minor adjustments to advertisements the campaigns were actually airing. Third, the advertisements were also presented to subjects in a setting that was as natural as possible. As the authors noted, "The viewing room was furnished with a couch, easy chairs, coffee table, and potted plants. Participants could snack on cookies and coffee while they watched the news, and in most cases participants came accompanied by a friend or co-worker."[13] Finally, the researchers were careful not to tell subjects about what they were studying until after the experiment was over. Instead, subjects were told that they were participating in a study about how individuals perceive the news. If subjects knew that they were participating in a study of television advertising effects, they may have paid more attention to the advertisements than would be typical. Indeed, in many political science experiments it is necessary to keep the goal of the experiment hidden from subjects until after they have completed the task.

A second threat to external validity in laboratory experiments is the nature of the subjects being studied in the experiments. Political scientists often rely on **convenience samples** for their studies, and most typically these convenience samples are made up of their own students. Students are in abundant supply on college campuses and researchers have discovered that many of them are more than willing to participate in research experiments in exchange for a small fee or extra credit. However, students also tend to differ from the general population of American adults in several important ways. For example, college students tend to have more malleable opinions and attitudes on issues and greater cognitive capacity than the general population.[14] As you

---

12 For more detail on how Ansolabehere and Iyengar address external validity, see pp. 20–22 of *Going negative.*

13 Ansolabehere and Iyengar, *Going negative,* p. 21.

14 David O. Sears, "College sophomores in the laboratory: Influences of a narrow data base on social psychology's view of human nature," *Journal of Personality and Social Psychology* 51 (1986): 515–530.

might imagine, these tendencies could influence the findings in many political studies. For example, political scientists often use laboratory experiments to examine whether framing an issue in different terms can cause citizens to take different positions on that issue. If, in fact, college students have weaker opinions on issues, then it may be easier to change their mind by framing an issue in a different way than it would be for a typical adult. Nevertheless, recent work by James Druckman and Cindy Kam suggests that the situations in which student subject pools pose a threat to external validity tend to be relatively limited, and that concerns about the use of this population in experiments may be over-stated.[15]

To increase the external validity of their studies, researchers often try to recruit non-student adult populations for their studies. Such an approach typically entails advertising the opportunity in local newspapers or websites and offering some non-trivial payment in exchange for participation. For example, for their experiments on negative advertising, Ansolabehere and Iyengar recruited participants by advertising in local newspapers, distributing flyers in shopping malls, making announcements at offices and churches, and even telephoning individuals from voter registration lists. However, recruiting a sample in this way can be challenging for a variety of reasons. First, the costs associated with such recruitment efforts can be substantial. In order to get adults to participate in laboratory studies, the fee must be non-trivial. For example, Ansolabehere and Iyengar paid $15 to each subject in 1992 (which would be over $20 today), with the typical experiment lasting approximately one hour. Since they recruited approximately 3,000 subjects for their experiments, this amounted to a cost of $45,000 just in payments to subjects. Advertising can also be costly, and there are substantial administrative costs involved in such an effort. Ansolabehere and Iyengar ran their experiments from two different three-room suite offices in different parts of Los Angeles. The researchers had to pay for the office space and for the furniture and other materials located in that space. They also had to pay individuals to run the experiments in each of those offices, with the experiments generally taking place between 10 a.m. to 8 p.m. every evening. And even with all this effort, the types of adults recruited in this way are still likely to be unrepresentative of the general population.[16]

---

15 James N. Druckman and Cindy D. Kam, "Students as experimental participants: In defense of the 'narrow data base'," in James N. Druckman, Donald P. Green, James H. Kuklinski, *et al.*, eds, *Cambridge handbook of experimental political science* (Cambridge, UK: Cambridge University Press, 2011), pp. 41–57.

16 In the Ansolabehere and Iyengar experiments, the individuals recruited were much more likely to have a college degree relative to the general population and they were also much more likely to be African American.

Survey Experiments

Survey experiments were initially conceived as a way of understanding what researchers mostly considered to be a nuisance for public opinion polling; namely, that those being polled tended to express different opinions depending on how a question was worded or what else had been asked earlier in the survey. For example, respondents asked about whether they approve of the job the president is doing in office tend to give somewhat different responses when the question is placed after an inquiry about economic conditions. Asking the question about the economy first tends to lead to lower approval ratings when the economy is doing poorly and higher ratings when the economy is doing well. Either way, the question about the economy is priming respondents to think more about the economy as they evaluate the president than they would have otherwise.

Pollsters used survey experiments to better understand some of these patterns. For example, they would randomly assign respondents into different conditions, where one-half would get the economy question first and the other half would get the approval question first. This would help a pollster to understand the nature and magnitude of the question order effects they were encountering, thereby making it possible to adjust for any bias. For a political scientist, the same type of experiment may yield important insights into how the public thinks about politics and how their opinions can be manipulated by elites.[17]

A question wording experiment can be used in a similar way. Take, for example, an experiment conducted by the Pew Research Center in 2002. The survey was conducted by telephone from August 14 to 25, 2002 with a national sample of 1,001 adults. At the time, the United States was debating whether to invade Iraq, and the survey asked respondents about that very issue. However, the pollsters at Pew were interested in understanding whether respondents would answer differently if given a differently worded question. One-half of the sample was randomly assigned to a version of the question that simply asked "Would you favor or oppose taking military action in Iraq to end Saddam Hussein's rule?" The other half of the respondents received a question that asked, "Would you favor or oppose taking military action in Iraq to end Saddam Hussein's rule, *even if it meant that U.S. forces might suffer thousands of casualties?*"

The differently worded questions led to very distinct responses from the public. When asked the shorter version of the question, which omitted the clause about the risk of casualties, 62 percent of respondents favored military

---

17 John Zaller and Stanley Feldman, "A simple theory of the survey response: Answering questions versus revealing preferences," *American Journal of Political Science* 36 (1992): 579–616.

action while 24 percent opposed it (14 percent were undecided). However, when the question wording included the phrase about the risk of casualties, support for military action dropped to 43 percent, with 42 percent opposed and 16 percent undecided. The different results produced by variations in question wording was important in its own right, particularly as it underscored how tenuous public support for an Iraqi invasion really was. However, the experiment had additional value to political scientists by demonstrating that Americans often fail to consider the risks inherent in policy actions unless specifically primed to do so.[18]

While survey experiments were a relatively uncommon research approach in much of twentieth-century political science, they are quickly becoming more widely used by political scientists for two main reasons. First, surveys are becoming an increasingly affordable way for political scientists to collect data. In the past, most survey data was collected by human interviewers either in person or by telephone. While many polls are still conducted in this manner, political scientists are increasingly turning to internet surveys. Such surveys can generally be conducted at a fraction of the cost of traditional polls because it is not necessary to employ individuals to ask respondents questions.[19] Second, the use of internet experiments also expands the types of treatments that political scientists can apply to respondents. With surveys conducted over the telephone, researchers were largely limited to changing the wording of a question and observing whether the different wording influenced the types of answers respondents provided. Internet surveys allow for a more dynamic and flexible survey where respondents can be shown different pictures or videos during the interview. Thus, to study advertising effects, a researcher could embed video of an advertisement during a survey and ask questions about the candidates featured in the ad following that video.[20]

Even with modern internet survey technology, survey experiments are typically more limited than laboratory experiments with regard to the types of treatments that can be employed. For example, it is far more difficult to set up an experiment where subjects interact with each other to reach collective decisions with a survey compared to the laboratory. Yet, while survey experiments tend to be simpler in their construction, they have the potential to improve external validity. The increased external validity for these experiments comes from the types of subjects used; survey experiments are most commonly performed on a random (or representative) sample of American adults. Accordingly, researchers need not be as concerned about whether the

18 David L. Eckles and Brian F. Schaffner, "Priming risk: The accessibility of uncertainty in public policy decision making," *Journal of Insurance Issues* 34 (2011): 151.
19 Brian F. Schaffner, "Innovations in survey research," in Stephen K. Medvic, ed., *New directions in campaigns and elections* (New York: Routledge, 2011), pp. 39–58.
20 Lynn Vavreck, "The exaggerated effects of advertising on turnout: The dangers of self-reports," *Quarterly Journal of Political Science* 2 (2007): 325–343.

findings they uncover with their survey experiments are generalizable to the larger public.

While it is generally true that survey experiments are conducted on representative samples, experimental political scientists have begun conducting these types of experiments on convenience samples as well. With this approach, a researcher programs a survey using some web-based survey software to place a survey experiment at some URL. Some of the most common software programs include Survey Monkey (www.surveymonkey.com), Survey Gizmo (www.surveygizmo.com) and Zoomerang (www.zoomerang.com). The researcher then uses a variety of platforms to recruit people to take the survey. For example, an advertisement on Google or Facebook may invite people to participate. Even more effective is recruiting from a community of individuals registered at sites like Amazon.com's Mechanical Turk site. Mechanical Turk is a platform that connects individuals interested in completing small tasks for payment with people or companies seeking such assistance. Initially, the types of tasks that individuals performed on Mechanical Turk included tagging images to indicate what appeared on those photographs or looking at websites to determine whether the content is unsuitable for children. However, social scientists soon discovered that individuals on Mechanical Turk were also willing to participate in online surveys for a nominal fee.

A political scientist seeking to use the Mechanical Turk community to conduct an experiment would start by using an online survey program to develop a short questionnaire. Depending on the length of the survey, the researcher would then decide how much to offer individuals registered on Turk to complete the survey. For example, for a survey of approximately five minutes, the researcher might offer between 25 and 50 cents. The researcher can then set a limit on how many responses she is willing to accept and whether individuals will be allowed to complete the task more than once (for most experiments, researchers will want to limit participation to one time). Depending on the length of the task and how much is offered, researchers are often able to collect hundreds of responses within a week.

Despite the fact that over 100,000 Americans have registered to complete tasks on Mechanical Turk, the population of Turk users is hardly representative of the adult population. Turk workers tend to be younger, more educated, and are more likely to be female compared with the American adult population. There is also some evidence that Turksters are more likely to identify as Democrats and independents than they are to be Republicans. Nevertheless, in comparison with other convenience samples (like college sophomores), the Mechanical Turk population is much more representative of the population and, even more importantly, produces variation on variables like age, education, and interest in politics. Thus, for researchers interested in quickly gathering data from a survey experiment of a convenience sample of American adults, Mechanical Turk has become a viable option. Several studies have even found that a Turk sample tends to be more representative and attentive than using college students as subjects.[21] Furthermore, for the student researcher without access to an experimental laboratory, an online survey using the Turk community may be an excellent option.[22]

Field Experiments

Until recently, **field experiments** had been used sparingly by political scientists. Yet, in many ways, they represent an ideal research design for demonstrating causal relationships with high levels of internal *and* external validity. A field experiment is an experiment that takes place out in the world, where the researcher lacks laboratory-like control over the environment. Individuals are generally selected to participate in such an experiment without their knowledge and often real-life political outcomes are observed. Perhaps the most famous recent examples of field experiments are those carried out by Don Green, Alan Gerber, and their colleagues.[23] Green and Gerber were interested in understanding whether candidates or parties could increase voter turnout by contacting voters and encouraging them to vote. Observational studies seeking to understand the effects of campaign contact on voter turnout suffered from some of the same issues mentioned above in the discussion of campaign advertising. Candidates and parties only target certain individuals for such appeals. Thus, Green and Gerber knew that they needed a way to randomize which voters were contacted and how they were contacted.

The Green and Gerber experiments have usually involved using lists of registered voters maintained by states or parties to randomly assign individuals into different conditions. They then cooperate with either political parties or interest groups to have some individuals receive an appeal to vote while others do not. After the election, they can return to the state's vote records to determine whether, in fact, the individuals who received contact were more likely to vote than those in the control condition. Because such a large number of individuals have been randomly assigned into different conditions, if they find differences between the treatment and control conditions, they can be confident that these differences can be attributed to the appeals. For the most part, Green and Gerber have found that face-to-face appeals are the most effective, while those sent by mail or by phone have only marginal effects.

---

21 Adam J. Berinsky, Gregory A. Huber, and Gabriel S. Lenz. "Evaluating online labor markets for experimental research: Amazon.com's mechanical turk," *Political Analysis* 20 (2012): 351–368.

22 Indeed, we have had much recent success advising undergraduate students who have used Mechanical Turk to conduct experiments for their research papers.

23 See, for example, Donald P. Green and Alan S. Gerber. *Get out the vote: How to increase voter turnout* (Washington, D.C.: Brookings Institution Press, 2008).

Green and Gerber have made a forceful case for field experiments as the "gold standard" of social science research:

> Random assignment ensures unbiased inferences about cause and effect. Natural settings ensure that the results will tell us something about the real world, not just some contrived laboratory setting. Field experimentation would therefore seem to recommend itself as the most solid and unobjectionable form of social science and program evaluation.[24]

Field experiments have been used to answer a wide array of research questions over the past several years. For example, one study randomly assigned individuals in Virginia to receive free subscriptions to either a conservative or liberal newspaper during a campaign to examine whether newspaper coverage influences how individuals vote.[25] In another field experiment, a researcher convinced candidates in Benin to make different types of appeals during a campaign (narrow versus broad appeals) to determine whether these different campaign messages led to different results.[26] Another set of researchers conducted a field experiment in Rwanda to examine whether using radio-based appeals to encourage citizens to be less deferential to authorities led those citizens to express more dissent with the government.[27]

A recent study even used a field experiment to address the influence of campaign advertisements on vote choice.[28] In 2006, Texas Governor Rick Perry (R) agreed to allow $2 million worth of his television and radio advertising decisions to be randomly assigned by political scientists. This control was ceded to researchers during a three-week period in the primary phase of his re-election campaign in eighteen of the twenty television markets in the state of Texas.[29] The political scientists involved in the study randomly assigned each market into different conditions so that decisions about when Perry's advertising would begin in that market (and how much advertising would appear) would be uncorrelated with other factors. They then conducted daily surveys

24 Green and Gerber. "The underprovision of experiments in political science," p. 94.

25 Alan S. Gerber, Dean Karlan, and Daniel Bergan, "Does the media matter? A field experiment measuring the effect of newspapers on voting behavior and political opinions," *American Economic Journal: Applied Economics* 1 (2009): 35–52.

26 Leonard Wantchekon, "Clientelism and voting behavior: Evidence from a field experiment in Benin," *World Politics* 55 (2003): 399–422.

27 Elizabeth Levy Paluck and Donald P. Green, "Deference, dissent, and dispute resolution: An experimental intervention using mass media to change norms and behavior in Rwanda," *American Political Science Review* 103 (2009): 622.

28 Alan S. Gerber, James G. Gimpel, Donald P. Green, *et al.*, "How large and long-lasting are the persuasive effects of televised campaign ads? Results from a randomized field experiment," *American Political Science Review* 105 (2011): 135–150.

29 The campaign did not want to cede control of Houston or Dallas–Fort Worth, the two largest markets in the state.

across the state to see how support for Perry fluctuated across each market. The authors did find that advertising had strong, but short-lived, effects on support for Perry. When advertising was introduced in a market, support for Perry increased, but that increase decayed after a few weeks.

It is not often that candidates are willing to turn over their advertising decisions to political scientists, but the opportunity was an excellent one for expanding what we know about advertising effects during campaigns. As the authors note:

> This research is not the first study to show advertising effects, but demonstrating these effects with a field experiment is an important advance because the research design sidesteps criticisms that are often levied against other research methods. The large effects that are observed in the laboratory are routinely challenged on the grounds that they fail to tell us how media exposure translates into votes in the context of an actual campaign. . . . The large effects found in observational studies are similarly open to the charge that campaigns target their ads strategically.[30]

Because this experiment was carried out during an actual campaign, it helps to bolster the findings from earlier laboratory experiments as well as those produced from observational studies.

Of course, field experiments can be difficult and often very costly to conduct. For example, it costs a lot of money to randomly send campaign mailings or some other information to hundreds (or thousands) of citizens. It can also cost a great deal of money to collect information on the dependent variable, particularly if doing so involves conducting a survey. Thus, for the average student, a field experiment is probably only viable when conducted in cooperation with either (1) a professor with a substantial research account or (2) an organization that would like to evaluate the effectiveness of its activities. Based on our informal assessments of most of our colleagues' research accounts, the latter situation is the one most likely to apply to the vast majority of students. But this possibility should be taken seriously by the enterprising student researcher. Think about groups (or politicians) for which you have an internship. The people at these organizations may very well be interested in a project that would help them understand how to persuade more citizens to support their cause. If you can design a study that would accomplish that goal, and you can explain how it would benefit their organization (as well as your own research goals), then they may very well allow you to have some control over their activities.

---

30 Gerber *et al.*, "How large and long-lasting are the persuasive effects of televised campaign ads?" pp. 147–148.

Box 5.2: Are Field Experiments Ethical?

While field experiments hold enormous potential for their ability to capitalize on high levels of internal and external validity, some scholars have questioned to what extent they are ethical. One ethical concern has to do with the fact that, in most field experiments, the subjects do not know they are participants in a study. This is not the case in laboratory or survey experiments, where individuals can opt out of a study (no individual can be forced to participate in an experiment or a survey). In field experiments, it is difficult, if not impossible, to inform subjects that they are participating in a study in the first place. Imagine researchers trying to contact every individual in the state of Texas before they conducted the advertising experiments there in 2006. Of course, if a field experiment has little chance of causing any harm to an individual, this inability to opt out may not be of concern. But what of an experiment like that conducted by Paluck and Green in post-genocide Rwanda? In that experiment, some communities were assigned to hear radio programs that would encourage people to be less deferential to authority and the researchers found that listening to these programs did make individuals more willing to express dissent. But what if these expressions of dissent led to some individuals being arrested or even just shunned by the community? Such an outcome could have significant social and economic consequences for those individuals.

A second (somewhat related) ethical concern is that a field experiment may hold the potential of influencing a social outcome, such as an election result. For example, imagine a field experiment designed to see whether voters could be mobilized by particular messages. If the mobilization was successful, and it succeeded mostly by mobilizing low-income voters who were more likely to vote Democratic, then a close election could be influenced by that effort. Then again, most field experiments generally produce rather small effects and, since they are randomized, they should not have a clear bias in any given direction. Furthermore, it is generally the case that scholars are cooperating with groups that would have made those same efforts anyway; the presence of the scholar in these situations is merely to persuade the organization to include some degree of randomization in the distribution of those resources. Nevertheless, scholars should make themselves aware of the potential ethical questions surrounding field experiments, and endeavor to produce experiments that are as ethical as possible. Following the proper Human Subjects Review process at your university will help to ensure that your experiments are as ethical as is warranted.

A few examples of successful field experiments executed at little (if any) cost by the researchers may help to illustrate this point. Daniel Bergan conducted a study of lobbying by convincing a coalition of interest groups in New Hampshire to randomly determine which state legislators would receive grassroots email appeals from their members and which would not.[31] The appeals were managed by the interest group and Bergan only needed to download the final

31 Daniel E. Bergan, "Does grassroots lobbying work? A field experiment measuring the effects of an e-mail lobbying campaign on legislative behavior," *American Politics Research* 37 (2009): 327–352.

roll call vote from the legislature's website to see whether the lobbying had an effect on how legislators voted on the relevant bill (it did). In another field experiment, Allison Dale and Aaron Strauss cooperated with interest groups to randomly determine whether individuals on their mobilization lists would get a text message reminder about voting and what kind of message they would receive.[32] The text message campaign was carried out by the organizations and the researchers needed only to work with a voter file firm to determine the percentage of individuals in each condition that actually voted. Even the $2 million television advertising experiment described above would have been utterly impossible for political scientists to carry out on their own, without the cooperation of one of the candidates. What these and other recent field experiments demonstrate is that, with a lot of initiative and a little luck, it is possible to conduct an excellent field experiment without breaking the bank.

DESIGNING THE EXPERIMENT

The design stage is make-or-break for an experiment. Unlike the analysis of observational data, which is a more dynamic process where the researcher can often add new variables or conduct more interviews to account for mistakes committed in the early going, a poorly conceived experiment is typically impossible to salvage. If something goes awry with an experiment, then there is usually no other choice but to try again.

On its face, an experiment may seem relatively straightforward to design. After formulating hypotheses, the researcher should be able to easily identify which independent variables need to be manipulated in the experiment. For example, if the researcher hypothesizes that seeing more of a candidate's advertisements will make an individual more likely to vote for that candidate, then exposure to advertising is the variable that needs to be manipulated in the experiment. Once this variable has been identified, then the researcher must focus on how much variation needs to be introduced on that variable. The researcher might decide that two conditions are sufficient—in one condition subjects would see one advertisement from the candidate and in the other condition subjects would not see any advertisements. This is the most simple experiment that a researcher could conduct, as it is limited to just two conditions. Of course, the researcher may decide that it is important to see how different amounts of advertising may have different effects. This can be tested by adding more conditions to the experiment; one additional condition may have a group of subjects see five advertisements from the candidate while another group might see ten.

To conduct a simple experiment like the one just described, the researcher would need to begin by developing the treatment (in this case, an advertisement

---

32 Allison Dale and Aaron Strauss, "Don't forget to vote: Text message reminders as a mobilization tool," *American Journal of Political Science* 53 (2009): 787–804.

for a hypothetical candidate). The next step would be recruiting subjects to participate in the experiment. As noted above, this could involve soliciting participation from students on a college campus or perhaps recruiting participants online at a site like Amazon's Mechanical Turk. The number of participants that a researcher must recruit for an experiment depends on a number of factors, including the type of statistics that will be compared (means or proportions), the size of the differences the researcher expects to find, and the number of conditions the experiment has. While there are formulas to help provide guidance on these matters, a good rule of thumb is to make sure that you have at least thirty to fifty subjects in each condition. Thus, for the hypothetical advertising experiment that includes four conditions, the researcher would want to try to recruit at least 200 subjects.

Once the subjects have been recruited for an experiment, the researcher must assign them to one of the conditions. As explained above, it is important that this assignment be done randomly to help ensure that any differences observed across the groups are attributable to the treatments imposed by the researcher rather than some other factor. The researcher can use a random number generator available online or through programs like Excel, Stata, SPSS, or SAS; the randomization could also be as simple as drawing numbers from a hat, flipping coins, or rolling dice.

It is worth noting that randomization does not always work as well in small samples, so, when subject pools are smaller, the researcher might pursue one of two different strategies. First, the researcher could do the randomization as planned and check to make sure the groups are roughly equivalent on the types of variables that might be correlated with the dependent variable. For example, in the advertising experiment, the researcher might want to make sure that each condition has a roughly similar percentage of Democrats, Republicans, and independents. Ideally, the researcher would discover significant unbalance before the experiment is executed; however, if this is not possible, then knowing the nature of the unbalance will at least allow the researcher to control for these rival explanations when analyzing the results.

A second possibility is to conduct what is called block randomization. Block randomization is a way of making sure that your groups will be balanced on some important variable (or variables). For example, if you are concerned about having a lack of balance on party identification, then you could start by taking four Democrats from your subject pool and randomly send one of these four Democrats to each of the four conditions. Then repeat this process until you have sent all the Democrats to one of the four conditions and follow by repeating the same process for Republicans and independents. Proceeding in this fashion will guarantee that your groups will be relatively even on that variable.

Once subjects have been assigned to a condition, they should be administered .the appropriate treatment (or lack thereof if they are in the control group). Following the treatment, it is necessary to measure the dependent variable of interest in some way. In the field experiments conducted by Green and Gerber, this was done simply by obtaining the official voter files from the state and then looking to see who voted and who did not vote. In a laboratory or survey experiment, the dependent variable is typically measured by asking questions of the subjects following the treatment. For example, after showing subjects a candidate's advertisements, you might ask how likely they would be to vote for the candidate who aired the advertisement. Subjects could place themselves on a scale ranging from 0 (not at all likely) to 10 (very likely). Additional questions could ask subjects how likeable and competent the candidate seemed (perhaps using similar scales). Once you have recruited a subject to take the time to participate, it generally makes sense to ask several questions of him after the treatment since you may find that the treatment influences some types of attitudes or opinions, but not others. The addition of such questions can also be useful in hiding the subject of the experiment.

ANALYZING AND PRESENTING RESULTS FROM AN EXPERIMENT

While experiments require a great deal of thought and planning to execute, they have the benefit of producing results that are relatively easy to analyze and present. The reason for this simplicity is that, by controlling the data generation process, the researcher has presumably removed the need to control for other variables or use complicated statistical techniques to establish a causal relationship. If the experiment was designed well, then to determine the effect of the independent variable on the dependent variable, one need only to compare values of the dependent variable across each of the conditions. The addition of a relatively simple statistical test will help to determine how confident you can be that these differences are more than just random fluctuations.

Once the experiment is completed, the researcher should generate summary statistics for each of the experimental groups. These summary statistics may be averages (if the variables are continuous) or proportions (if the variables are categorical). Once calculated, the statistics can be compared across groups to determine whether any differences exist. In these comparisons, the control group serves as the baseline, since this group did not receive any treatment at all. Then each treatment group can be compared with the control group as well as to each other.

Suppose we executed the experiment described above, where subjects were shown either no advertisements, one advertisement, five advertisements, or ten advertisements and then asked how likely they would be (on a scale of 0 to 100) to support the candidate featured in the ads. We would begin by taking each individual's score on the 0 to 100 scale and then averaging them to generate a mean value for each group. These mean scores are presented in Table 5.1. The interpretation of these results would be rather straightforward. The average support for the candidate was only a few points higher for the group that saw just one advertisement, but support was about 15 points higher among subjects who viewed five advertisements.

TABLE 5.1 Average Scores in Hypothetical Advertising Experiment

	Control	One advertisement	Five advertisements	Ten advertisements
Average support	50.6	54.2	65.8	72.4

While a table like Table 5.1 is a perfectly reasonable way of presenting this information to someone reading about your findings, visual representations of results tend to be more impactful on readers. Thus, we might easily convert our findings from Table 5.1 into a figure like Figure 5.4. We chose a bar chart for this figure rather than a line graph because the line graph implies that we have data across the range of values on the *x*-axis. However, we really only know how subjects react to seeing either no, one, five, or ten advertisements, so a bar chart would be more appropriate here. We might have spaced the *x*-axis so that rather than each condition being next to each other there would be gaps between one and five, and five and ten, to account for the jump in the number of ads between those conditions. But the tradeoff of such an approach is that the bars would no longer be close enough to each other to easily gauge their relative sizes, so in this figure we kept the bars next to each other. Ultimately, this figure shows quite clearly that the biggest increase in support comes from moving from one advertisement to five advertisements. In other words, there are diminishing returns with increasing advertising; the first five advertisements are much more influential than the next five.

To this point, we have merely examined the mean values for all subjects across conditions. However, there are often reasons to expect that the treatment effects might be larger for some groups than they are for others. For example,

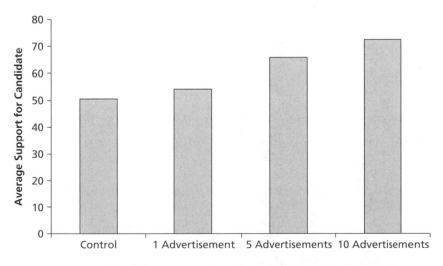

FIGURE 5.4 Example of the Presentation of Results from a Simple Experiment

people who pay less attention to politics may be easier to influence with political rhetoric; similarly, individuals who do not identify with either political party may be easier to persuade with advertising. Exploring the way that treatments affect some groups more than others is an excellent way to push the analysis beyond the simple reporting of differences across conditions and uncover additional results worthy of discussion. In many experiments, the treatment effects are small when comparing the effects among all respondents, but, when subgroups are analyzed, larger and more significant differences may be revealed. For example, if independent voters are strongly influenced by advertisements, but neither Democrats nor Republicans are moved much, then looking at all subjects together could be a bit misleading. After all, the advertisements have a strong effect on independents, but independents might have only comprised about one-third of our subject pool.

Figure 5.5 presents how results for our advertising experiment might work differently among Democrats, Republicans, and independents who had viewed an advertisement from a Democratic candidate. Note that in this figure it is clear that advertising matters little for Democrats and Republicans. Democratic subjects already liked the Democratic candidate quite a bit, while Republicans already disliked her. More advertising from that candidate did little to change these predilections. Independents, on the other hand, were more influenced by the candidate's advertising, with their support being about 30 percentage points higher in the 10 advertisements condition compared with the control condition. The lesson here is that delving deeper into the findings to examine different treatment effects for different subgroups is often a rewarding exercise.

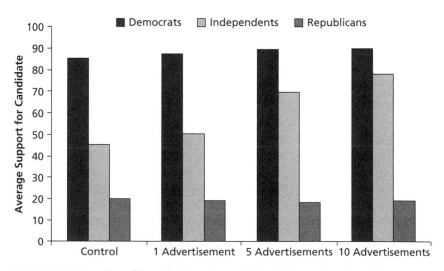

FIGURE 5.5 How the Effect of Advertising Might Differ by Partisanship in a Hypothetical Experiment

AVOIDING MISTAKES IN YOUR EXPERIMENT

There are many reasons why an experiment may fail. Recall that the strength of an experiment is in the creation of different groups that are essentially equivalent on everything other than the variable (or variables) being manipulated. To understand what effect the independent variable has on the dependent variable in your experiment, it is important to consider what the control condition should look like. Constructing a good control condition is often more difficult than it might initially sound. For example, what should a control group look like in a campaign advertising experiment? Should individuals assigned to the control group watch no advertisements at all? Or should they watch advertisements for some consumer product rather than the political advertisements? If you follow either of these strategies, then subjects in the control condition may be quite confused when you start asking them about candidates they have never heard of (since they never saw any of the relevant advertisements).

Political scientists Rebecca Morton and Kenneth Williams point out, "Many experiments do not have a clear baseline and in some cases it is not necessary."[33] While this is certainly true in many situations, one should always take as much care as possible to create conditions that will produce as much variation in the key variable(s) as is warranted to draw useful conclusions. Thus, in an advertising experiment, it may in fact make sense to have a condition where some subjects see no advertisements at all. To deal with the problem mentioned above, all subjects could be asked to read an identical brief description of the candidates before watching ads. Thus, all subjects will start with the same baseline information about the candidates, and the only difference will be what advertisements the subjects see after reading that information.

A related issue that can arise in the design of an experiment is when more than one variable is allowed to vary across conditions. Consider a relatively simple experiment designed to determine whether female candidates are perceived differently than male candidates. A researcher might design an experiment where subjects read a brief description of a candidate for office and then evaluate the candidate along several dimensions. In one condition the candidate would be male, but in the other condition the candidate would be described as female. However, what if the researcher also designed the experiment so that the male candidate was a Republican and the female candidate was a Democrat. If the experiment was designed in this way, the variables for party and gender would be perfectly correlated and there would be no way to

---

33 Rebecca B. Morton and Kenneth C. Williams, "Experimentation in political science," in *Oxford handbook of political methodology* (Oxford: Oxford University Press, 2008), pp. 339–356.

differentiate their effects. Thus, the researcher would not be able to determine whether any differences in subjects' evaluations across conditions were attributable to the different gender of the candidate or the different party label.

While the example above is a relatively simple one that seems easy enough to avoid, it is remarkable how many experimental designs we have seen where this rule has been violated. This often happens when experiments become more complicated and there are many different pieces of information that have to be accounted for. At the same time, researchers are always cognizant of the limited number of subjects that they may be able to recruit for their experiments, so there is often a strong preference to create as few conditions as possible in order to avoid having too many conditions with too few subjects. Pre-testing is generally not useful for uncovering instances where too many variables vary across too few conditions. Instead, it is imperative on the researcher to think carefully about what pieces of information vary across conditions. It may even be useful to create a table or grid to ensure that every piece of information that changes has its own conditions.

Another common mistake made in the design of an experiment happens when the researcher develops a treatment that does not produce the variation in the independent variable that the researcher intended. Often this happens because the treatment is not strong enough and possibly goes unnoticed by the subjects. As an example, imagine an experiment that is designed to determine whether negative campaign advertisements make citizens less interested in politics. The researcher might design an advertisement that she thinks is clearly a negative attack on the candidate's opponent and then show this advertisement to subjects. But what if the experimental subjects do not perceive the advertisement in the way the researcher intended; perhaps they do not see the ad as negative at all. In this case, the experiment cannot be used to draw conclusions about the effects of negative ads since the subjects did not actually perceive the ads as negative. In essence, the treatment is not operationalized in a way that really represents the theoretical concept the researcher is attempting to understand.

Researchers often take several different approaches to ensure that they do not create an experiment that fails to properly operationalize the key concepts. These strategies are best used in conjunction with one another for full effect. First, it is useful in an experiment to use a validity check to see whether subjects perceived the treatment in the way it was intended to be perceived. In the example of negative advertisements, respondents might be asked whether they thought the advertisement they just viewed was positive, negative, or neutral in tone. If most subjects correctly identified the advertisement as negative, then this would bolster the researcher's confidence in the results. Of course, if the researcher only does this when he runs the experiment, it will be too late if he discovers that most subjects do not see the advertisement as negative. Thus, a second strategy is to use a small subsample of subjects for a pre-test of the experiment. These subjects can participate in the experiment and then

Box 5.3: Studying Corruption with Experiments

The issue of corruption is an important one, and a wealth of political science and economic research has focused on understanding what mechanisms work for discouraging corruption. While many of these studies are large-n observational analyses, some scholars have used clever experimental approaches to gain a better understanding of this question. Benjamin Olken wanted to understand to what extent monitoring (with the threat of a sanction) could reduce the amount of corruption observed in the building of public works projects.[a] To do this, he cooperated with the Indonesian government to conduct a field experiment in conjunction with the government's allocation of block grants to construct roads in 608 different villages. Local officials receiving these grants may have an incentive to embezzle some of the funds allocated for the road projects. However, Olken assigned villages to different conditions. The control group was in a condition where the possibility of a government audit was normal (4 percent chance); villages in the experimental group had a 100 percent chance of being audited and were told this before they received their funds. Olken did find that less money was missing from projects in villages assigned to the treatment condition; however, more jobs were given to family members in these villages, suggesting that the nature of the corrupt acts simply changed.

a. Benjamin A. Olken, *Monitoring corruption: Evidence from a field experiment in Indonesia*, No. w11753 (Cambridge: National Bureau of Economic Research, 2005).

be fully debriefed by the researcher. During the debriefing, the researcher can ask these test subjects whether they viewed the treatments in the way that was intended and whether anything else about the experiment was confusing or otherwise problematic. Using the information gleaned from this debriefing, the researcher can then tweak the experiment before running it with the larger sample of subjects.

NATURAL EXPERIMENTS

To this point in the chapter, we have discussed experiments as research designs where the researcher has control over the data-generating process. Specifically, the researcher is able to manipulate the extent to which subjects are exposed (or not exposed) to some treatment. However, political scientists are also increasingly making use of what are often called **natural experiments**. Natural experiments differ from experiments in that the researcher actually does not have control over assignment of the independent variable. However, good natural experiments can be analyzed as if they are experiments because some exogenous, approximately random process creates variation in the independent variable in a way that is unlikely to be correlated with any other rival explanations. As Robinson, McNulty, and Krasno explain, "The hallmark of a natural experiment is a circumstance that creates some sort of arbitrary or random division of an observed population."[34]

To illustrate what makes a natural experiment different from both an experiment and a large-n observational study, we will use the example of a study conducted by Bob Erikson and Laura Stoker.[35] As you likely know, during the Vietnam War the United States drafted young men into military service. While the method of drafting individuals was initially idiosyncratic to local draft boards, in 1969 a standard national system was developed. This system was based on randomly assigning each day of the year a number between 1 and 366; individuals would receive the number that had been assigned to their birthday. Lower numbers were at high risk of being drafted while those with high numbers were at low risk of being drafted. Ultimately, individuals holding numbers 1 through 195 were called up in the draft.

Erikson and Stoker were interested in understanding how the risk of being drafted influenced the types of opinions young Americans developed towards the war and ultimately how it affected their vote choices and party identification in the long run. In a true experiment, the researchers would have to manipulate the variable of interest. Of course, it is quite unrealistic to expect researchers to be able to assign individuals to different conditions where they have a higher or lower risk of being drafted, especially for a war that occurred several decades ago. Yet, even though the researchers did not have any control of the data generation process themselves, draft status was still determined by a random lottery and, therefore, should not be correlated with any other competing explanations. In essence, nature produced a quasi-experimental intervention that could then be exploited by the authors.

Erikson and Stoker took advantage of the fact that scholars had conducted a political socialization survey on young adults during the same time period, and they had re-interviewed these same individuals later in life. Because lottery status was randomly determined, Erikson and Stoker did not need to rely on sophisticated statistical techniques to determine whether draft status had an effect on political attitudes—they could simply compare the attitudes of those with lower draft numbers to those with higher draft numbers. Doing this, they demonstrated that "Males holding low lottery numbers became more antiwar, more liberal, and more Democratic in their voting compared to those whose high numbers protected them from the draft."[36]

---

34 Gregory Robinson, John E. McNulty, and Jonathan S. Krasno, "Observing the counterfactual? The search for political experiments in nature," *Political Analysis* 17 (2009): 341–357, p. 349.

35 Robert S. Erikson and Laura Stoker, "Caught in the draft: The effects of Vietnam draft lottery status on political attitudes," *American Political Science Review* 105 (2011): 221–237.

36 Erikson and Stoker, "Caught in the draft," p. 221.

A strong natural experiment can be a very powerful approach to answering a research question. After all, natural experiments share many of the advantages of field experiments, particularly with regard to promoting high levels of external validity. If the internal validity is also high, then a great deal can be learned. However, the key to utilizing a natural experiment is to ensure that the intervention is truly exogenous to the relationship being studied. In the case of a draft lottery, the exogeneity of the treatment is quite clear. An individual's risk of being drafted was assigned to him randomly, just as a researcher would have done it in a true experiment. But, in other natural experiments, the exogeneity of the treatment may not be quite as strong.

One dynamic that political scientists often capitalize on to construct natural experiments are how jurisdictional borders are drawn. For example, every ten years congressional redistricting means that many voters are moved from one congressional district to another. Stephen Ansolabehere, Jim Snyder, and Charles Stewart took advantage of this process to determine the extent to which members of Congress were able to build a personal vote for themselves.[37] They did this by comparing how well the incumbent performed in new parts of his district compared with those portions of his district that did not change. Of course, redistricting may not always be an entirely exogenous (or random) process. In many states, politicians themselves are responsible for drawing district lines and members themselves may have some influence on what their districts will look like over the next decade. Thus, in cases where the independent variable is not clearly exogenous and random, it is imperative on the researcher to make a case for why the intervention can be treated as if it is random and to demonstrate that the treatment is not correlated with other variables that could be alternative explanations for any patterns uncovered.

Let us return once more to the question of whether campaign advertising can persuade voters to support a candidate. We have already elaborated on how scholars have studied this question through various experimental designs, but Greg Huber and Kevin Arceneaux have shown that it is also possible to address the question using a natural experiment. Specifically, Huber and Arceneaux took advantage of the fact that television advertisements cannot be targeted by campaigns in the same way as direct mail and phone calls. As the authors note, "Fortuitously, television broadcast signals, unlike campaign workers, have little regard for state boundaries. If a campaign purchases advertising in the Philadelphia media market to target voters in Pennsylvania, these broadcasts also appear on televisions in parts of Delaware and New Jersey."[38]

37 Stephen Ansolabehere, James M. Snyder, Jr, and Charles Stewart III, "Old voters, new voters, and the personal vote: Using redistricting to measure the incumbency advantage," *American Journal of Political Science* 44 (2000): 17–34.

38 Gregory A. Huber and Kevin Arceneaux, "Identifying the persuasive effects of presidential advertising," *American Journal of Political Science* 51 (2007): 957–977, p. 961.

Thus, if a candidate targeted advertisements to persuade voters in Pennsylvania, those advertisements would still be seen by citizens in Delaware, even though voters in Delaware were not the intended target of the ads.

The authors take advantage of this mismatch between market and state boundaries to examine whether advertising is persuasive. For example, Indiana was by no means a battleground state during the 2004 presidential election, but neighboring states like Michigan and Ohio were. Thus, when candidates aired advertisements in those states, some of those advertisements were inevitably seen by people living in Indiana near the borders of those states. Since exposure to these ads among people in Indiana was accidental, it was unlikely to have been correlated with other factors that would typically drive campaign decisions (such as pre-existing support for the candidates). Indeed, the authors went the extra step of demonstrating that, in fact, the presence of advertising in these non-battleground states was entirely uncorrelated with previous support for either party. Ultimately, this allows them to discover that "advertising does a little to inform, next to nothing to mobilize, and a great deal to persuade potential voters."[39]

Another limitation with natural experiments is even more fundamental; by their very nature, natural experiments cannot be produced on demand. Furthermore, it is often difficult or even impossible to derive a set of hypotheses and then go about searching for a natural experiment that would be useful for testing them. Natural experiments simply do not exist for all (or even for most) research questions. Indeed, it is far more common for scholars to see random or approximately random interventions in the world and then think about what questions those interventions could be used to answer. Thus, when it comes to natural experiments, the research design is often executed before the research question is even posed. As we have often stressed in this book, the research process is very often not a linear one. Sometimes research questions are re-conceived to match the type of research design that is actually practicable, and sometimes research questions come directly from the discovery of excellent research designs. It is very possible that you may find a natural experiment that leads you to a research question you are interested in answering. The key strategy when looking for interesting natural experiments is to think about shocks that may have affected some portions of a population in different ways than others. Such shocks may be actually caused by nature—like extreme weather or earthquakes—or they may be induced by humans—like redistricting or draft lotteries. But as long as the shock is exogenous, it has the potential to be used as a natural experiment.

---

39 Huber and Arceneaux, "Identifying the persuasive effects of presidential advertising," p. 961.

Box 5.4: The Nonlinear Research Process: How Experiments Often Make Us Rethink Our Theory

As we stress throughout this book, it is often the case that, once we begin to analyze our empirical data, we are forced to rethink the theory we have developed or even refine our question. Experiments typically offer the best opportunities to do this, largely because of the strong causal inferences they allow us to make. Unlike with observational data where theory is crucial for directing us toward competing explanations we must account for, our confidence in experimental results is not dependent on a strong theoretical understanding of the process generating those results. For example, we might conduct an experiment where we heat a pot of water to 212 degrees Fahrenheit and find that it begins to boil when we do this. We do not need to have a theory about why the water boils at this temperature to be confident that it boils. Likewise, we need not have a theory of why advertising influences the vote preferences of individuals to be confident in experimental results that show that the relationship exists.

If experimental results do not produce the findings you expect, then it often makes sense to rethink the theory you developed to generate your hypotheses. For example, you may run an experiment and discover that advertising produces no increase in support for the candidate featured in the ads. Perhaps this finding indicates that people are impervious to advertising effects, or perhaps it makes sense to think more carefully about the nature of those effects. If you are confident that the experimental design is sound, then it is sometimes the theory that must be re-evaluated.

CONCLUSION

For maximizing internal validity, experiments offer the most ideal research approach. By controlling the data generation process, researchers can rule out competing explanations and ensure that any associations between the independent and dependent variables are the result of a causal relationship. Field experiments attempt to maintain the internal validity of a laboratory experiment while also increasing external validity by pulling the research out of the lab and into the real world. Of course, these also tend to be the most challenging types of experiments to execute.

It is often assumed by political scientists that there are substantial limits to the types of questions that experiments can be used to answer. Indeed, experiments have traditionally focused on addressing questions related to political psychology, such as how voters make decisions and the extent to which they are subject to elite manipulation through framing and persuasion. However, just because these are the types of questions that have been addressed by experiments thus far does not necessarily mean that they are the only questions amenable to experimentation. In fact, a little imagination can make it quite possible for a researcher to apply experimental methods to a wide variety of questions. For example, recall that with field experiments the experimental subjects are unaware that they are participating in a study at all. Thus, it may be possible to conduct field experiments where politicians are the subjects, as Daniel Bergan did in his examination of lobbying effects in the New Hampshire legislature. Additionally, it may be possible to use incentives to make it so that normal citizens act as if they were political elites, as Elinor Ostrom has often done in her decision-making experiments.

The point is that it is never wise to fully write off an experimental approach without giving the method considerable thought. At a minimum, we think it is a useful exercise for students to think about how they might analyze a question they are interested in using an experimental approach. The student may ultimately decide that such an approach is either inappropriate or unworkable for her particular question, but the mere process of thinking systematically about how an experimental approach might work will help the student think more carefully about how she should undertake an observational approach to answering the question at hand.

KEY TERMS

control group   122

convenience samples   127

data-generating process   118

external validity   125

field experiments   132

internal validity   125

laboratory experiment   122

natural experiments   143

spurious relationship   120

survey experiments   129

treatment groups   124

CHAPTER 6

Large-n Observational Studies

Large-n observational studies have been a mainstay of political science research since the mid-1900s. Such studies became increasingly more attractive to political scientists as (1) new quantitative sources of data became available and (2) computers made it easier for social scientists to analyze those data. More to the point, large-n research offers an invaluable tool in drawing both descriptive and causal inferences. Without large-n observational data, we would not know what percentage of Americans favor a certain policy, political view, or candidate. We would not be able to compare measures of literacy, infant mortality, corruption, inequality, or economic development across countries. To understand why the political world works the way it does, we must first understand how it works, and, without large-n studies, we would not know nearly enough about the *how*. But the value of the large-n observational approach is not limited to making descriptive inferences. For many research questions, we might not be content with determining if one country has greater corruption than another or if corruption is increasing or decreasing with time. We might want to go further and ask *why*. Why is corruption higher in some countries than in others, and why is it increasing or decreasing?

In Chapter 5, we discussed how experiments are powerful tools for generating causal inferences because of their high internal validity. By using random assignment to hold constant other potential explanatory factors between control and condition groups, experiments allow us to make reliable inferences about the impact of an independent variable on a dependent variable. Instead of relying on control and experimental groups, large-n studies use statistical methods to mathematically control for alternative explanations.

In this chapter, we will explore several statistical methods that allow researchers to control for potential rival causes and reduce the risk of omitted variable bias. We will begin with a basic means comparison, which we will use to explain the logic of statistical control. From there we will graduate to more sophisticated techniques, including linear and logistic regression. While most of the chapter focuses on overcoming the challenges posed by systematic and random sampling, and measurement error and omitted variable bias, the chapter also delves into the problem of reverse causality and explores how longitudinal techniques, or comparing data over time, can be used to address this challenge. The chapter concludes by considering some ways that you can incorporate large-n approaches into your own research.

THE LOGIC OF LARGE-N STUDIES: A MEANS COMPARISON

Large-n observational studies can to some extent attempt to replicate the logic of control and experimental groups. Say, for example, that a researcher is interested in explaining why some countries have high levels of corruption while other countries have low levels. She hypothesizes that democracies will have lower levels of corruption than authoritarian regimes. She bases this hypothesis on the theory that elections allow voters the means to punish corrupt officials and that democracy is conducive to a free press, which can expose corruption. It would certainly be possible to divide countries into two groups—democracies and autocracies—and then see which group has a higher level of corruption.

While this method is similar to an experiment in that we can divide countries into groups, it is very different because the researcher does not control which countries are in the control group (autocracies) and which are in the condition group (democracies); there is no random assignment. This produces several important challenges to making causal inferences, one of which is omitted variable bias, which happens when the relationship between two variables is spurious. Given that the groups are not randomly assigned, there is a risk that those countries that are democracies also have other factors in common *vis-à-vis* those countries that are autocracies. For example, many of the democracies with low levels of corruption, such as Denmark and New Zealand, also have high levels of economic development; whereas many authoritarian countries, such as Zimbabwe, have low levels of economic development. It could be that economic development, not democracy, is driving differences in corruption. By failing to take economic development into account, we might be erroneously attributing explanatory power to "democracy" when the actual factor driving variation in the dependent variable is "economic development."[1] We might have omitted an important explanatory variable and biased our conclusion: hence the term **omitted variable bias**.

Large-n studies offer a solution to this problem. Because there are many observations, the researcher can further divide her sample into those with low, medium, and high levels of economic development. If she continues to observe that democracies have lower levels of corruption, regardless of whether they are at low, medium, or high levels of economic development, then she will be more confident in her findings. So while experiments use random assignment to ensure that their control and experimental groups are the same across all other potential explanatory factors, large-n studies use statistical techniques to simulate such control.

Let's see how this works with real data. As we know from Chapter 4, there are several different ways to conceptualize and measure both democracy and corruption. For illustrative purposes, let's use Cheibub, Gandhi, and Vreeland's measurement of regime type and group countries into democratic and authoritarian regimes based on the presence or absence of free and fair elections.[2] For corruption, we can use Transparency International's Corruption Perception Index (CPI), whose strengths and weaknesses were discussed in Chapter 4.

In Chapter 4, we also discussed how the nature of data determines what statistical techniques we use. We divided quantitative data into interval and categorical data, the latter of which we further divided into ordinal- (able to be put in an order) and nominal- (unable to be put in an order) level data. In this case the CPI score, which ranges from 1–10, can be treated as an interval-level variable and democracy as a categorical-level variable. As we know, for interval-level data, we are able to calculate a mean, or average score. Thus, it is very easy to divide countries between democracies and autocracies, and calculate and compare the average CPI score for each group, a process known simply as a **means comparison**.

The means comparison pictured in Figure 6.1 shows the average corruption score among countries that were democratic and countries that were authoritarian in 2008. As evident in the figure, democracies on average have a higher CPI (4.7) than autocracies (3.0), which means they have lower levels of corruption than their authoritarian counterparts. The data appear to support our researcher's hypothesis!

Of course we are not done there. We have to consider if we can draw valid inferences from this information. As we did in Chapter 4, we have to first ask ourselves if there are any concerns related to conceptualization, measurement,

---

1 Consider how this is similar to the process we described in Panel D of Figure 1.1.
2 José Antonio Cheibub, Jennifer Gandhi, and James Raymond Vreeland, "Democracy and dictatorship revisited," *Public Choice* 143 (2010): 67–101.

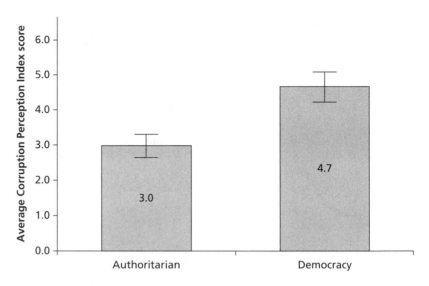

FIGURE 6.1 Average Corruption Perception Index Score among Democracies and Dictatorships (10 = Low Corruption)

Source: Author's analysis using Cheibub, Gandhi, and Vreeland's 2008 classification of regime type and Transparency International's CPI for 2008.

Note: n = 189.

or sampling. Since we already covered these issues, we will not go into them again in detail here. Nonetheless, we would want to ask ourselves if our measures of democracy and corruption are consistent with our conceptualizations and if there are any systematic problems in the way that these variables are measured. Because we are examining nearly every country, sampling error is not a concern. Even so, we still would want to calculate confidence intervals around our two sample statistics as a means to take random measurement error into account. If you will recall from Chapter 4, there is considerable random measurement error in the CPI. The I-shaped lines at the top of the bars in Figure 6.1 represent the 95 percent confidence intervals for the two means. For example, we calculate an average CPI score among authoritarian countries of 3.0 (on a 1–10 scale) and a margin of error of approximately 0.3.[3] Assuming no systematic error in measurement (a big assumption), once we take random error into account, we are 95 percent confident that the true average CPI is between 2.7 and 3.3.

These error bars help provide a better test of our hypothesis that democratic countries are more likely to have low levels of corruption than authoritarian

3 In this case the standard error would be calculated as the standard deviation (1.3) divided by the square root of the total number of authoritarian countries (69). This yields a standard error of .16. Doubling this produces a margin of error of 3.2.

countries. We observe a difference of 1.7 between the two means (4.7–3.0), but are we confident in this difference once random error is taken into account? The foil of our hypothesis, what is referred to as the **null hypothesis**, posits that there is *no difference* in the CPI scores between democracies and authoritarian countries. If the error in the data is greater than the observed difference of 1.7, then we would *not* be able to conclude that democracies and autocracies have different levels of corruption. Nonetheless, we can see in the bar chart that the upper bound of the authoritarian error bar is about 3.3 and the lower bound of the democracy error bar is 4.3. Because there is no overlap, we are very confident that the difference observed is not due to random chance. We call this a **statistically significant relationship**, because the relationship observed is greater than the random error in the data.[4]

But we are not done yet. What about omitted variable bias? Because the groups are not randomly determined as in an experiment (not many political scientists have the political capital to randomly determine the regime type of countries), we cannot yet make the causal inference that regime type causes corruption. To make a strong causal inference, we must develop an approach that allows us to account for potential omitted variables. As mentioned above, it might be economic development—not regime type—that is driving the difference in corruption scores.

As a result, Figure 6.2 controls for the level of economic development using an ordinal-level variable of low, medium, and high Gross Domestic Product (GDP) per capita. This is simply referred to as a **controlled means comparison** because it adds a control variable: economic development. The controlled means comparison clearly shows that the level of economic development is an important predictor of corruption. Low-income countries have much lower CPI scores (higher corruption) than their high-income counterparts. But what does the figure say about our democracy hypothesis? Among the low-income and middle-income countries, the average corruption scores for democracies are only slightly higher than for dictatorships. Further testing (not presented here) reveals that the relationship between regime type and corruption is still statistically significant, which means that we are confident that there is a relationship even once random error is taken into account; however, the impact is small. Only among the high-income countries does democracy appear to have a substantial effect on corruption levels. The impact of regime type appears to matter, but the magnitude of the effect depends on the level of economic development, and it matters far less than suggested by Figure 6.1. Clearly, by omitting economic development from our study in Figure 6.1, we biased our results.

4 The fact that there is no overlap between the bars means that we are much more than 95 percent confident. Because of the way a standard error of the difference between two means is calculated, material that is not discussed here, it is possible for there to be some overlap in the error bars and still be 95 percent confident in the difference.

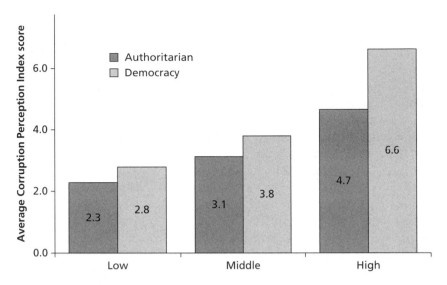

FIGURE 6.2 Average Corruption Perception Index Score among Democracies and Dictatorships Controlling for Low, Middle, and High Levels of Economic Development (10 = Low Corruption)

Source: Author's analysis using Cheibub, Gandhi, and Vreeland's 2008 classification of regime type, Transparency International's CPI Index, and the World Bank's GDP per capita.

In summary, the controlled comparison presented in Figure 6.2 attempts to replicate the logic of control used in an experiment. We cannot ignore other factors like income levels, but, because we have many observations, we are able to divide the sample into groups and control for income mathematically. Controlled means comparisons are, nonetheless, limited in that we can really only control for one factor at a time. There might be other factors that could explain variation in corruption and whose exclusion might bias our results. For example, some scholars have argued that religious tradition, colonial tradition, natural resource endowments, and the size of government all help explain corruption. The bad news is that our means comparison cannot control for all of these factors at the same time; however, the good news is that a more sophisticated statistical tools, known as regression analysis, allows us to do just that.

MULTIVARIATE LINEAR REGRESSION

Students will need to refer to other texts for a more complete understanding of how linear regression works; however, some explanation of this important statistical tool is required to understand the basics of making causal inferences with large-n studies. Figure 6.3 offers a scatterplot of the relationship between economic development, measured by the natural log of GDP per capita, and

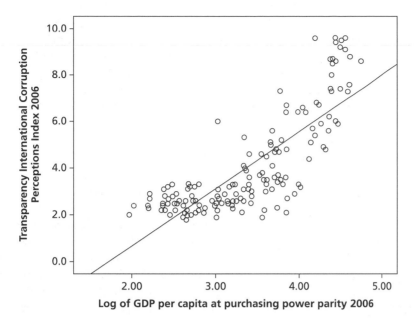

FIGURE 6.3 Scatterplot of the Relationship between the Log of GDP Per Capita and the Corruption Perceptions Index

Source: Author's calculations based on data compiled by Pippa Norris using World Bank 2006 GDP per capita at purchasing power parity and Transparency International's CPI.

corruption perceptions.[5] Again, the level of measurement determines the type of statistical tool that we use. In this case, a scatterplot is preferable to a means comparison because both of the variables are interval level. Because each country has a unique GDP per capita, the average CPI for each value of GDP would not tell us very much.

Each of the circles in the scatterplot represents an individual country at its particular level of development and level of perceived corruption. The relationship is not perfectly linear, but one can see that high-income countries almost always have low levels of corruption (a high CPI score) and most of the low-income countries have high levels of corruption (a low CPI score). Clearly, there is a correlation, or relationship, between these two variables. The scatterplot also includes a line running through the data known as a **bivariate regression line**, or a line that estimates the relationship between two variables. The slope of this line is summarized by a **regression coefficient**, which provides researchers with an estimate of the precise nature of that relationship.

5 In this case, the log of GDP per capita is used to produce a linear relationship between the two variables. Because of the uneven distribution of GDP per capita, this variable would otherwise have a curvilinear relationship with the CPI.

The regression line can be represented by the same mathematical function taught in high school algebra classes: $y = mx+b$, where "x" is the value of the independent variable, "m" is the slope of the line, "b" is the value of y when x equals zero (the y-intercept), and "y" is the predicted value of the dependent variable. The slope of the line, or the regression coefficient, tells us how much change in y we expect from a one unit change in x. Positive values imply a positive relationship; negative values indicate a negative relationship; larger absolute values signify steeper slopes; and smaller absolute values represent weaker relationships. In statistics we use slightly different terminology, however, and rewrite this equation as either $y = \beta(x)+\alpha$ or as $\hat{y} = b(x)+a$.

This is potentially confusing to students because "b" or the β (Greek beta) is used to represent the slope rather than the y-intercept. In the former equation, we use the Greek letters β and α to represent the population parameters, or the slope and y-intercept in the population. Of course, we do not know the true slope of the relationship between x and y, so the latter equation uses Latin letters to symbolize sample statistics or estimates of the population parameters.

Interestingly, in the same way that we can estimate the amount of random error in an average corruption score, we can also estimate the amount of sampling error in the slope of a regression line. We are able to do this by calculating a standard error for the regression coefficient (b). In the means comparison, the null hypothesis posited that there was no difference in the CPI between democracies and autocracies. In the scatterplot and bivariate regression, the null hypothesis posits that the slope of the regression line is really zero, or as GDP increases there is no change in the predicted value of corruption. Therefore, a statistically significant regression coefficient implies that, even once we take random error into account, we are confident that the regression coefficient is not equal to zero—that there is a relationship between economic development and corruption.

Scatterplots with a regression line make an excellent graphical tool to present data. Even without any statistical background, a reader can look at the scatterplot in Figure 6.3 and quickly understand the bivariate relationship between economic development and corruption. Slight modifications such as shading plots from a region of interest, labeling countries, or highlighting interesting outliers provide additional tools to portray important information to readers (see Figure 6.4). Nonetheless, while the scatterplot and bivariate regression line appear to be more sophisticated tools than a means comparison, they suffer from the same basic limitation. Because the scatterplot only looks at the relationship between two variables, it could suffer from omitted variable bias.

Multivariate linear regression, or regression with more than one independent variable, continues the logic of the regression line, but instead of describing the relationship between just the independent and dependent variable, what is known as a bivariate relationship, it estimates the independent effect of each variable on the dependent variable while controlling for other

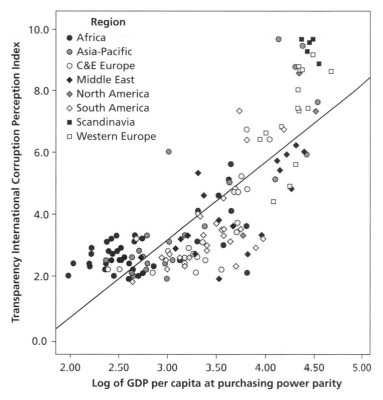

FIGURE 6.4 Scatterplot of the Relationship between the Log of GDP Per Capita and the Corruption Perceptions Index with Regional Shading

Source: Author's calculations based on data compiled by Pippa Norris using World Bank 2006 GDP per capita at purchasing power parity and Transparency International's CPI.

factors. Peter Kennedy uses Venn diagrams to describe the logic behind multivariate regression analysis.[6] The Venn diagram in Figure 6.5 summarizes the hypothetical effect of democracy and economic development on corruption. As can be seen in the figure, the democracy and economic development circles together cover more than half of the corruption circle. This implies that by knowing the level of economic development of countries and whether or not they are democracies, we can explain more than half of the variation in corruption. Basic multivariate linear regression analysis (there are various other regression techniques) produces a measure of the association called an R^2, which tells us the percentage of variation in the dependent variable that is explained by all the independent variables in the analysis. In this case it would be over .5 or 50 percent.

Multivariate regression, like a bivariate regression, also produces a regression coefficient; however, rather than describe the bivariate relationship between an

6   Peter Kennedy, *Guide to econometrics* (New York: Wiley-Blackwell, 2008).

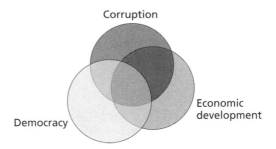

FIGURE 6.5 Venn Diagram Explanation of Regression

independent variable and the dependent variable, it tells us the **independent effect** of each independent variable on the dependent variable while controlling for other factors. As can be seen in the figure, each circle overlaps within one another. This reflects the fact that economic development correlates with both corruption and democracy. This overlap between the two independent variables is the reason why separating out the effect of just one variable on corruption is very difficult. If both Sweden and Finland are observed to have low levels of corruption, it is impossible to know if this is because of strong democratic traditions in these countries or because of high economic development. In Figure 6.5, the independent effect of economic development is represented by the area that overlaps with corruption, but does not overlap with democracy. This area would include cases like Singapore and Qatar, which are authoritarian, highly developed, and have low corruption rankings, suggesting that economic development has an independent effect on corruption, irrespective of democracy. The smaller area, where democracy overlaps with corruption but not economic development, represents the independent effect of democracy on corruption. Here we would find fewer countries that are democratic, have a low level of economic development, and have relatively low levels of corruption. In sum, regression tells us both the cumulative effect of all the independent variables through the R^2 and the partial effect of each factor through the regression coefficients. This same logic can be extended to additional independent variables.

Regression techniques have been employed in a number of cross-national studies of the causes of corruption. Now that we have the tools to understand the challenges of inference in large-n studies, let's consider how recent scholarship has sought to explain variation in corruption across countries. Much like our simplified study, Gabriella Montinola and Robert Jackman conducted a regression analysis to test the impact of democracy on corruption.[7] They have cross-sectional data for sixty-six countries, and they use an indicator similar to the CPI, and a measure of democracy that is continuous, this is to say

7 Gabriella R. Montinola and Robert W. Jackman, "Sources of corruption: A cross-country study," *British Journal of Political Science* 32 (2002): 147–170.

along a continuum rather than just democratic or authoritarian. In addition to economic development, they also control for the size of the government, and whether or not a country is a member of the Organization of the Petroleum Exporting Countries (OPEC). These variables are included because the authors hypothesize that larger governments and countries with extensive natural resources will experience higher levels of corruption. Interestingly, they find that there is no "linear" relationship between democracy and corruption once economic development and other factors are controlled for; however, they do find a curvilinear relationship. Specifically, they find that weak democracies are just as corrupt, or possibly even more corrupt, than authoritarian countries; however, strong democracies have statistically significantly less corruption even when controlling for economic development. As discussed above, "statistically significant," means that the authors are confident in the relationship even when random error is taken into account. Having taken into account more factors than our simple bivariate regression, Montinola and Jackman are able to reduce the threat posed by omitted variable bias.

So have Montinola and Jackman settled the issue and provided a clear test of the democracy–corruption hypothesis? What concerns should we have? First, we know that good causal inference begins with good descriptive inference. So we would want to make sure that the authors' measurements reduce the risk of measurement error. Second, the authors have a relatively small sample size: only sixty-six countries. Therefore, even though the authors take random error into account in their tests of statistical significance, there is still a risk of systematic sampling error. Are these sixty-six countries representative of the population of countries? The authors do not discuss this issue (as they should), but the answer is probably not. As in many cross-national studies, the authors were limited to the countries they had data for. Missing data are a serious problem in cross-national research, producing an effect akin to the non-response bias discussed in Chapter 4. Third, although the authors include three control variables, they do not control for a host of other factors that researchers have argued are important to explaining corruption. As a result, there is still a risk of omitted variable bias.

In his 2000 study, Daniel Treisman tested a larger set of variables against corruption.[8] While he still confronts problems of measurement error and sampling error, he runs less of a risk of omitted variable bias. He too is concerned with the relationship between democracy and corruption, and he finds evidence that "uninterrupted democracy" corresponds with reduced corruption levels. He also finds that economic development, Protestant religious culture, and British colonial heritage have statistically significant, independent, and negative relationships with corruption.

---

8 Daniel Treisman, "The causes of corruption: A cross-national study," *Journal of Public Economics* 76 (2000): 399–457.

You and Khagram are concerned with how omitted variable bias inhibited studies about the relationship between inequality and corruption.[9] Prior to their research, several studies had found that inequality did not have an independent impact on corruption.[10] This surprised You and Khagram, who theorized that in unequal societies the rich have a great deal to lose from fair political, administrative, and judicial processes, particularly given that the demand for redistribution is likely to be high in an unequal economy. Under a corrupted system, however, the wealthy are able to buy influence. The authors argue that previous studies found that inequality had no impact because prior research had failed to control for a legacy of a socialist legal system. You and Kagram contend that socialist systems bred both corruption and greater equality, but, in the rest of the world, inequality exacerbated corruption. Failing to control for a legacy of a socialist legal system masked this effect of inequality, and, in fact, once this factor is controlled for, the authors find that inequality has an independent, statistically significant effect on corruption. Their analysis highlights that *omitted variable bias can work in either of two directions.* Absent adequate controls, an observed relationship might be spurious or an unobserved relationship might be overlooked.

The authors also point out another potential flaw in many regression analyses. Linear regression assumes additive relationships between the independent variables and the dependent variable. Consider the independent variables of democracy and inequality, and the dependent variable of corruption. An additive relationship would suggest that (1) democracy has an independent effect on corruption and (2) inequality has a separate, independent effect. An interactive relationship, however, would suggest that the relationship between inequality and corruption *depends* on the level of democracy in the country, and vice versa. This interactive relationship is similar to the means comparison we showed in Figure 6.2, where regime type only had an effect on corruption in nations with high levels of economic development.

Regression techniques can be used to explore interactive relationships; however, it is necessary for analysts to create and test interaction variables. You and Khagram explain the surprisingly inconsistent findings regarding both democracy and inequality by testing for just such an interaction. They argue that, in an authoritarian regime, elites can maintain power through repression. In a democracy, elites have fewer repressive tools at their disposal and corruption offers an alternative means to influence policy decisions in their favor. While the method that they use to test this interactive hypothesis is somewhat

---

9 Jong-Sung You and Sanjeev Khagram, "A comparative study of inequality and corruption," *American Sociological Review* 70 (2005): 136–157.

10 For example, see Bryan W. Husted, "Wealth, culture, and corruption," *Journal of International Business Studies* 30 (1999): 339–360 and Martin Paldam, "Corruption and religion: Adding to the economic model," *Kyklos* 54 (2001): 383–413.

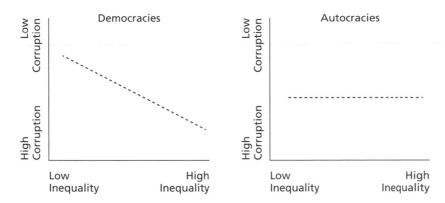

FIGURE 6.6 Hypothesized Interactive Relationship

different, one could imagine dividing the sample of countries between democracies and authoritarian countries. Then, as presented hypothetically in Figure 6.6, one could generate a scatterplot of the relationship between inequality and corruption among democracies and a separate scatterplot of this relationship among autocracies. You and Khagram find evidence consistent with their interactive theory: that inequality is an important determinant of corruption among democracies but not among autocracies.

One final large-n corruption analysis worth profiling is Danila Serra's study, which attempts to address a problem heretofore not discussed.[11] After two decades of large-n statistical analyses of the causes of corruption, Serra reviews seven such studies and finds that their results are somewhat contradictory, even though the different authors use many of the same variables. She's particularly concerned about a very worrisome problem for large-n quantitative research: robustness. **Robust** findings mean that statistical analyses consistently reveal the same relationship between the independent and dependent variables regardless of what control variables are included in the analysis, or, in the terminology of many social scientists, how the model is specified. There is a concern that unethical scholars will selectively present regression models to best support their theories. Serra quotes Ronald Coase as saying "If you torture data long enough, Nature will confess."[12] Most scholarship goes through a peer review process that is supposed to discourage such selective data presentation, but the process is not foolproof, and, of course, sometimes researchers just make mistakes. Regardless, of the cause, when different scholars run slightly different models and come up with divergent conclusions, this suggests that the findings are not robust.

11 Danila Serra, "Empirical determinants of corruption: A sensitivity analysis," *Public Choice* 126 (2006): 225–256.
12 Serra, "Empirical determinants of corruption," p. 229.

Box 6.1: Ethical Issues in Large-n Research

There are several ethical issues in large-n research. Here we briefly consider three such issues.

Picking and choosing: Large-n scholars often deal in complex statistical models with large data-sets of thousands of observations. As humorously reflected in Figure 6.7, there is a concern that unethical scholars will selectively pick and choose data and statistical models that best support their theories. Most scholarship goes through a peer review process that is supposed to discourage such selective data presentation, but the process is not foolproof and depends on the professionalism and good judgment of scholars. Politicians, pundits, and activists are not necessarily bound by such professional norms, and students should always consider the objectivity of their source. Students themselves are often subject to the tendency for selective data presentation. In many classes, students are asked to take a side in a debate or argument and then back up their arguments with support. Scientific social science research does not work in this manner. Instead, a social scientist

"That's the gist of what I want to say. Now get me some statistics to base it on."

FIGURE 6.7 Ethical Issues in Data Presentation

Source: Joseph Mirachi/The New Yorker Collection/www.cartoon bank.com

LARGE-N OBSERVATIONAL STUDIES

should view his role as objectively testing hypotheses—not trying to support an argument. Complex statistical models may make political science appear more "scientific"; however, model specification and interpretation still depends on the good judgment of the researcher. To avoid disappointing null results, it is usually a good idea to select and design research projects whose results will be interesting regardless of whether or not the tested hypothesis is supported.

Anonymity: Another ethical issue in survey research is ensuring the anonymity of study participants. In the course of this book we have discussed surveys that ask respondents if they have paid bribes and if they have consumed drugs. Both of these are illegal activities, and surveyors can only reliably obtain honest answers to such questions by guaranteeing the anonymity of survey results. This is an even larger issue in panel data, where study participants are contacted over time and researchers have to maintain databases with names and contact information. As a result, many university research review boards set very strict protocols for the handling of personal information to ensure that such information is well protected.

The non-linear research process vs. data mining: Throughout this book we have argued that the research process is non-linear. It frequently occurs that researchers will go back and rethink their research question, theory, or hypothesis based on their data. The same holds for large-n studies. For example, in observing the scatterplot in Figure 6.4, we would observe that Middle Eastern countries are comparatively less corrupt than other countries at their same level of economic development. We would also observe that Singapore is far less corrupt than any other country in Asia. These interesting empirical puzzles might take our research in a new direction. These are natural and desirable adjustments; however, there is a risk of what is often pejoratively referred to as **data mining**. Rather than begin with a theory and hypothesis, a researcher might randomly explore correlations between variables in a dataset until she finds a strong relationship and then build a theory and hypothesis around the findings. In other words, she might take a fully inductive approach to analyzing data. We recommend against such an approach. Students should keep in mind that stunning findings are often too good to be true and are frequently the result of data errors, spuriousness, or some other challenge to inference. Building a model around such findings often results in embarrassing errors.

As a result, Serra runs what is called a sensitivity analysis. This means that she runs numerous regression models, 299 to be precise, specified in slightly different ways to see which variables show a consistent relationship with corruption perceptions as measured by both the CPI and the World Bank's corruption index. She finds that economic development, for example, has a *robust* relationship with the dependent variable. Regardless of how the model is specified, it consistently shows a relationship to corruption, as does political instability, uninterrupted democracy, and a Protestant religious tradition. Other factors, such as government intervention into the economy, are not robust.

Box 6.2: Interpreting Linear Regression Results

Regression tables are often very intimidating; however, once you know what you are looking at, they are actually fairly simply to interpret. Table 6.1 below presents one of many regression outputs from Treisman's article on corruption. In the left-hand column we are presented with all of the independent variables in the study. The dependent variable, the CPI, is mentioned in the title. The top number to the right of the independent variable name is the regression coefficient. If the number is negative, the model predicts a negative relationship with the dependent variable. This number can be understood as the amount of change in "*y*" that is predicted to occur with a one unit change in "*x*." In the case of the variable "uninterrupted democracy," the model predicts that, controlling for

TABLE 6.1 One of Treisman's (2000) Many Regression Models Explaining Transparency International's Corruption Perception Index in 1997

Uninterrupted democracy (1950–1995)	−.81*
	(.47)
Common law system	.98*
	(.51)
Former British colony or the UK	−2.31***
	(.62)
Never a colony	−.27
	(.47)
Percentage Protestant 1980	−.003***
	(.01)
Ethnolinguistic division	.01
	(.01)
Fuel, metal, and mineral exports	.01
	(.01)
Log GDP per capita	−3.63***
	(.66)
Federal	.66**
	(.29)
Imports/GNP (%)	−.01**
	(.01)
R^2	.8987
N	42

note: *$p < 0.10$; **$p < 0.05$; ***$p < 0.01$.

Source: Daniel Treisman, "The causes of corruption: A cross-national study," *Journal of Public Economics* 76 (2000): 399–457.

other factors, a country with uninterrupted democracy will have .81 less corruption on a 1–10 scale than a country that has had interrupted democracy.

We have to be somewhat careful in interpreting this number, however, as this is what the model predicts based on the sample. This number does not take into account the random error in data. As a result, below this number in parentheses is the standard error of the regression coefficient; this is our measure of random error in our data. What we want to know is that, once we take this error into the account, do we still observe a relationship between the independent variables and the dependent variable? Or is it possible that the regression coefficient is really 0: that there is no relationship? The stars to the right of the coefficient provide us with the answer to this question. If there is no star, it means that we are less than 90 percent confident that there is a relationship; one star means that we are 90 percent confident in the relationship; two stars mean we are 95 percent confident in the relationship, and three stars mean that we are 99 percent confident in the relationship. At the bottom of the table we are presented with the R^2, which tells us that together all of the variables explain 89 percent of the variation in the CPI. We are also presented with the sample size of 42 countries, which should raise some alarms about potential sampling error.

TOOLS FOR CATEGORICAL DATA: CROSS-TABULATION AND LOGISTIC REGRESSION

Let's consider the role of large-n studies in addressing some of this book's other research questions. In Chapter 5, we discussed the use of experiments to test the impact of advertisements and outreach on voting and vote choice. While experiments are increasingly more common, the primary means to test the effects of advertisements and outreach on voter behavior has traditionally been through large-n observational studies. For example, since 1996, the Wisconsin Advertising Project has been collecting an impressive supply of data on the campaign advertisements aired in U.S.'s largest television markets. Each advertisement is coded for its tone (positive, negative, or otherwise), the issues mentioned in the ad, and the types of appeals and images seen in the ad. Additionally, the dataset includes a measure of each date and time that the advertisement aired and on which stations and programs it aired. These data have revolutionized the study of advertising effects by providing scholars with an independent measure of which ads individuals were likely exposed to depending on where they live.

In addition, surveys such as the American National Election Study (ANES) ask survey respondents if they have been contacted by someone urging them to vote or to register to vote, and it also asks respondents if they voted in the previous election. Unlike the previous dependent variables that we have examined in this chapter, the decision to vote is not an interval-level variable but a two-category nominal-level variable. Therefore, a means comparison and linear regression would be inappropriate statistical methods; one cannot really find an average score for a dependent variable or create a scatterplot when there are only two possible values. Instead, we require different tools to analyze categorical-dependent variables. One simple tool for categorical data is a cross-tabulation. A **cross-tabulation** merely divides the sample into those who were urged to vote and those who were not. Then, it compares the percentage of those who were contacted and voted with the percentage of those who were not contacted but voted anyway. If the former percentage is higher, it would suggest that outreach matters.

Such a cross-tabulation is presented in Table 6.2 using data from the ANES 2010. The cross-tabulation shows that, of those who were not contacted, 72.4 percent reported voting, and, of those who were contacted, 80.1 percent reported voting: an observed difference of 7.6 percent. Again, the data appear to support our hypothesis, although the relationship is not particularly strong.

As in the previous examples, however, we have to consider our challenges to inference. Again we would want to consider conceptualization, measurement, and sampling concerns. There is a negative stigma attached to not voting, and, as mentioned earlier, survey respondents tend to state that they voted when in fact they did not, a form of systematic error that we called a social desirability bias. Furthermore, given that the question about outreach preceded the question about voting in the survey instrument, individuals who experienced outreach efforts might be more inclined to be dishonest about their actual voting behavior. Furthermore, unlike the above comparison of countries, data in Table 6.2 are based on a sample, and as such it is subject to sampling error.

Again, we can take random error into account with a test of statistical significance. The null hypothesis would predict that the percentage who voted is the same regardless of whether a respondent was urged to vote or not. It is possible that the small difference observed, only 7.6 percent, is smaller than

TABLE 6.2 Cross-Tabulation between Contacted to Vote or Register and Vote Behavior

	Contacted	Not contacted	Total
Did not vote	210	289	499
	19.9%	27.6%	23.8%
Voted	843	759	1,602
	80.1%	**72.4%**	76.2%
Total	1,053	1,048	2,101
	100%	100%	100%

Source: American National Election Survey 2010.

the amount of error in the data. In other words, it is possible that the difference we observe in the sample does not exist in the population. In this case, we would use a different statistical test than we used with the mean comparison and the regression coefficient: a Chi-square (x^2) test. Again, we will not go into the specifics of how the x^2 is calculated, but essentially the x^2 asks what the cross-tabulation would look like if the null hypothesis were correct—that is, if there was no relationship between the variables—and then compares that hypothetical cross-tabulation with our actual cross-tabulation. While we do not present the calculations here, the result would tell us that we can be at least 95 percent confident that the observed difference is not due to random chance. Nonetheless, given that the true difference between these groups might be less than 7.6 percent, we have to conclude that there is possibly only a very weak relationship between outreach and voting.

An additional concern is of course omitted variable bias. Because survey respondents were not randomly assigned to receive an outreach message (as in a field experiment) and because we are not controlling for other factors, the observed relationship could be spurious. In fact, there are many factors that we might want to control for, including interest in politics, the type of outreach method, the message of outreach efforts, education levels, the nature of the political race, etc. . . . As with a controlled means comparison, we are able to add one control variable and conduct a **controlled cross-tabulation**. For example, we could divide our sample into high- and low-education respondents, and then examine the relationship between outreach efforts and voter turnout among each of these two groups. Nonetheless, as with the means comparison, we are limited to one control variable, and there are many factors we might want to control for. Fortunately, just as multivariate linear regression allowed us to control for the effect of numerous independent variables on an *interval*-level dependent variable, we have another regression tool that will allow us to control for the effect of additional factors on our *categorical* dependent variable: **logistic regression**.

Logistic regression offers a similar tool to linear regression that can be used for examining **dichotomous** dependent variables, or dependent variables with just two values. Of course, a dependent variable with only two values does not permit us to develop a scatterplot and run a regression line through the data points. What logistic regression does, therefore, is transform this dichotomous dependent variable into an interval-level variable. It does this by transforming the choice to vote or not vote into a probability of voting, which is in fact interval. It actually goes a couple of steps further and transforms the probability of voting into the odds of voting and then the logged odds of voting. The term "logistic" regression comes from this process of studying the logged odds.

Again, the math is not particularly important for our purposes here. While we certainly hope that you will learn these techniques in detail, as you might imagine each technique requires considerable time and effort to understand and master. Unfortunately, in this process, it is often easy to lose sense of the

Box 6.3: Experiments vs. Large-n Studies: The Effect of Negative Campaign Advertising

In contrast with the results of large-n observational studies, in a series of laboratory experiments discussed in Chapter 5, Ansolabehere and Iyengar found that individuals who viewed negative ads were less likely to report that they will vote.[a] The experiments were innovative because the negative campaign ads were imbedded in news broadcasts, much like they would be in real life, and respondents thought that they were participating in an experiment about the news. Nonetheless, there were still limits to external validity. In particular, the authors were only able to measure a study participant's intention to vote—not his or her actual behavior.

Wattenberg and Brians's study, discussed below, overcame this external validity problem by asking participants if they had seen campaign ads and if they had voted in the past election.[b] Nonetheless, while Wattenberg and Brians had overcome the external validity challenge to inference, their research was subject to other internal validity challenges. Ansolabehere, Iyengar, and Simon, in a response to Wattenberg and Brians, argued that relying on individuals to remember advertisements they had seen was not only unreliable, but also potentially biased.[c] In other words, Wattenberg and Brians's study suffered from measurement error. They noted that, when they conducted their initial experiments on negative advertising, over 50 percent of their experimental subjects could not recall having seen a campaign advertisement they had been shown

a. Stephen Ansolabehere and Shanto Iyengar, *Going negative* (New York: Free Press, 1995).
b. Wattenberg and Brians, "Negative campaign advertising: demobilizer or mobilizer?"
c. Stephen D. Ansolabehere, Shanto Iyengar, and Adam Simon, "Replicating experiments using aggregate and survey data: The case of negative advertising and turnout," *American Political Science Review* 93 (1999): 901–909.

forest in examining the trees. Our goal here is to convey the big picture. Your take away should be the following:

- Different types of data require different statistical tools. If we know a little bit about our data, such as whether they are interval, ordinal, or nominal, then we can select the appropriate tool.
- Regardless of the tool at hand, all of these tests attempt to isolate the independent effect of an independent variable on a dependent variable while controlling for other factors.
- They then go a step further and tell us (1) if we can be confident that the relationship is not zero when we take random error into account and (2) the strength of the observed relationship.

In this case, we use logistic regression because we are attempting to explain a dichotomous dependent variable. There are also several other regression just a half hour earlier. Using a sophisticated regression procedure called two-stage least squares to attempt to address this bias, the authors re-analyze the same data as Wattenberg and Brians and conclude that negative advertising does in fact have a negative impact (albeit small) on the probability of voting. They argue that their experiments and their analysis of survey data point in the same direction: negative advertising suppresses the vote.

Nonetheless, the debate is not over. In addition to other scholars who jumped into the fray, Krasno and Green sought to answer the research question using a natural experiment.[d] The U.S. electoral college system creates incentives for presidential campaigns to focus their advertising resources on swing states. However, the television markets are not entirely fixed at the state lines. As a result, New Jersey voters living in eight counties near the Pennsylvania border were inundated with ads while those near the New York border barely saw any ads. By comparing aggregate voter turnout across media markets (their unit of analysis) in states like New Jersey in the 2000 presidential election, the authors sought to measure the impact of negative campaign ads on voter turnout. They argue that focusing on aggregate voter turnout is preferable because of the aforementioned tendency of survey respondents to say they had voted when in fact they had not, a serious measurement problem. The result of their study: negative ads were found to have no effect.

Krasno and Green probably do not have the final word, however. Although they agree with the conclusions, Franz, Freedman, Goldstein, and Ridout raised a number of concerns with the Krasno and Green study, including issues of measurement error and concerns over the statistical techniques that they employed.[e] The issue is hardly settled and scholars will continue to develop research designs to gain a better understanding of the effects of negative advertising on citizen participation in elections.

d. Jonathan S. Krasno and Donald P. Green, "Do televised presidential ads increase voter turnout? Evidence from a natural experiment," *Journal of Politics* 70 (2008): 245–261.
e. Franz *et al.*, "Understanding the effect of political advertising on voter turnout."

techniques that have been developed for studying diverse forms of categorical data.[13]

Martin Wattenberg and Craig Brians used logistic regression to study the effects of advertisements on voter turnout using data from the 1992 and 1996 ANES.[14] Wattenberg and Brians examined whether individuals who recalled seeing a negative ad were more or less likely to vote compared to those who recalled seeing no advertisements or a positive advertisement. Because recalling an advertisement and reporting voting could be correlated with many other factors that might also explain voter turnout, the authors controlled for as many possible explanations as possible, including how much attention the respondents paid to news about the campaign, the respondents' levels of

13 Ordered logit or ordered probit is used to study ordinal dependent variables, and multinomial logit or multinomial probit is used with nominal-level dependent variables.
14 Martin P. Wattenberg and Craig Leonard Brians, "Negative campaign advertising: Demobilizer or mobilizer?" *American Political Science Review* 93 (1999): 891–899.

education and income, and a variety of other political and demographic indicators. After controlling for these factors, Wattenberg and Brians found that when respondents recalled a negative advertisement they were *more* likely to vote in the 1992 election but no more likely to vote in the 1996 election. Thus, the results were inconclusive. In a subsequent study, Kenneth Goldstein and his colleagues used data from the Wisconsin Advertising Project and found that negative advertising has little effect on making individuals either more or less likely to vote.[15]

REVERSE-CAUSALITY AND LONGITUDINAL ANALYSIS

Thus far we have discussed systematic and random sampling and measurement error as well as omitted variable bias at length. We have also addressed the issue of robustness. There is, however, another *major* challenge to inference in large-n studies: **reverse-causality** (see Panel B in Figure 1.1). Let's return to our example from earlier in the chapter to illustrate this concept. Above we hypothesized that democratic regimes would have lower levels of corruption than authoritarian regimes. In other words, regime type *affects* corruption. But couldn't the reverse also be true? Couldn't corruption help determine regime type? In fact, several military coups in recent history have been partially justified as a response to corruption in the political system. Take for example military takeovers in Pakistan in 1999, Thailand in 2006, and Bangladesh in 2007.

Consider another research example from above: whether being urged to vote has an impact on voting. In this case, we asked if a "get out the vote" campaign influences vote behavior, but, again, couldn't the reverse also be true? Wouldn't it make sense for a vote campaign to focus on communities with low voter turnout? In other words, voter turnout might determine who is reached by a campaign, rather than vice versa.

Just as with omitted variable bias, the problem of reversal-causation stems from the inability of large-n observational researchers to randomly assign study participants to control and condition groups as in experimental research. While large-n researchers can divide between those who have been contacted and urged to vote and those who have not, they do not determine who falls into which group. With reverse-causality, the intended "dependent variable" in a given research project might actually be a factor in determining who ends up in which group.

How then can we solve this dilemma? There are different potential answers to this question, but a simple one is to look at data over time. To use the example above, if we saw that countries tend to become authoritarian first and

15 Michael M. Franz, Paul Freedman, Ken Goldstein, *et al.*, "Understanding the effect of political advertising on voter turnout: A response to Krasno and Green," *Journal of Politics* 70 (2008): 262–268.

then become more corrupt later, then this would support our hypothesis that authoritarian regimes foster corruption. In other words, for an independent variable to cause a dependent variable, a change in the independent variable must have preceded a change in the dependent variable. Temporal ordering is easy to establish in experiments, where the researcher assigns a value of the independent variable first and then measures for the dependent variable, but such temporal ordering is generally not possible with cross-sectional data, since all variables are measured at the same point in time.

Studies on the influence of gender on the behavior of elected officials are illustrative of both this problem and the longitudinal solution to the problem. Several studies have argued that female legislators bring different experiences and viewpoints to the policymaking process than their male counterparts. A simple way to test this hypothesis using cross-sectional data would be to compare the behavior of male and female legislators. In fact, such a comparison would show that women legislators introduce more bills related to women's issues and that they do more to support such bills throughout the legislative process. Nonetheless, such cross-sectional studies suffer from our reverse-causality problem. It might be that women legislators are brought into office and do more to support women's issues because they represent districts that prioritize women's issues. Cross-sectional studies can attempt to control for district-level differences by including variables for demographic factors, attitudinal characteristics measured in survey data, and party identification, but they cannot control entirely for district-level differences or preferences.

Gerrity, Osborn, and Morehouse Mendez address this problem by using longitudinal data of congressional behavior over several legislative sessions.[16] Rather than study legislators as their unit of analysis, they study seats that have turned over and compare differences in seats where (1) a woman has replaced a man with seats where (2) a woman has replaced a woman with seats where (3) a man has replaced a man. They limit their sample to seat changes within the same party to control for any partisan differences. They find that women replacing men are in fact more likely to support bills dealing with women's issues but that they are no more likely to discuss women's issues in floor speeches.

The reverse-causality problem can be found in a great deal of cross-national research or any research where a geographical division is the unit of analysis. Consider for example the strong cross-sectional relationship that we can observe between democracy and economic development. Wealthy countries are almost all democratic and many lower-income countries are authoritarian. Observing this relationship, however, doesn't tell us whether democracy drives economic development or whether economic development causes democracy. To address this problem, several scholars, such as Acemoglu and his colleagues, have used a method known as fixed-effects estimation. If country is the unit

16 Jessica C. Gerrity, Tracy Osborn, and Jeanette Morehouse Mendez, "Women and representation: A different view of the district?" *Politics and Gender* 3 (2007): 179–200.

of analysis, rather than look at differences *between* countries, **fixed-effects estimations** look at differences *within* countries over time. The authors explain:

> Consider, for example, the comparison of the United States and Colombia. The United States is both richer and more democratic, so a simple cross-country comparison . . . would suggest that higher per capita income cause democracy. The idea of fixed effects is to move beyond this comparison and investigate the "within-country variation," that is, to ask whether Colombia is more likely to become (relatively) more democratic as it *becomes* (relatively) richer.[17]

Longitudinal analyses using fixed-effects models are also better able to address omitted variable-bias problems. For example, in cross-national research, there are so many differences between countries that no study can control for all of them. While there are general variables that can be included in such an analysis, there are also a number of country-specific factors that cannot be included, such as historical factors or cultural norms. Without taking these into account, however, cross-sectional studies might suffer from omitted variable bias. By comparing within-country data over time, fixed-effects models automatically control for idiosyncratic factors specific to a given country.

Fixed-effects models are so powerful because they do not just perform this analysis for one country, but they do it for all countries simultaneously. The estimation then combines all the separate in-country analyses together to determine if—generally speaking—countries become more democratic as they become wealthier. Of course, using this method requires having panel data, or data that can be analyzed both longitudinally and cross-sectionally. Fortunately, there are periodic measures of democracy and economic development for almost all countries, so in this case such a study is feasible. Perhaps surprisingly, and despite the strong cross-sectional relationship, Acemoglu and his colleagues looked at changes within countries over a hundred-year period and found that increases in income *do not* correspond with increases in democracy.

CONDUCTING YOUR OWN LARGE-N STUDY

Large-n studies offer an attractive tool for student-led research. Unlike experiments, which are often expensive for students to conduct on their own, and small-n studies, which might require extensive field research, students can get started with a large-n study simply by downloading a dataset. Rather than design their own survey or collect their own data, students can take advantage of the detailed and expensive work of the many researchers that have come before

---

17 Daron Acemoglu, Simon Johnson, James A. Robinson, *et al.*, "Income and democracy," *American Economic Review* 98 (2008): 808–842, p. 810.

them. The amount of data that are readily available is astounding, and yet most of it goes completely unused by university students. The largest obstacle is often inadequate statistical training to understand techniques like regression and a lack of familiarity with data management tools such as Stata, SPSS, SAS or R. On the other hand, even students who have been trained in these techniques and software packages are so used to thinking qualitatively that they are often hesitant to take advantage of such quantitative resources.

While we encourage students to pursue more detailed statistical training than this book allows for, even students without a strong statistical background can take advantage of quantitative resources. Even if one does not feel comfortable with some of the sophisticated tools of causal inference, he or she can certainly use large-n quantitative data for descriptive inferences. How does a country of interest compare with others in terms of corruption perception? What is the president's approval rating and how has it changed over time? What do Americans think about the 2010 health care law? These are all questions of descriptive inference that thoughtful students without an extensive background in statistics can use quantitative data to answer.

Even in terms of causal inference, cross-tabulations, means comparisons, and scatterplots offer relatively easy-to-use tools that do not require detailed statistical or mathematical knowledge beyond a thorough understanding of the logic of inference. One particularly easy-to-use resource for cross-national data available to students without any statistical background is Gapminder. Available at www.gapminder.org, the Gapminder software allows students without knowledge of statistical software packages to develop scatterplots using an enormous quantity of cross-national indicators. Consider the scatterplot presented in Figure 6.8 from Gapminder. Not only does the figure clearly show the bivariate relationship between GDP per capita and life expectancy, but individual countries are also labeled, the size of the plot shows population size, and the shading of the plot indicates region. This one picture communicates an enormous amount of information and is an excellent example of good data presentation. The software even allows users to animate data and see changes over time.

For students who do have statistical training, there is a host of additional resources. There are numerous survey datasets that are available with a simple click of a button. The World Values Survey, for example, is publicly available and offers students access to numerous survey questions tapping into culture, politics, and economics in close to 100 countries (www.worldvaluessurvey.org). Pew's Global Attitudes Project offers access to similar surveys conducted by Pew (www.pewglobal.org). Gallup provides a searchable database on their website where one can search for results from all of their public opinion polling and articles (http://brain.gallup.com). Consortiums of scholars produce regular public opinion surveys across many regions of the world, including the Latinobarómetro (www.latinobarometro.org), AmericasBarometer (www.vanderbilt.edu/lapop), Eurobarometer (ec.europa.eu/public_opinion/index_en.htm), Afrobarometer (www.afrobarometer.org), and Asian Barometer (www.asianbarometer.org).

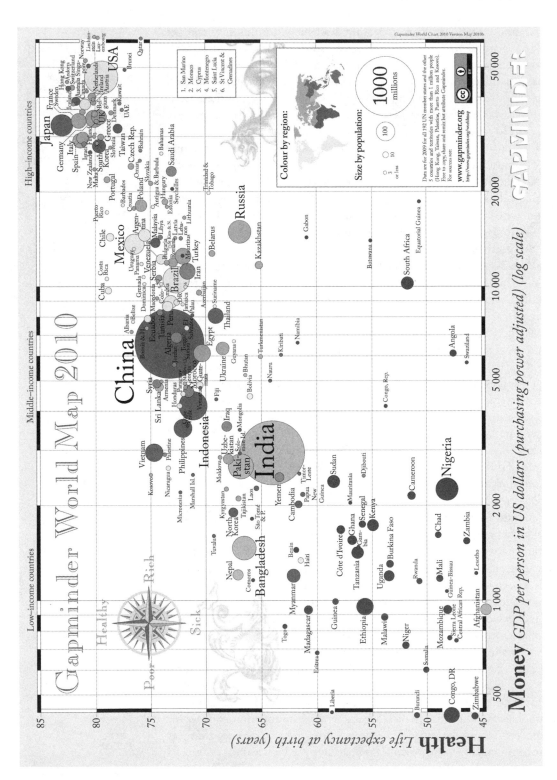

FIGURE 6.8 Gapminder Scatterplot of the Log of GDP Per Capita and Life Expectancy

Source: Gapminder.org.

In the United States, we have already discussed the ANES, whose public opinion data are also available online (www.electionstudies.org/). Many universities have access to the Roper Center for Public Opinion Research, which provides access to a wealth of public opinion polls.

There is also a wealth of non-public opinion data available. The Inter-University Consortium for Political and Social Research (ICPSR) archives data from a wide variety of research studies and the Dataverse (described in the concluding chapter) is also becoming an increasingly common place for scholars to archive their datasets. The U.S. Census Bureau is a great source for U.S. information (www.census.gov). Until recently it was difficult to access statistical information from the World Bank and the United Nations. Now, however, both multilateral institutions offer impressive data portals with access to a host of cross-national indicators (data.worldbank.org, data.un.org). Think tanks and nonprofit organizations can also be a good source for topic-based data. Environmental data are available through Earth Trends (earthtrends.wri.org). For those interested in democracy, freedom, and press freedom, Freedom House (www.freedomhouse.org) offers a number of resources. Students interested in immigration issues in the United States should consider the Pew Hispanic Center (www.pewhispanic.org). The Brookings Institution offers a regularly updated Iraq Index with numerous quantitative indicators on Iraq from the 2003 U.S. invasion to the present (www.brookings.edu/iraqindex). In addition, many university professors post data from their research online. Students can find databases about terrorist attacks, civil wars, globalization, cross-national indicators, regime changes over time, and a host of other topics. In short, the tools are available.

CONCLUSION

As this chapter has shown, large-n observational studies have their strengths and their weaknesses. True, they cannot match the internal validity of experimental research nor achieve the qualitative depth of small-n research. Furthermore, they run the risk of measurement and sampling error, omitted variable bias, reverse-causality, and generalizing from non-robust results. Nonetheless, scholars conducting large-n analyses have numerous tools at their disposal to reduce (although not eliminate) these challenges to inference. Random measurement and sampling error can be taken into account in tests of statistical significance. Systematic measurement error can be reduced by selecting accurate measurements and systematic sampling error through random sampling. In some cases, both can be addressed through weighting. The threat of omitted variable bias can be reduced by controlling for additional factors and by using fixed-effects models where longitudinal data are available. The problem of reverse-causality can also be addressed by examining changes over time. The problem of generalizing non-robust findings can be minimized through running multiple models, ethical scholarship, and the replication of results by other scholars. The flexibility offered by a growing body of increasingly sophisticated statistical techniques and the ever increasing availability of datasets make and will continue to make large-n observational studies an attractive research method in political science.

The increasing sophistication of statistical techniques is, however, something of a double edged sword. Students of political science run the risk of falling into two camps, those who blindly accept quantitative work as inherently authoritative and those who reject it entirely. Hopefully this chapter has illustrated that both approaches are incorrect. As with other research methods, large-n observational studies confront numerous challenges to inference. By recognizing these challenges and taking steps to confront them, scholars can make valid and reliable inferences. By developing an understanding of the logic of inference, students of political science can become more knowledgeable consumers of research as well as scholars in their own right. Admittedly, it is difficult for students not to become bogged down or confused by complex statistical analyses; however, by focusing on the logic of inference, students will at least know the right questions to ask in evaluating a piece of scholarship. Rather than try to understand all the complexities of a nuanced statistical argument, students should ask: Did the authors address problems of sampling and measurement error, omitted variable bias, and reverse-causality?

In his book *Damned Lies and Statistics*, Joel Best sums up both the problem and the solution when he writes:

> The solution to the problem of bad statistics is not to ignore all statistics, or to assume that every number is false. Some statistics are bad, but others are pretty good, and we need statistics—good statistics—to talk sensibly about social problems. The solution, then, is not to give up on statistics, but to become better judges of the numbers we encounter. We need to think critically about statistics. . . .[18]

▌ KEY TERMS

bivariate regression line   155

controlled cross-tabulation   167

controlled means comparison   153

cross-tabulation   166

data mining   163

dichotomous   167

fixed-effects estimations   172

independent effect   158

logistic regression   167

means comparison   151

multivariate linear regression   156

null hypothesis   153

omitted variable bias   151

regression coefficient   155

reverse-causality   170

robust   161

statistically significant relationship   153

18 Joel Best, *Damned lies and statistics: Untangling numbers from the media, politicians, and activists* (Berkeley: University of California Press, 2012), p. 6.

Small-n
Observational
Studies

A small-n observational study, as the name suggests, typically either entails a comparison of a small number of cases, known as a comparative case study, or an analysis of one case, referred to simply as a case study. The use of the term observational means that such research is not experimental, but rather based on an observation of political phenomena as they naturally occur in the real world.[1] Small-n observational studies are commonplace in political science, particularly in the fields of comparative politics and international relations, but also in the study of American politics and public policy. They are a particularly important tool for exploring complex macro-level phenomena, such as wars, revolutions, and regime change, or aggregated units of analysis, such as a city, region, organization, agency, or country. For example, students of international relations might want to know the causes of wars; researchers in comparative politics might be interested in the causes of military coups; and scholars of U.S. politics the effect of financial crises on regulation. Because financial crises are relatively rare events, it is often difficult to study a large number of such observations using statistical techniques. Likewise, it is certainly difficult to imagine setting up a field experiment involving war.

---

1 Throughout this chapter, we interchangeably use the terms "small-n observational study" and "small-n study."

In addition, small-n research often employs qualitative rather than quantitative research methods. Advocates of such methods contend that in-depth interviews and direct observation allow researchers to avoid over-simplifying and missing many of the nuances of the way politics plays out in the real world. The work of Nobel Laureate Elinor Ostrom and her colleagues on governing the commons is illustrative. As mentioned earlier in this book, these scholars were frustrated with contradictory policy prescriptions that advocated either privatization or central government control as the only way to manage common-pool resources (CPRs), such as fisheries, forests, pasture land, and water basins. Before undertaking the experiments discussed in earlier chapters, she and her colleagues sought to test if communities were able to effectively self-govern CPRs, and, if so, under what conditions. They were interested in the impact of a variety of factors that could not be easily tested in an experiment or in a large-n statistical study, including different types of rules, cultures, and physical environments. Given the complexity of their topic and the difficulty in measuring many of the concepts they were interested in, delving deeply into individual cases offered an attractive means to explore how a diverse set of variables interacted with one another to impact governance outcomes. Selecting from a large pool of existing case studies from throughout the United States and the world, Ostrom was able to identify a number of potentially important variables in predicting successful self-governance.[2]

While small-n studies offer a means to explore aggregated, macro-level phenomena and while they embrace nuance and complexity, from a deductive social science perspective, they confront a serious challenge to inference that is often summed up as: "too many variables and too few cases." For example, we might observe changes in economic policy following the U.S. subprime mortgage crisis in 2007, but we would not know for sure if these changes could be attributed to the mortgage crisis or to some other factor—such as rising unemployment. The only way to know with confidence would be to rerun history without the mortgage crisis—a theoretical proposition known as a counterfactual (which we introduced in Chapter 1). Because we cannot rerun history and because we do not know the counterfactual, we will have a hard time confidently making causal inferences. If we argue that a given change in economic policy was due to the mortgage crisis, our conclusion might suffer from omitted variable bias—this is to say that any observed relationship could in fact be spurious. As we will see in the course of this chapter, small-n researchers have taken different approaches to overcoming this challenge to inference.

---

2 Ostrom's work does not stand alone; many of political science's most famous studies involve in-depth analyses of a small number of cases. In American politics, Robert Dahl explored how local government works in one American city in his book *Who governs?*. In international relations, Graham Allison's *Essence of decision* explored a single event, the Cuban Missile Crisis. In comparative politics, Theda Skocpol compared revolutions in France, Russia, and China in her book *States and social revolutions*.

The discussion that follows can be divided into three parts. The first part explores how, even with a small number of cases, researchers can still effectively test hypotheses and draw inferences. In the second part, we consider a wider array of small-n research studies, which can be used to refine theory, explore causal mechanisms, and examine complex, interactive relationships either in cases that typify or deviate from a trend. These studies, which frequently benefit from in-depth qualitative research methods, provide a necessary and important complement to large-n and experimental research designs. The final part of the chapter explores some of these qualitative research methods and discusses approaches to designing small-n research studies.

MIMICKING EXPERIMENTS THROUGH A "MOST SIMILAR SYSTEMS DESIGN"

In an ideal world, a small-n study mirrors the logic of an experiment. As discussed in Chapter 5, the hallmark of a laboratory or field experiment is that the researcher controls the data-generating process. Rather than just observe naturally occurring phenomena, the researcher randomly assigns study participants into control and condition groups. Because the only difference between the control and experimental group is the independent variable of interest, the researcher is able to test if this factor has an impact on the dependent variable. Small-n studies can seek to mimic the logic of such experiments through purposeful case selection. Often referred to as a most similar systems research design, scholars using the comparative method select cases that are extremely similar to one another and only differ substantially on the value of the independent variable that the researcher is interested in studying.[3] As a result, such a design is able to mimic the logic of an experiment to study phenomena that could not be easily studied using an experiment (e.g. wars, military coups, mortgage crises).

In this section, we will use the example of research into ethnic division and conflict to explore how small-n studies work. We will begin with an example of a natural experiment, such as those discussed in Chapter 5, and then discuss a most similar systems design to highlight the differences. Daniel Posner's study of African ethnic fragmentation asks: Why do some cultural cleavages matter for politics while others do not?[4] To help answer this question, he explores an interesting natural experiment. When the African countries of Malawi and Zambia were formed, the new international border ran right through the

3 Adam Przeworski and Henry Teune, *The logic of comparative social inquiry* (New York: Wiley Press, 1970).

4 Daniel N. Posner, "The political salience of cultural difference: Why Chewas and Tumbukas are allies in Zambia and adversaries in Malawi," *American Political Science Review* 98 (2004): 529–545.

territory of the Chewa and Tumbuka ethnic groups. This division left majorities of these two groups in Malawi and minorities in Zambia. Surprisingly, in Malawi there was considerable ethnic tension and competition between the two groups, whereas in Zambia the groups were actually politically allied with one another. The somewhat arbitrary delineation of the border produces an interesting natural experiment. On one side of the border, two groups conflict with one another and, on the other side of the border, the same groups cooperate.

What could explain such a surprising difference in the value of the dependent variable—conflict or cooperation between ethnic groups? For Posner the finding is the product of demographic explanatory variables. Because the Chewas and Tumbukas are large groups in Malawi, they are able to serve as a political base to contest power. As a result, there is an incentive for ethnic political entrepreneurs to mobilize and politicize these groups. In Zambia, by contrast, because the ethnic groups are relatively small, there is no such incentive, and no such mobilization occurs. The result of these demographic differences is that ethnic tension arises in Malawi and not in Zambia. Posner's conclusions are strengthened by the fact that he is comparing the same ethnic groups, which by random chance (i.e. the arbitrary delineation of the border) find themselves in two different political environments.

Selecting on the Dependent or Independent Variable in Most Similar Systems Designs

A most similar systems research design can attempt to simulate the logic of such natural experiments. A small-n researcher interested in explaining ethnic conflict could look for two similar countries that differ in the degree of ethnic tension or conflict. For example, these two countries might have a similar political history, level of economic development, degree of ethnic and religious heterogeneity, and demographics. With a smaller number of potential explanatory variables, the researcher would have an easier time explaining divergent ethnic relations. This is an example of selecting on the dependent variable, or choosing cases that exhibit variation on the factor that the research wants to explain. For example, Zurcher, Baev, and Koehler wanted to know why the southern Russian republic of Chechnya was a center of major conflict while there had been far less fighting in neighboring Dagestan, despite many similarities, including similar grievances.[5] They also analyzed a parallel situation in Georgia, where South Ossetia and Abkhazia had fought to separate from the Republic of Georgia, yet where the Adjaria autonomous region had avoided

5   Christoph Zurcher, Pavel Baev, and Jan Koehler, "Civil war in the Caucasus," in Paul Collier and Nicholas Sambanis, eds, *Understanding civil war: Evidence and analysis* (Washington, D.C.: World Bank, 2005), pp. 259–298.

such violence. In both these cases, the authors select on the dependent variable: the presence or absence of conflict.

Alternatively, a researcher could select on the independent variable, or look for two cases that are similar in most ways but differ in the value of the hypothesized explanatory variable. Any subsequent differences observed in ethnic conflict could perhaps be attributed to differences in the independent variable. To illustrate, imagine two countries that are similar in terms of economic wealth, regime type, and ethnic make-up, but one country has adopted electoral rules designed to ease ethnic tensions and the other has not. If we observed divergences in the levels of ethnic tensions, the differences could be due to the electoral rules. Edward Miguel employed a related research design in his comparative study of Kenya and Tanzania.[6] Miguel selected a region in Tanzania and one in Kenya with similar geography, degree of ethnic division, and population size, but the two regions differed in terms of public policy. Tanzania had promoted a national language (Swahili), a public school curriculum that fostered a national identity, and reformed its local governments, while Kenya had not taken any comparative measures. Finding lower levels of ethnically related governance problems in Tanzania than in Kenya, Miguel uncovers convincing evidence that better public policy deserves the credit.[7]

There is an interesting debate on whether it is preferable to select cases based on the independent or dependent variable. Conventional methodological wisdom posits that selecting cases based on the independent variable is more desirable, as this more closely matches the deductive logic of the experimental method.[8] In an experiment, random assignment of the independent variable ensures that the only difference between the control and condition groups is the independent variable of interest. This approach leaves open the possibility that there will be no subsequent difference in the dependent variable between the two groups, a result that would disprove the hypothesis. In short, the hypothesis is easier to falsify. Alternatively, if we select cases based on variation in the dependent variable, then we might erroneously attribute the observed difference to the wrong explanatory variable. Small-n research in the real world cannot ensure that there are no differences between the cases selected besides the main independent variable of study. For this reason, a researcher might attribute a change to a hypothesized independent variable when in fact it was due to some other difference between the cases.

6   Edward Miguel, "Tribe or nation?" *World Politics* 56 (2004): 327–362.
7   Miguel actually presents his study as a natural experiment. In fact, the line between natural experiments and most similar systems research design might often appear blurred. For us, the natural experiment requires an event that randomly divides a population of study into condition groups, simulating random assignment in an experiment. In Miguel's case, the ethnic groups studied are different in Tanzania and Kenya, suggesting a most similar systems research design rather than a natural experiment.
8   Gary King, Robert O. Keohane, and Sidney Verba. *Designing social inquiry: Scientific inference in qualitative research* (Princeton: Princeton University Press, 1994).

Other scholars, however, note that selecting on the independent variable is at times impractical. Scholars often know the value of both the independent and dependent variable ahead of time, particularly when studying salient topics such as revolution, conflict, democratic transition, or election to office. If one already knows the value of both variables, then he could be tempted to choose cases—or be accused of choosing cases—that match his hypothesis. Kaarbo and Beasley argue that it is justifiable and at times preferable to select on the dependent variable.[9] Furthermore, selecting on the dependent variable is often an outgrowth of an empirical puzzle. In the above mentioned case of conflict in former communist countries, Zurcher, Baev, and Koehler wanted to know why some regions experienced conflict and others did not.[10]

Regardless of whether a scholar selects his or her cases based on the independent or dependent variable, it is important that the selected cases allow for variation in the values of the political phenomena being studied. Say, for example, that a student wanted to explain the dependent variable of democratic transitions in North Africa and the Middle East during the Arab Spring, which began in 2010. It would be tempting to study Libya, Egypt, and Tunisia, all of which experienced a democratic transition, and to look for commonalities among these cases. While such a study might be interesting, it would offer no way of knowing if any identified commonalities also existed in countries that did not experience regime change. As a result, a meaningful study of the Arab Spring would not only need to include cases where regime change occurred, but also cases where regime change did not occur.[11] The same logic applies to uncovering the causes of ethnic conflict. To make valid causal inferences, one would have to study cases where ethnic conflict occurred and cases where ethnic conflict did not occur. When selecting cases based on the independent variable, adequate variation is also needed. For example, if we are interested in the effect of inequality on conflict, then we would need to select cases with varying degrees of inequality. Indeed, a failure to do so would be akin to running an experiment with two groups but with just one condition (lacking a control condition, for example).

How Many Cases?

Once we have resolved whether to select on the dependent or independent variable, the next question is how many cases are needed to make valid inferences. Provided that the researcher is testing the effect of one independent variable using a most similar systems research design, he needs, at the very

9 Juliet Kaarbo and Ryan K. Beasley, "A practical guide to the comparative case study method in political psychology," *Political Psychology* 20 (1999): 369–391.
10 Zurcher, Baev, and Koehler, "Civil war in the Caucasus."
11 Of course, a study of Libya, Egypt, and Tunisia could still be used to rule out hypothesized explanatory variables.

TABLE 7.1 Example of Hypothetical 2×2 Research Design

	Low inequality	High inequality
Low fragmentation	Case 1 Low inequality Low fragmentation	Case 2 High inequality Low fragmentation
High fragmentation	Case 3 Low inequality High fragmentation	Case 4 High inequality High fragmentation

least, two cases—one case with one value of the independent variable (e.g. low inequality) and another with a different value of the independent variable (e.g. high inequality). If he is interested in the effect of an independent variable with more than one value, then additional cases can be added to accommodate additional values (e.g. low, medium, and high inequality).[12]

If, however, the analyst is interested in testing the impact of two independent variables using a most similar systems design, then he needs, at the very least, four cases. Such a research design produces a commonly used 2×2 table, with each cell representing a different combination of the four possible combinations of the variable values. For example, if we were interested in the effect of inequality and ethnic fragmentation on conflict, then we might look for four comparable countries that vary on these two variables. As shown in Table 7.1, one case would have low inequality and low fragmentation, another low inequality and high fragmentation, a third high inequality and low fragmentation, and a fourth high inequality and high fragmentation.

Herbert Kitschelt developed such a research design in his study of political opportunity structure on social movement organization.[13] Kitschelt wanted to test the argument that social movements could only emerge and be effective if there was sufficient opportunity. He understood "opportunity" in two ways: the opportunity to impact policy design, what he calls "political input structures," and the opportunity to impact policy implementation, or "political output structures." He compared four cases, one with high opportunity on both criteria, one with low opportunity on both criteria, and two cases with differing opportunities.

Unfortunately, small-n research is not well equipped to test hypotheses involving more than two independent variables. Once we start adding additional variables, the research design quickly becomes messy and better suited for

12 Of course, the minimum number of cases is just that, a minimum. Our inferences will improve when we are able to add more cases to our analysis, even if we have only a single independent variable to examine.

13 Herbert Kitschelt, "Political opportunity structures and political protest: Anti-nuclear movements in four democracies," *British Journal of Political Science* 16 (1986): 57–85.

large-n statistical analysis. For example, adding a third variable would produce a $2 \times 2 \times 2$ table of possible variable combinations, requiring at least eight cases.

The Continued Risk of Omitted Variable Bias

While a most similar systems design allows for a degree of control, such studies still confront the risk of omitted variable bias. It is difficult to find cases that have only one theoretically important difference between them. For example, while Posner makes a compelling argument in his study of ethnic conflict in southern Africa, because Zambia and Malawi are not identical it is possible that observed differences in ethnic tension could be explained by some other factor besides Posner's explanatory variable of demographics. This challenge is slightly greater in the most similar systems design employed by Miguel, as the regions he studied in Tanzania and Kenya contain somewhat different tribal groups, introducing another point of variation between the two cases that could offer a rival explanation for different outcomes. In their study of conflict in former communist countries, Zurcher, Baev, and Koehler have the advantage of comparing regions within the same country, controlling for important political factors (e.g. electoral rules, laws, central government actors); however, there are still differences between Chechnya and Dagestan and between South Ossetia and Adjaria. In fact, while it is possible to find two regions or countries that are very similar along a key set of variables, it is highly unlikely that these two countries or regions would be comparable in the way a control and experimental group would be. In sum, while natural experiments and most similar systems designs attempt to mimic the logic of an experiment, it is important to remember that they represent an imperfect substitute with lower levels of internal validity.

Comparing across Time: A Means to Compare Even More Similar Systems?

One potential solution to the problem of finding most similar systems is to compare a unit of analysis across time. All of the above examples compare two geographical regions at one point in time, what some authors refer to as a **cross-sectional** or **spatial comparison**.[14] However, it is also possible to make comparisons across time, a **longitudinal comparison**, or comparisons across time and space, what Gerring and McDermott call a **dynamic comparison**.

To illustrate, several scholars have noted that majoritarian electoral systems, whereby the loser of an election is locked out of power, are problematic in countries with ethnic tensions. If party formation overlaps with ethnicity in a

14 John Gerring and Rose McDermott, "An experimental template for case study research," *American Journal of Political Science* 51 (2007): 688–701.

majoritarian system, the victory of a given party means that ethnic minorities might be entirely cut out of the policy process. As a result, several scholars have recommended consensual electoral systems for such divided countries, whereby electoral minorities will still be allowed a continued say in the policy process.[15] Consider the possibility that an ethnically conflictive country, say Kenya, follows this policy advice and changes its form of government from a majoritarian system to a consensual one. A scholar could then measure ethnic tensions before the change and after the change. In theory, any observed differences could be attributed to the new political system. This longitudinal comparison is particularly attractive because the research subject, Kenya, does not change, holding constant a whole variety of factors that could be expected to affect ethnic conflict.[16] In a sense, one could think of the pre-system change period as a condition group and the post-system change period as a second condition group.

This same logic of comparing a given research subject before and after some event could be applied to a host of issues: Did violence in Iraq decrease after the 2007 U.S. military surge? Did murder decline as a result of gun control legislation enacted in Chicago in the 1970s? Did increases in security along the United States–Mexico border in the late 2000s create a drop in migration? Unfortunately, longitudinal approaches in small-n research still confront serious limitations. By now, you should be able to pick out two familiar flaws: reverse-causality and spuriousness. Consider our hypothetical country that changed its electoral system. One should consider why this country decided to change its electoral system in the first place. Unlike an experiment, the country was not randomly assigned its electoral system. The fact that those in power in a majoritarian system were willing to surrender some of their authority to accommodate minorities suggests a possible resolve to reduce ethnic tensions. In other words, the change in the electoral rules could have been *the result* of a desire to reduce tensions rather than a *cause* of reduced tension. Or, put another way, the change was reciprocal.[17]

Small-n longitudinal comparisons also do not control for other temporal changes, yielding a risk of omitted variable bias. While dramatic declines in migration across the United States–Mexico border in the late 2000s coincided temporally with the massive growth of the U.S. Border Patrol and improved fencing and border infrastructure, the decline also coincided with a downturn in the U.S. economy, contraction of the construction industry, and reduced

---

15 Arend Lijphart, *Patterns of democracy: Government forms and performance in thirty-six countries* (New Haven: Yale University Press, 2012).

16 In fact, Kenya recently underwent some constitutional reforms in 2010 in response to ethnic violence following the controversial 2007 elections. A study could compare ethnic tensions before and after the constitutional change.

17 Consider how this is similar to the hypothetical choices we described in Chapter 5 about which voters candidates would advertise to.

job opportunities for migrants. As a result, there was no way to confidently tell if the drop was due to improved deterrence along the border or reduced incentives to migrate.

This omitted variable bias problem applies to our ethnic conflict example as well. Say, for example, that we observe far less ethnic-related violence after a constitutional change to a consensual system, but also imagine that the political change coincided with an improvement in the global economy and the country's economic situation. We would have no conclusive way to determine whether the drop in violence was due to the new constitutional rules or to the improved economic situation.

For an even stronger research design, it is also possible to combine the spatial and longitudinal comparison and compare cases across both geography and time. One could imagine two countries with ethnic tensions, whereby one of the countries changes to a consensual system and the other does not, as is presented in the 2×2 table in Table 7.2. If both countries experienced economic improvements due to the change in the global economy but only the country with the consensual system saw a decline in violence, then we would be more confident that the change was due to the constitutional rules. While desirable, the challenge with this dynamic comparison research design is finding the cases that allow for such control. We see that the same fundamental dilemma of small-n work applies for longitudinal comparisons as well: few cases with many potential variables create a risk of omitted variable bias.

Absent the strong internal validity of an experiment, and lacking the ability to control for alternative explanations using statistical techniques, one might be tempted to question the desirability of small-n research to test hypotheses and make causal inferences. However, as has been emphasized throughout this book, each methodology has both strengths and limitations. As discussed in the introduction to this chapter, issues such as conflict, war, revolution, common-pool resource governance, and a transition to democracy are all macro-level phenomena that are at times difficult to study through experimental methods and large-n studies. Of course, political scientists do not have the political influence to randomly assign one ethnically diverse country one set of institutions and another country a different set. While one can still conduct quantitative studies comparing large numbers of common-pool resources, conflicts, countries, and regions, it is important to remember that

TABLE 7.2 Example of Hypothetical 2 × 2 Dynamic Research Design

	Time 1	Time 2
Country 1	Worse economy	Improved economy
	Majoritarian system	Consensual system
Country 2	Worse economy	Improved economy
	Majoritarian system	Majoritarian system

large-n studies also have their drawbacks. As discussed in Chapter 4, aggregating data to the national level might obscure important regional variation. In many cases, quantitative data might not exist, or it might be plagued by sampling and measurement errors. It also might not be possible to quantify all variables of potential importance. For all these reasons, small-n research is still a commonly used tool for studying aggregated units of analysis in political science. Of course, as we discuss in Box 7.1, the line between large-n and small-n research is not always as clear as we might expect.

Box 7.1: Is It Small-n or Large-n?

Is a study of 1,000 survey respondents in the city of Cleveland, Ohio a large-n or a small-n study? At first blush, such a survey would appear to be a clear example of a large-n study—it's a comparison of 1,000 observations after all! Nonetheless, from another point of view, it is also a case study of just one city: Cleveland. The answer to the question depends on the unit of analysis. Cleveland can be examined at the city level of analysis or it can be disaggregated into its component parts (i.e. the people who live in Cleveland). For example, a survey of 1,000 Clevelanders could be used in a large-n study of individuals or in a small-n case study of the city of Cleveland.

As discussed in the previous chapter, large-n analyses always use quantitative, or statistical, research tools. Small-n studies, however, can be either qualitative or quantitative. Traditionally, most people—and even most scholars—associate small-n research with qualitative research methods, such as interviews, focus groups, and observation. But King, Koehane and Verba, among others, argue that one of the easiest ways to overcome the problem of "too many variables, too few cases" in small-n research is to disaggregate the unit of analysis being studied. In fact, both the Posner's and Miguel's studies of ethnic tension in African countries, which were profiled above, include analyses of survey data. Given the limitations of individual methods, mixed-methods approaches are often necessary to make valid and reliable inferences. Perhaps a more useful way to think about the different types of research studies would be to divide by the methodological technique used and the unit of analysis analyzed as in Table 7.3. A study might entail one quadrant within the table, or, as in the Posner and Miguel studies, it might overlap multiple quadrants.

TABLE 7.3 Typology of Observational Studies

	Individual unit of analysis	Aggregated unit of analysis
Quantitative research techniques	E.g. surveys of many individuals	E.g. large-n statistical comparison of many countries
Qualitative research techniques	E.g. in-depth interviews with individuals	E.g. case study and comparative case study of fewer countries

▮ OTHER APPROACHES WITH OTHER OBJECTIVES

Beyond deductive hypothesis testing, there are additional reasons why scholars employ small-n research methods. Because small-n methods using qualitative methods often emphasize depth rather than breadth, many scholars use such research not necessarily to test hypotheses, but to generate new hypotheses, refine theory in complex arenas, consider complicated interactions between variables, and otherwise elucidate causal mechanisms. A focus on causal mechanisms goes beyond observing a relationship between two variables, as it explores in detail the precise way in which an independent variable affects a dependent variable. In this section, we will explore this alternative focus of small-n research.

The Case Study Project on Civil Wars exemplifies these alternative objectives.[18] The project has used as its point of departure two large-n studies of civil wars by Fearon and Laitin and Collier and Hoeffler that had found (perhaps surprisingly) that conflicts are not driven so much by ethnic divisions or legitimate grievances but by opportunities for rebellion, which are exploited by opportunistic political entrepreneurs.[19] Investigators in the Case Study Project did not intend to retest this hypothesis; instead they sought to explore its causal mechanisms, refine the theory, and examine deviant cases.

As we have seen in the previous chapter, large-n research is particularly good at finding a correlation, or relationship, between two variables. What it is not good at doing is clearly explaining how or why those two variables relate to one another, particularly if we are lacking strong theory. For example, if contrary to Fearon and Laitin's and Collier and Hoeffler's findings, a large-n statistical analysis suggested a relationship between high levels of ethnic diversity and conflict, such a finding would not necessarily tell us why diversity and conflict are related. Is it because language divisions inhibit communication? Or perhaps it is because different groups distrust people that look different than they do? Maybe opportunists exploit divisions to rise to power? Or perhaps it is for all of these reasons? Quantitative analyses typically cannot answer these questions, and it is frequently necessary to dig into concrete cases to flush out these causal mechanisms. By exploring the relationships present in a **typical case**, or a case representative of a general causal trend, scholars can refine and improve their theories, derive new hypotheses from these theories, and develop new research designs to test them.

Scholars of institutional analysis have been particularly concerned with causal mechanisms and have relied heavily on case studies to elucidate such

18 Nicholas Sambanis, "Using case studies to expand economic models of civil war," *Perspectives on Politics* 2 (2004): 259–280.

19 James D. Fearon and David D. Laitin, "Ethnicity, insurgency, and civil war," *American Political Science Review* 97 (2003): 75–90; Paul Collier and Anke Hoeffler, "On the incidence of civil war in Africa," *Journal of Conflict Resolution* 46 (2002): 13–28.

relationships. Influenced heavily by game theory and rational choice theory, these scholars have developed simplified models, or games, explaining the strategic interactions among self-interested actors with the aim of clarifying potential causal mechanisms. While traditional game theorists have sought to test their theoretical models largely through computer simulations, other scholars have attempted to see how well these games explain real-world outcomes. Using the term **analytical narratives**, several political scientists have sought to combine the well-delineated theoretical approach of rational choice with the case study method.[20] While the term would come later, Ostrom and her colleagues in many ways pioneered this approach in their studies of common-pool resource governance. For example, Ostrom, Gardner, and Walker use the logic of games in their analysis of water appropriation in three Californian basins.[21] They find that one basin illustrates the traditional prisoner's dilemma game, whereby appropriators face perverse incentives to use as much of the resource as possible and in so doing deplete the resource. However, in two other basins, rules delineating use and monitoring regimes ensuring compliance altered the game to one whereby appropriators had strong incentives to cooperate with one another and sustainably use the resource. By focusing on the importance of rules, Ostrom, Gardner, and Walker were able to clearly establish the causal mechanisms separating a failed case of resource governance from successful cases.

Theory can be improved and refined in other ways as well. Instead of focusing solely on typical cases, or cases that fit a general trend, the Case Study Project on Civil Wars has also explored several **deviant cases**, or examples that defied the trends identified in large-n studies. It is important to note that generally speaking the existence of a single case (or a handful of cases) that support or do not support a hypothesis is (are) insufficient grounds on which to accept or reject a hypothesis.[22] This is one of the primary criticisms leveled at scholars using small-n methods, who have been accused of studying a "tree" in great detail and then making generalizations about the "forest." Because not all cases will support a general trend, we have no way of knowing if a selected case is representative of a trend or a deviation from it. The Case Study Project was able to use large-n, quantitative studies to identify typical and deviant cases and then use more in-depth research methods to explore these deviant cases.

20 Robert H. Bates, *Analytic narratives* (Princeton: Princeton University Press, 1998).
21 Elinor Ostrom, Roy Gardner, and James Walker, *Rules, games, and common-pool resources* (Ann Arbor: University of Michigan Press, 1994).
22 Arend Lijphart contends that case studies can be either theory "confirming" or theory "infirming," but he nonetheless would agree that a single case is not sufficient evidence to support or reject a hypothesis. Eckstein, however, contends that there is such a thing as a "critical case study," or a case that offers such unfavorable conditions for a given theory that evidence of support for a hypothesis would in fact offer a meaningful test. See Harry Eckstein, "Case study and theory in political science." In Roger Gomm, Martyn Hammersley, and Peter Foster, eds, *Case study method* (London: Sage, 2000), pp. 119–164.

By using case studies, the project was able to determine when outliers deviated from the trend for idiosyncratic reasons and when they revealed flaws in the theoretical models employed by previous research.[23] In other words, scholars can be served best by studying both the forest (through large-n quantitative methods) and the tree (through qualitative small-n methods). We expand on the benefits of these types of mixed-methods approaches in the concluding chapter (Chapter 8).

Qualitative, small-n methods are also an attractive option for research topics where measurement is difficult or where we do not understand the research topic well enough to develop strong hypotheses, robust measurements, or an effective research design. If our theory, measurements, and design are inadequate, then we will not be able to effectively test our hypotheses and advance understanding—regardless of how impressive our experimental and statistical techniques appear. Exploratory, qualitative research allows scholars to propose new hypotheses, measurements, and research designs. Interestingly, even when there is a large body of scholarship on a topic, scholars might miss important changes or over-look valuable perspectives. Under such conditions, an exploratory study, or in-depth examination of a case or a series of cases, is a particularly valuable tool.

Small-n research is particularly amenable to inductive approaches. As discussed earlier in this book, inductive research does not seek to test a hypothesis derived from a political theory. Instead, inductive research reverses the order of the scientific method and derives hypotheses and theories from observation of the political world. Inductive research techniques that do not presume to know all relevant variables offer an important complement to enrich and ensure that the deductive techniques of experiments, large-n studies, and most similar systems designs stay on track. Richard Fenno, who famously accompanied members of Congress in their home districts and authored the subsequent book *Home Style*, used a qualitative research methodology that he called "soaking and poking," or—more simply—direct observation.[24] Rather than deductively approach a research project with a series of theories, hypotheses, and variables, **inductive observation** requires the researcher to approach her research subjects with an open mind, allowing the theory, hypotheses, and variables to emerge from the data and the research itself. Fenno notes that such a method entails a loss of control over the research process, but, "It brings you especially close to your data. You watch it being generated and you collect it at the source."[25]

---

23 Sambanis, "Using case studies to expand economic models of civil war."

24 Throughout this text we have used the term "observational research" as a contrast to "experimental research." This commonly accepted distinction differentiates between phenomena that can be observed in the natural world and a research setting controlled by the researcher. However, other scholars use the term "observation" to refer to data directly observed by the researcher. To avoid confusion we use the term "direct observation." Richard F. Fenno, *Home style: Representatives in their districts* (Boston: Little, Brown, 1978).

25 Richard F. Fenno, "Observation, context, and sequence in the study of politics," *American Political Science Review* 80 (1986): 3–15, p. 3.

Advocates of inductive research note that there is a certain humility in the approach. Some have provocatively—yet validly—asked if middle-class university students and/or university professors in an advanced industrial country can really understand major social problems, poverty, revolution, corruption, and so on, absent personalized contact with these issues. In his defense of observation as a research tool in the study of political campaigns, Fenno challenges scholars to learn their subjects better:

> Can we be satisfied that we know enough about the ways in which strategic options open up and close down over the course of the campaign, or about the kinds of choices that lead a campaign down one path rather than another, or about the choice points at which such branching decisions get made, when we have yet to follow a single campaign from start to finish? With so little closely detailed investigation of so common a context as the constituency and so common a sequence as a campaign, it seems unlikely that we have yet given these variables the close, hard study they deserve.[26]

To illustrate the importance of inductive approaches, consider our research questions regarding corruption. Because corruption is an illegal activity, it is a difficult concept to measure and even specialists might not fully understand how it functions. Rather than rely on surveys or corruption perception indices, authors such as Maria Eugenia Suárez de Garay and Elena Azaola Garrido and her colleagues have tried to answer complex research questions related to police misconduct in Mexico through direct observation, focus groups, in-depth interviews, and even interviews with former officers convicted and serving time for criminal involvement.[27] In one controversial study that would probably not meet today's strict ethical research standards, a researcher actually embedded himself within a police force for two years to document gross corruption and misconduct (see Box 7.2 on ethics in qualitative research).[28]

---

26 Fenno, "Observation, context, and sequence in the study of politics," p. 6.

27 Maria Eugenia Suárez de Garay, "La ruta pirata del asfalto. Trayectorias femeninas y delictivas en el mundo policial," *Revista de estudios de género. La ventana* 24 (2006): 258–296; Elena Azaola Garrido and Miguel Ángel Ruíz Torres, *Investigadores de papel: Poder y derechos humanos entre la Policía Judicial de la Ciudad de México* (Mexico City: Fontamara, 2009).

28 Nelson Arteaga Botello and Adrián López Rivera, *Policía y corrupción: El caso de un municipio en México* (México: Plaza & Valdés, 1998). In a similar vein, in-depth qualitative work can also be used to identify problems in quantitative measurement and operationalization of concepts. For example, many studies of conflict are interested in the role of valuable export commodities, such as diamonds, gold, or oil on conflict. This is for good reason. First, grievances by ethnic groups that do not get their desired share of revenues might fuel rebellion. Second, both governments and rebels alike are able to use export revenues to sustain conflict. In large-n studies, this factor is often operationalized as the percentage of GDP that comes from export commodities. Using findings from the case studies, however, Sambanis contends that this measurement is problematic and does not offer an effective test of the

Box 7.2: Ethics in Qualitative Research

Ethical guidelines require researchers to obtain the informed consent of study participants. Typically, study participants must receive and sign a document that outlines the goals of the study and any risks to the study participant. The document also informs the participant that his participation is voluntary and that he can conclude the interview at any time. It further states whether or not responses are confidential and might ask permission to record the interview. Confidentiality extends beyond actual publication, and researchers must even be careful about how they store their data and who has access to it.

Informed consent emerged out of medical studies where participants are often exposed to physical risks. Because of the differences between social science and medical research, some social science researchers view ethical guidelines as an unnecessary imposition. They might argue that high-level political leaders, for example, are frequently interviewed by journalists who follow no such informed consent and confidentiality guidelines. Nonetheless, even when the risks are minimal, it is simply good practice to be clear about what the study is for and to clarify the rules regarding confidentiality.

Furthermore, there are many research topics where participation in an academic study might confront real risks. An interviewee participating in a study on ethnic conflict or corruption, for example, should give some thought to those risks before participating in a study. Consider for example, a researcher conducting a study on ethnic conflict in a violence-prone region. While taking a taxi to an interview, the researcher asks her driver about the violence. Unaware that his fare is a researcher, the taxi driver relates in detail a violent episode that he witnessed, implicating prominent local leaders in the violence. The story appears to be accurate and is corroborated by other sources. How should the researcher treat this information? On the one hand, the narrative provided is rich and would be helpful to the study. On the other hand, the information provided is sensitive, and there is the potential that the story could be traced back to the driver—even if his name is omitted and details of the story changed. What would you do?

So when should we use small-n observational research? This discussion suggests several different answers to this question. Small-n research is useful to test hypotheses concerning aggregated units of analysis (e.g. countries, events, organizations) and make causal inferences using a most similar systems research design. Nonetheless, the researcher must bear in mind the risk of potential omitted variable bias, choose her cases thoughtfully, and be systematic

hypothesis. He discusses several cases where conflicts in high-export commodities countries had nothing to do with the commodity (e.g. Maitatsine rebellion in Nigeria in the 1980s, Azeri-Armenian conflict in the early 1990s) and where conflicts in low-export commodity countries or time periods were closely related to the commodity (e.g. Biafran rebellion in Nigeria in 1967). These findings do not necessarily refute the hypothesis, but they do suggest a problem with the measurement used to test the hypothesis in large-n studies.

in her measurement. Furthermore, as mentioned in Box 7.1, a study of a few cases can be transformed into a large-n study by disaggregating the unit of analysis, for example by converting a country study into a study of individuals in that country.

In addition, and perhaps most importantly, small-n research can and should be employed to complement other methods and to explore causal mechanisms. Focusing on a small number of observations is extremely useful in environments of complexity and where there is a risk of over-simplification. Small-n qualitative work is the preferred method to really dig deep into either a typical or deviant case, which can be essential for strengthening existing theories or generating new hypotheses. Qualitative studies of a limited number of observations are particularly useful when quantifiable indicators are inadequate or flawed. There are ways to overcome the problem of too many variables and too few cases, but, perhaps more importantly, in-depth analyses offer a much needed complement to overcome the limitations of and improve experimental and large-n research.

TOOLS OF THE TRADE IN QUALITATIVE RESEARCH

While small-n research can certainly use quantitative indicators and data, case studies and comparative case studies are often associated with qualitative research methods, which allow researchers to dig deeply into their cases. There are numerous tools that are employed in qualitative research, and here we profile and consider the strengths and weaknesses of four such tools: interviewing, focus groups, direct observation, and document analysis.

Interviewing

Interviewing is perhaps the core research methodology used in most small-n research. Interviews might be held with political leaders, social movement participants, civil servants, or any variety of public and/or political actors. (See Box 7.3 for more details on the nuts and bolts of interviewing.) The unquestionable advantage of interview research is that it allows analysts an opportunity to learn about their research topic straight from the mouths of their study participants. Nonetheless, Jeffrey Berry points out that interviews risk a number of measurement errors.[29] Because interview questions are typically not standardized in the way that survey questions are, readers of such studies have no way of knowing if questions were well written, impartial, and not leading. Furthermore, as in a survey, interviewees might hide their true

---

29 Jeffrey M. Berry, "Validity and reliability issues in elite interviewing," *PS: Political Science and Politics* 35 (2002): 679–682.

Box 7.3: Interviewing

Interviewing is one of the primary tools used in qualitative, small-n research. In some interviews, researchers might only be concerned with the attitudes and perspectives of research participants. In others, however, the researcher might seek factual information about an event, policy, or problem. In both cases, researchers should ensure that they have prepared properly for the interview. Interviews should only be used to obtain information that cannot be obtained elsewhere, such as from reports, media sources, or government documentation. Exchanges are far more profitable when time does not have to be wasted on rudimentary material, and interviewees are often impressed when researchers demonstrate that they have done their homework. For example, high-level officials who typically give stock answers to the press and to citizens will often delve deeper into a topic with academic researchers who know their subject well.

Interviews vary in their degree of structure and the extent to which the researcher controls the interview. In the case of a close-ended survey question, the interviewee only responds to the questions asked and she is limited by the answers offered. The main advantage to such a technique is that the answers of one interviewee can be easily compared with those of another. There are, however, disadvantages to such a method. The approach presumes that the interviewer has asked the right questions and identified the correct possible responses. Moreover, such an approach cannot accommodate more nuanced or complex questions and answers. While surveyors might see their job as measuring attitudes of respondents, interviewers often want to learn from their research subjects.

At the opposite extreme is an open-ended, unstructured, in-depth interview. While the interviewer will ask questions, they will typically be open-ended, and many of the subsequent questions will be follow-up questions based on the statements of the interviewee. Jeffrey Berry, for example, states that he typically goes into an interview with only eight questions—compare this with a survey that might contain 200 questions.[a] Such a method tailors the interview to the interviewee. In fact, a researcher might ask entirely different questions to different interview participants. This offers the researcher considerable flexibility, but the success of the method is dependent on good interviewing skills that are not typically taught (and difficult to teach) in research methods classes. Good interviewers need to be able to ensure that an interviewee is engaged, develop a level of trust in a short time, encourage the interviewee to talk openly but politely head off long-winded monologues, separate out good/accurate information from potentially false information, think up and properly phrase follow-up questions on the fly, and effectively direct the interview. Jeffrey Berry quotes his mentor to say that "the best interviewer is not one who writes the best questions. Rather, excellent interviewers are excellent conversationalists."[b]

There are numerous approaches between these two extremes, including the commonly used semi-structured interviews. Such an approach might offer close-ended survey-style questions

a. Berry, "Validity and reliability issues in elite interviewing."
b. Berry, "Validity and reliability issues in elite interviewing," p. 679.

that can be compared with other interview respondents, but then follow such questions up with open-ended inquiries. If an interesting topic comes up, the researcher might go off script and ask additional questions. Such an approach seeks to obtain a degree of structure and comparability while also learning from the research participant. The interview approach adopted should be determined by the objective of the research. For a most similar systems research design, comparability and structure are extremely important. For exploratory studies seeking to refine theory, generate hypotheses, or explain a given case, then more open-ended approaches are desirable.

Interviewers confront a logistical challenge in documenting the interview. Many researchers like to record and transcribe interviews; however, recording might make some interviewees nervous and transcribing often takes two to four times the time of the interview. Because of this, other researchers prefer to simply take notes on an interview, but it is extremely important that such notes are formalized and typed up before the researcher begins to forget important details. Some researchers prefer a mixed strategy, taking notes and quickly typing up sensitive, non-recorded interviews, while recording and transcribing the remainder.

thoughts and preferences or misrepresent events. Particularly on sensitive subjects, such as our examples of corruption or ethnic conflict, interviewees might intentionally mislead researchers. On the one hand, interviewers can respond to this problem by disregarding information that they consider to be inaccurate. In fact, given the copious amount of information that is collected through qualitative techniques, researchers have to be selective in what data they present. On the other hand, however, how do qualitative researchers know what is inaccurate? What is to stop them from consciously or unconsciously disregarding information that does not support their theories and hypotheses? Of course, this challenge exists in all inferential work; however, qualitative researchers have to be particularly cognizant of the choices that they make.

Furthermore, just like large-n research, interview methodologies also confront sampling challenges. In some cases, when the population of research subjects is sufficiently small, qualitative researchers might be able to avoid sampling problems by interviewing the population of relevant actors. In other cases, however, the researcher will only be able to interview certain members of a larger population, and it might be difficult or impractical to obtain a random sample. The issue of non-response bias may also be an issue with small-n interviewing, particularly if the people who refuse to participate may be systematically different than those who agree to be interviewed. Qualitative researchers should give careful thought to who they select to interview, employ the same methodology across their cases of study (if there is more than one), and be thoughtful about any potential sampling errors.

Focus Groups

Focus groups represent a less commonly used method in political science research; however, in certain situations they can offer an efficient and useful research tool.[30] Focus groups are researcher-led discussions with a homogeneous group of research subjects. In terms of efficiency, they allow researchers to interact with more individuals in less time. They are particularly appropriate when the researcher is interested not just in individuals' attitudes but also groups, group dynamics, and group norms. Perhaps paradoxically, there are many times when focus groups are more effective in eliciting sensitive information than interviews. Provided a homogeneous group whose members can relate to one another, just one honest focus group participant can encourage other individuals to offer information that they would otherwise be hesitant to provide. For example, one of the authors, Sabet, in his study of police misconduct in Mexico, frequently conducted focus groups with police officers.[31] As long as the officers were of the same rank (i.e. homogeneous), they would often open up and discuss the challenges they confronted in far greater depth than in one-on-one interviews.

As with interviews, focus groups also confront sampling and measurement errors. Focus group participants might not be representative of a larger population and information provided might be inaccurate. Given that each participant does not typically answer every question asked, focus groups present an additional sampling concern: there might be biases in which participants answer which questions. More importantly, charismatic and dominant participants might influence the responses of others and cause a researcher to incorrectly infer that a consensus exists among the group. As a result, successful focus groups are best led by a well-trained and experienced focus group team or leader. Because of their limitations, focus groups are usually employed as one of a number of other qualitative and quantitative research tools. For example, survey firms often use focus groups in conducting preliminary research prior to developing a survey instrument.

Direct Observation

A researcher using direct observation techniques can either do so as a nonparticipant, literally an observer, or as an active participant. In this latter case, a researcher might study a social movement by participating in the movement over time. Ethical research principles require that observation be **overt**, whereby the

---

30 Nathaniel Copsey, "Focus groups and the political scientist," *European Research Working Paper Series* No. 22 (2008). European Research Institute. www.download.bham.ac.uk/govsoc/eri/working-papers/wp22-copsey.pdf.

31 Daniel Sabet, *Police reform in Mexico: Informal politics and the challenge of institutional change* (Stanford: Stanford Politics and Policy, 2012).

study participants are aware of the research being conducted. However, historically there are certainly cases of **covert** observational research, whereby the research subjects are unaware that they are being studied. This was the case in the above mentioned example of a researcher joining a municipal Mexican police force to study police corruption in Mexico. The strength of direct observation is that it offers researchers a means to immerse themselves in a case and inductively learn about their topic of study. Direct observation is therefore less useful in hypothesis testing and making causal inferences, and far more appropriate in making rich descriptive inferences, refining theories, and generating hypotheses.

There are downsides to the approach, however. Researchers might lose their objectivity and come to identify too much with their research subjects. Alternatively, observation might suffer from measurement and sampling bias. First, research subjects might respond to the presence of a researcher and either consciously or unconsciously alter their behavior. Second, despite the enormous amount of data generated through direct observation techniques, many important phenomena might still go unobserved. For example, a scholar studying police corruption who fails to observe bribery during a ride-along with police would certainly not be able to claim the police are corruption free. While perhaps less controversial, the same problem exists in studying members of Congress, social movements, or public meetings, where many important phenomena might occur away from the eye of the researcher.[32]

If you are studying political phenomena in other nations, then direct observation may be too costly or time consuming for an undergraduate research project. However, direct observation is a real possibility for students in a study abroad program or for research on domestic politics or public policy. Students might attend party conventions to learn more about the internal workings of political parties or attend city council meetings to examine how local policy is made. In fact, we have found that many of the best student papers have been based on observation-based research.

Document Analysis

Government documents, archives, media sources, correspondence, and a variety of other written documentation offer a wealth of information to scholars. The documents analyzed in a particular research project will vary dramatically from research question to research question. For example, in international relations, scholars of U.S. foreign policy have often relied on *Foreign Relations of the United States*, a collection of declassified State Department documentation released thirty years after their use. In addition, groups such as the National Security Archive at George Washington University have assembled massive

---

32 To some extent this problem can be ameliorated through a clear sampling methodology that establishes when observation will occur.

archives with both hard and electronic copies of important documents in U.S. foreign policy. While controversial, some students and researchers have even taken advantage of WikiLeaks documentation.

While students are generally good at using library resources to find secondary sources, they tend to be less certain about how to find primary sources. This is mainly because sources vary dramatically from research topic to research topic. University librarians can be very helpful in helping students and researchers identify resources specific to their topic. The amount of primary source documentation that can be found online is somewhat astounding, even when compared with the recent past. Government studies and reports are often a great place to start. In the United States, U.S. government data can be found on www.data.gov and government publications in the U.S. Government Printing Office's Federal Digital System at www.gpo.gov/fdsys. Even outside of the United States, close to one hundred countries have passed freedom of information laws and increasingly this information is available online.

The strengths and weaknesses of document analysis vary considerably based on the source, which might range from environmental impact statements, to party platforms, to transcripts of public meetings, to editorials in a sample of newspapers. If the researcher is able to analyze only a sample or subset of documents or if only a portion of what is being studied is documented, then the researcher will have to consider the potential for sampling error. This is certainly the case if particularly important documents are considered classified. There is also the possibility of measurement error in interpreting documents. For example, a study of party platforms in many countries might offer a better measure of the image that a party wants to portray than their actual position on important political issues.

In summary, all of these tools offer the advantage of greater depth. Nonetheless, they also confront risks. As the above discussion should make clear, qualitative data, just like quantitative, risk sampling and measurement errors. Unlike quantitative data, however, the amount of error in qualitative information is harder to measure and estimate. In fact some scholars, including King, Keohane, and Verba, criticize some qualitative researchers for failing to provide reasonable estimates of the degree of uncertainty in their data and their subsequent descriptive and causal inferences.[33] To be sure, there are limitations to the extent that they can make such estimates, but the critique is a valid one. Can qualitative scholarship be more thoughtful about the error in its data and the uncertainty in its conclusions? Many scholars think that it can be. As King, Keohane and Verba write, "All good research can be understood—indeed, is best understood—to derive from the same underlying logic of inference. Both quantitative and qualitative research can be systematic and scientific."[34]

33 King, Keohane, and Verba, *Designing social inquiry.*
34 King, Keohane, and Verba, *Designing social inquiry*, p. 5.

To offer a few concrete examples, Alexander George suggests that qualitative researchers should give preference to standardized, structured interviews, which will aid in comparability.[35] Yin advocates for creating databases of qualitative data similar to those used in qualitative analyses. He argues, "too often, the case study data are synonymous with the evidence presented in the case study report, and a critical reader has no recourse if he or she wants to inspect the database that led to the case study conclusions."[36] In one interesting case of qualitative research transparency, Innovations for Successful Societies, a research institute at Princeton University focused on governance issues, has gone so far as to make available hundreds of recorded interviews on their website. And we discuss another emerging archive for qualitative data in the conclusion. In short, while qualitative researchers maximize the benefits of in-depth research, they should be cognizant of the importance of a transparent, replicable, and systematic method of implementation.

DESIGNING SMALL-N RESEARCH STUDIES

In designing you own small-n research project, you should first be clear about the goal of the study. If the goal is to make strong causal inferences and test hypotheses, then you would best be served by a most similar systems research design that compares similar cases or the same cases over time. Ideally, you would look for natural experiments, where the differences between your cases are determined by some exogenous intervention, simulating the logic of random assignment in a laboratory or field experiment. Absent a natural experiment, you can mimic the logic of an experiment through case selection. By selecting cases that either vary on a key independent or dependent variable—but are similar or the same on other important explanatory variables—small-n research can lead to valid causal inferences. While the threat of omitted variable bias cannot be entirely eliminated, careful case selection allows researchers to minimize this threat.

There is a debate on the criteria one should use to select such cases. Traditionally, many scholars have relied on geography as a principal mechanism of control, hence the development of area studies that focus on Latin America, or South Asia, or Western Europe. This often makes a good deal of sense. To be sure, countries such as Chile and Argentina, with similar language, colonial tradition, level of economic development, culture, religion, and a history of both military dictatorship and democratic traditions, have a great deal in common. In fact, there are many research questions for which these factors

35 Alexander L. George, "Case studies and theory development: The method of structured, focused comparison," in P.G. Lauren, ed., *Diplomacy: New approaches in history, theory, and policy* (New York: Free Press, 1979), pp. 43–68.
36 Robert Yin, *Case study research* (Beverly Hills, CA: Sage, 1994), p. 95.

would be important to control for. Nonetheless, many scholars have argued that two countries should not be treated as comparable just because they are proximate to one another.[37] For example, despite similarities in many of the variables stated above, a comparison of Venezuela and Colombia during the 2000s would be inappropriate to address many political research questions given the radically different nature of their governments. During this time period, the rightwing Alvaro Uribe headed the Colombian government and the leftwing Hugo Chávez governed Venezuela. The key intuition is that scholars should look for cases that are comparable across variables that offer alternative explanations of the dependent variable. For example, given the important role that valuable commodities (e.g. diamonds, oil) have played in funding civil wars in Africa, a comparative case study of the effect of ethnic fragmentation should ensure that selected cases are comparable in terms of their resource endowments rather than in terms of their geography.

By contrast, if the goal of our small-n study is to make strong descriptive inferences about a given case, to elucidate causal mechanisms in a representative case, to sharpen our theory through an explanation of deviant cases, or to develop theory and generate hypotheses, then we do not necessarily need a natural experiment or a most similar systems research design. Nonetheless, we still have to be careful in case selection. Unfortunately, many students and scholars are tempted to pick cases based on their personal interests rather than on strong theoretical or methodological grounds.

So how should these cases be selected? Seawright and Gerring point out that *quantitative* methods can be helpful in systematically selecting cases for *qualitative* study.[38] Causal mechanisms, for example, are best explored in representative or typical cases, which, as suggested above, can be identified through large-n regression analyses. For example, if I was interested in exploring the causal mechanisms linking freedom of the press to corruption, then I could run a regression between quantitative measures of press freedom and corruption, as shown in Figure 7.1. Countries that score closest to the global trend at low, medium, and high levels of press freedom could be considered representative cases. In like fashion, such a method could be useful in identifying deviant cases for further study. As the figure illustrates, many Middle Eastern countries, such as the Qatar (represented as QAT in the figure), have far less corruption than the general trend would predict based on their low levels of press freedom. Why is this? Is it because of their Islamic religion, Arab culture, resource endowments, or some other factor? A qualitative exploration of these cases would be useful to help answer this question.

Once the cases have been selected, the researcher then has the task of fine tuning the research design and determining data collection techniques. The tools of

37 Przeworski and Teune, *The logic of comparative social inquiry.*

38 Jason Seawright and John Gerring, "Case selection techniques in case study research," *Political Research Quarterly* 61 (2008): 294–308.

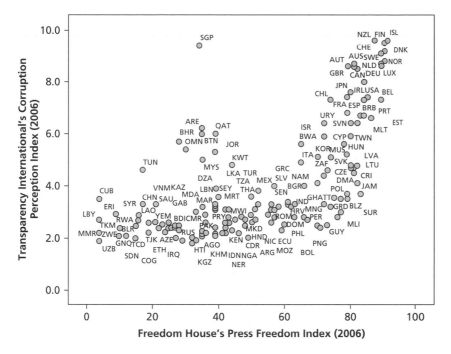

FIGURE 7.1 Scatterplot to Aid in Case Selection

qualitative research methods, including interviews, focus groups, direct observation, and document analysis, offer powerful means to delve into the details of a case or cases. Nonetheless, as discussed above, a case study or a comparison of a few cases can still benefit from quantitative methods in making descriptive inferences about the case or cases and for observing within-case causal mechanisms.

Regardless of whether the researcher relies on qualitative or quantitative measures, she has an important obligation to be thoughtful about and seek to minimize sampling and measurement error. This can be done by developing a clear methodology that is replicable across research cases and can be transparently included as part of the research results. Sampling errors can be reduced by thoughtfully considering how to best sample interview or focus group participants and considering any potential biases in the final pool of research subjects. Measurement error can be reduced—to the extent possible—by standardizing well-developed questions, systematically transcribing and recording research activities, and deriving conclusions from the totality of the data rather than the most salient interviews.

Presenting Results

Data presentation is admittedly more difficult in the case of the qualitative research methods frequently employed in small-n studies. Qualitative researchers are unable to boil their data down to summary measures such as proportions, means, or regression coefficients like their peers using quantitative methods. Instead, the most powerful data presentation tool in the qualitative researcher's toolkit is the narrative. Through a brief but compelling narrative, the small-n researcher can, for example, clearly illustrate a causal mechanism underlying the theory being tested. Arteaga Botello and López Rivera in their research into Mexican police corruption are able to offer vivid narratives illustrating how norms of corruption perpetuate themselves. They tell the story of one officer, Eduardo, who was assigned the worst possible shifts until he was told by a fellow officer, "You're here for one simple reason, which is because you have not paid off the commander. José must have told you that, shift after shift, you must pay off the commander."[39] Just as a quantitative researcher must choose from among different indicators and different statistics in the presentation of her data, so too must the qualitative researcher carefully select her narrative. Just as the quantitative researcher should not selectively choose data that supports her hypothesis, qualitative researchers should not selectively choose narratives that support theirs. While it is tempting to present a story that is dramatic and will engross the reader, the qualitative researcher must resist this urge if such a story is not representative of the findings of the research.

Illustrated simplified models of human interaction offer another tool to help present research findings. In his comparisons of ethnic conflict in Africa, Robert Bates argues that three factors help explain a political leader's decision to exploit his people: the level of public revenues, the reward from predation, and the political leader's rate of discount (the extent to which the leader prefers short-term rewards).[40] He uses the simple figure reproduced in Figure 7.2 to sum up his argument. Political leaders can either benefit from a small amount of public revenues, which over time constitute a reasonable profit, or they can engage in predation, and earn a large amount in a short time at the risk of major losses in the future. The key variable is how much the political leader "discounts" the future (the discount rate). If the leader's time horizon is short-term, then predation makes the most sense. Using simple graphics or flow charts to illustrate causal mechanisms offers qualitative scholars an important means by which to present their argument and their results.

Of course, because small-n research can still use quantitative methods at disaggregated levels of analysis (e.g. surveys of individuals in a case country or city), quantitative data presentation is still an option for small-n researchers to make descriptive inferences. In the above mentioned example, Posner uses a series of bar charts to very starkly illustrate the differences among Chewa and Tumbuka survey respondents in Malawi and Zambia.[41] For example,

---

39 Arteaga Botello and López Rivera, *Policía y corrupción*, p. 68.
40 Robert H. Bates, *When things fell apart* (Cambridge, UK: Cambridge University Press, 2008).
41 Posner, "The political salience of cultural difference."

Figure 7.3 aggregates survey data to compare responses in the two countries and show that Chewas and Tumbukas are far less likely to consider marrying or voting for a presidential candidate from the other ethnic group in Malawi than in Zambia.

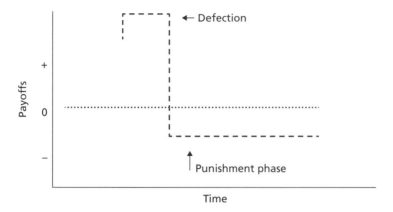

FIGURE 7.2 Example of Visual Presentation of a Qualitative Argument

Source: Robert H. Bates, "The logic of state failure: Learning from late century Africa," *Conflict Management and Peace Science* 25 (2008): 297–314.

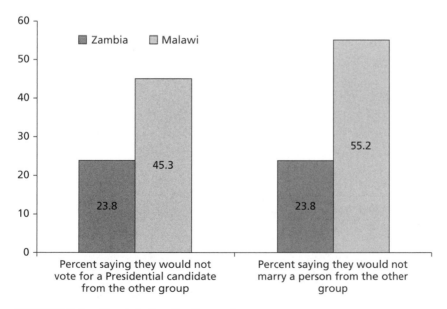

FIGURE 7.3 Bar Charts in Small-n Research

Source: Daniel N. Posner, "The political salience of cultural difference: Why Chewas and Tumbukas are allies in Zambia and adversaries in Malawi," *American Political Science Review* 98 (2004): 529–545.

CONCLUSION

In summary, small-n observational studies have both strengths and weaknesses *vis-à-vis* experiments and large-n studies. Even in the case of a most similar systems research design, small-n studies lack the internal validity of experiments and the ability to statistically control for rival factors as in large-n studies. Given these constraints, they risk the problem of too many variables and too few cases, and subsequent omitted variable bias. Nonetheless, small-n studies are better able to study macro-level phenomena than experiments and are arguably better able to cope with complexity and real-world politics than either experiments or large-n studies. As a result, even when small-n studies cannot draw robust causal inferences, they still offer a necessary complement to experimental and large-n work, providing narratives, exploring causal mechanisms, explaining deviant cases, improving theory, and generating hypotheses.

KEY TERMS

analytical narratives   189

covert observation   197

cross-sectional comparison   184

deviant cases   189

dynamic comparison   184

inductive observation   190

longitudinal comparison   184

spatial comparison   184

typical case   188

Conclusion

In the Introduction to this book, we began by discussing the difference between the production of information and the advancement of knowledge. "Advancing knowledge" may seem an intimidating project, and perhaps one beyond the reach of undergraduate or new graduate students. Yet, by calling attention to the challenge of inference and by providing guidelines for best practices when facing that challenge, we hope we have made the possibility of making an intellectual contribution more accessible.

Naturally, it is important to keep in mind that most political science scholarship "moves the ball forward" *incrementally*; in other words, grand theories or substantial revisions to findings in the literature are far less common than, for example, re-visioning a way to approach a long debated puzzle with a new formulation of a question or a clever method, or ferreting out under-tilled yet significant areas of inquiry in which you can take advantage of "low-hanging fruit." Areas ripe for more analysis can consist of basic questions that have wider import but have not been studied extensively or studies that come to dramatically different conclusions on a particular question. But researchers can often make an important contribution simply by working to replicate the results from another study or examining whether a particular theory applies to other cases.

Whatever question you decide to ask, this book has provided guidance about how to choose an appropriate research question, how to engage with the existing research that is relevant to that question, how to elucidate a theory that can provide potential answers to that question, and, ultimately, how to select an appropriate approach to make inferences that will allow you to provide an answer to that question. But this is only part of the research process. In the discussion that follows, we provide some guidance for the "next steps" you will want to take as you embark on conducting your own study. We then conclude with a final note of advice about your responsibility as a political scientist.

DEVELOPING SKILLS IN THE APPROACH YOU CHOOSE

In this book, we have focused on outlining different types of broad approaches that students and scholars may use to make causal or descriptive inferences. You should come away from this text with the ability to consider the relative advantages and disadvantages of utilizing experiments, large-n observational analysis, or small-n observational analysis to answer any given research question. While this text has provided the basic intuition behind these different types of approaches, it does not provide the reader with the skills to implement different methods within those approaches. For example, we explain the logic behind regression analysis in Chapter 6, but we do not provide sufficient detail to allow you to use that tool effectively. We introduce you to various qualitative methodologies in Chapter 7, but we do not provide you with the skillset needed to do elite interviewing or document analysis.

No political scientist is an expert on every method; in fact, most political scientists know only a few methods very well. This book provides general information that every scholar needs to know to decide which approach is most appropriate and feasible for the study you wish to conduct. However, once you have chosen a particular approach, you will need to seek training in that particular method before you engage in your research. Your professors can be particularly helpful in this regard. Free online training guides and courses are abundant for both quantitative and qualitative methods, and a library of books exists to provide students with guidance about particular techniques. Additionally, many campuses offer training sessions for students to learn how to work with statistical or qualitative analysis software or even for training students on the methods themselves.

CONSIDERING A MULTI-METHOD (OR MIXED-METHOD) APPROACH

If the goal is inference, then the researcher should be prepared to employ the most appropriate tool in the researcher's tool kit. However, it is also worth noting that in many instances it may be worthwhile to use multiple methods in answering a particular research question. Indeed, the choice of approaches need not be mutually exclusive, and much of the best scholarship employs a **mixed-methods** approach. We have described in this book how the weaknesses of one approach are often the strengths of another. What lab or survey experiments sometimes lack in external validity can be complemented with the strong external validity of large-n observational analyses. And where quantitative analyses may lack detail, qualitative studies can often help to elucidate the causal mechanisms at play.

Frequently, there are ways to easily expand your study to incorporate a multi-method approach. For example, while case studies are commonly associated with qualitative methods, there is no reason why they cannot employ quantitative methods—particularly for descriptive inference. Because many case studies occur at the macro-level, these cases can often be disaggregated and explored at lower levels of analysis, what some scholars refer to as **within-case analysis**. For example, in the study of comparative politics, a "case" is often a country; however, a country can be divided into regions, into time periods in its history, and into the individuals within it. By moving down to these lower levels of analysis the researcher can often turn one observation into many observations. Robert Putnam's famous *Making Democracy Work: Civic Traditions in Modern Italy* is at first blush a study of Southern and Northern Italy: a comparison of two cases.[1] However, Putnam disaggregates these cases and studies the twenty administrative regions of Italy separately, increasing the number of observations. Furthermore, his research uses large-n survey data to help support its conclusions.

Seawright and Gerring find other complementarities between small- and large-n research.[2] They contend that qualitative small-n researchers should use quantitative methods to aid in case selection. For example, if a small-n researcher wanted a typical case study to explore the causal mechanisms behind a well-tested empirical relationship, she could use quantitative regression analysis and select cases that fit the model well. In a similar vein, if the scholar is interested in deviant cases, then she could look for cases that do not fit the model well. The authors even argue that statistical matching techniques can be used to select cases for a most similar systems research design. Rather than use proxies such as geography for the basis of case selection, Seawright and Gerring contend that countries should be matched based on relevant quantifiable variables.

It is also the case that in-depth qualitative research can provide a much needed complement to large-n studies. The Case Study Project on Civil Wars is a perfect example of such an approach, as it sought to round out the quantitative findings of Collier and Hoeffler.[3] Hodson contended that exploring cases as a complement to his large-n work allowed him to put "some flesh on

1 Robert D. Putnam, *Making democracy work: Civic traditions in modern Italy* (Princeton: Princeton University Press, 1993).

2 Jason Seawright and John Gerring, "Case selection techniques in case study research," *Political Research Quarterly* 61 (2008): 294–308.

3 Paul Collier and Anke Hoeffler, "On the incidence of civil war in Africa," *Journal of Conflict Resolution* 46 (2002): 13–28.

the bones of regression coefficients," an expression that vividly illustrates how qualitative and quantitative data can complement one another.[4]

Political scientists are also increasingly turning to experiments as a complement to both small- and large-n observational studies. It should be easy to see why experiments provide a good complement to observational research. A researcher may discover a relationship between two variables in a large-n observational data set and suspect that one variable causes the other. For example, perhaps the dataset shows that African American candidates for Congress do not receive as many votes as white candidates who run for Congress and the researcher suspects that this happens because some individuals refuse to support African American candidates out of prejudice. While the observational data provide support for the researcher's claim, there are other reasons why this result might occur. For example, African American candidates may run in different types of districts or they may take different issue positions than white candidates. Thus, a researcher might look to design an experiment that provides a way to test the suspected causal relationship. In this example, a simple experimental design would be to describe a fictional candidate for Congress and have subjects indicate whether they would be likely to support that candidate. The randomized treatment would be that half of the subjects would be shown a picture of a white candidate while the other half would be shown a picture of an African American candidate. If support for the African American candidate is lower than for the white candidate, then the difference can be clearly attributed to the race of the candidate (since the candidates would have been described identically in every other way). The researcher's paper could then present both the observational data and the experimental results to provide both clear evidence for causation (from the experiment) and external validity (from the large-n observational analysis). Such a paper would be able to make stronger inferences than one that included results from only one of the two methods.

Some research programs expand to incorporate all three different types of approaches. The work of Elinor Ostrom and her colleagues on commons governance is an exemplar in this regard. While Ostrom's 1990 book *Governing the Commons* only addressed a relatively small number of cases, Ostrom and her colleagues created an enormous database drawn from literally thousands of case studies on common-pool resource governance. After systematically screening these cases and selecting a subset for analysis, Ostrom and her team coded the case studies on a variety of variables of interest. For example, they created variables to measure and signify the structure of the resource system, the attributes and behaviors of the resource appropriators, the rules used by the appropriators, and the outcomes on the resources. It was then possible to treat these cases not as a small-n qualitative study but as a large-n quantitative

---

4 Randy Hodson, "Coding ethnographies for research and training: Merging qualitative and quantitative sociologies," *Sociological Perspectives* 54 (2011): 125–132, p. 125.

study.[5] Furthermore, as discussed in the previous chapter, these scholars took hypotheses developed in the field and tested them extensively in laboratory experiments. Thus, this research program ultimately expanded to include each of the three main approaches we have described—small-n observational analysis, large-n observational analysis, and experimental analysis—and the research became highly influential because of the strong inferences that could be drawn from the multi-methods approach.

Thus, multi-methods research can often help to strengthen the inferences we draw, but it is worth noting that adding a multi-method component to one's project is only as useful as the care with which the methods are employed. In many cases, the effort of expanding a project with a multi-method design may not be worth the payoff, particularly if the question is not well-suited to other approaches or alternative approaches are not feasible for practical reason (such as the lack of available data). Indeed, it is worth noting that the overwhelming majority of political science scholarship is based on single-method studies.

YOU'VE COMPLETED YOUR STUDY, SO NOW WHAT?

Once you have posed a question, developed your hypotheses, crafted and executed your research design, and written your paper detailing all of these steps and your results, you might wonder what comes next. Far too often, that is where the project ends. The student submits the paper for a class grade or to satisfy a thesis requirement and then moves on to other things. Yet, when your professors finish their research papers, it is often just the first step in the process of adding to the body of knowledge on a particular subject. What comes next can often take months or years. And whether you take these next steps will almost certainly make the difference between simply satisfying a course requirement and truly adding to the cumulative body of knowledge that exists on a particular subject matter.

Step 1: Seeking Input from Others

It is not always easy for people to share their work with others, but the scientific enterprise depends on sharing. Indeed, each of the "final steps" we discuss in this section involve some form of sharing. When we first share our work, we do so in order to improve what will ultimately be the final product. Indeed, even the most accomplished social and political scientists do not write a paper and immediately send it off to be published. Rather, all scholars first seek

---

5 Shui Yan Tang, *Institutions and collective action: Self-governance in irrigation* (Richmond: Institute for Contemporary Studies Press, 1992).

feedback on their papers once they have completed a preliminary "final" draft. They do this for many reasons.

First, peers and colleagues often will find ways to improve your research. For example, a peer who reads your work may have an idea about how you could construct your research design differently to better test your hypotheses (or to test them in different ways). In many cases, it will be possible to incorporate these suggestions in a revised version of the same paper. For example, a colleague might suggest another data set that could be used to conduct additional tests of your theory. It might then be possible for you to acquire that data set and add it to the analysis in your paper. If you have conducted a qualitative study, a colleague reading your paper may be able to direct you toward additional documents you could analyze for that analysis.

In some cases, however, it may not be feasible to incorporate your colleague's suggested changes to your research design. For example, your colleague might suggest a different type of condition or treatment you could have used in your experimental design. However, if you have already conducted the experiment, there is little you can do to address this suggestion without fielding an entirely new experiment. Likewise, your colleague may suggest that you include a new variable in your regression model, but if you cannot find a data set that includes that variable, then it will simply not be possible to make this change.

Even if it is too late in the process to alter your research design to address the suggestions from your colleagues, it can still be useful to address these critiques in your paper. As we have often noted in this book, every research design has its limitations, and, rather than ignore these limitations, the best research studies often make note of them. Indeed, many published research studies will raise, often in the conclusion, potential limitations of the research design employed and then attempt to address these limitations. Take, for example, the conclusion from Shanto Iyengar's book *Is Anyone Responsible?*[6] The book draws entirely on experiments, like those described in Chapter 5, to examine the effect of framing on how citizens understand news events. In the conclusion of his book, Iyengar raises several ways in which his experimental approach might limit his conclusions:

> some comments concerning the distinctiveness of experimental evidence are in order. First, each study was carried out within a span of two hours. Therefore, no conclusion can be drawn concerning either the effect of repeated exposure to particular news frames or the rate at which framing effects decay. . . . Second, the experimental manipulations involved only

---

6 Shanto Iyengar, *Is anyone responsible? How television frames political issues* (Chicago: University of Chicago Press, 1994).

television news. The nature of the print media makes it likely that thematic framing will occur more frequently in newspaper and magazine articles than in television news stories.[7]

Iyengar clearly lays out two ways in which his experimental design is limited in terms of how it answers his research question. Why would Iyengar wish to draw attention to the limitations of his own study? One reason to do this is that these limitations are often obvious to many readers, and failing to address them honestly may cause those readers to become more suspicious of other parts of the study. Recall that one of the tenets of social science research is that the method is described as clearly and as openly as possible. This openness includes not just explaining the method the researcher used, but also the limitations of that method.

A second reason Iyenar raises these possible critiques is to give himself the opportunity to tell the reader why his study is still valuable despite the limitations in his design. Indeed, Iyengar followed the passage cited above with such a defense:

> The short time period spanned by the experiments and the absence of exposure to alternative news sources might suggest either that the evidence of media effects is exaggerated or understated. While it might be argued that the effects are exaggerated because of the immediacy of exposure, it is also true that a single two-minute story is a small stimulus in the context of a lifetime of political socialization. Seen in this light, it is perhaps remarkable that *any* framing effects were detected.[8]

Iyengar does not know precisely how his findings would differ if he measured for framing effects over a longer period of time or with a variety of different types of media sources. However, he makes a compelling argument that there is some reason to expect that the effects would be even larger if such an alternative design were pursued. While settling this question is left to future work that other researchers could chose to pursue, social scientists will appreciate that Iyengar was honest about the possible limits of his study and made a case for why his findings are still useful despite these concerns.

A second reason to seek feedback from peers and colleagues is that they often have suggestions for new ways of framing the contribution of your work. Indeed, it is frequently the case that the research we conduct can be valuable for informing knowledge in areas far beyond what we initially intended. Sometimes the connection is relatively straightforward. A study on campaign advertising in the United States may actually be able to speak to scholars who

7 Iyengar, *Is anyone responsible?* p. 129.
8 Iyengar, *Is anyone responsible?* p. 129.

study campaigns in other countries. But in other cases the connection might be less expected. For example, a significant body of economics research has focused on the most efficient institutional structures for ensuring that employees can be held accountable by their employers.[9] Political scientists have found this research useful for thinking about how elected officials can be held accountable by citizens.

So what is the best way to share your work? Start by showing it to some of your friends and professors. Ask for their feedback and, when you receive it, take it seriously. This does not mean that you have to incorporate every suggestion you receive, but you should give each suggestion serious thought and consider whether it is something you want to address in the paper. Some comments may necessitate only a footnote to address. Others may require a complete re-analysis of your data. But most comments you receive will be valuable because they will preview the concerns that other readers will have when they read your paper in the future. And the best papers are those that proactively address concerns that readers might have raised rather than remaining silent about those concerns.

Once you have had an opportunity to collect feedback from your peers and colleagues, the next step is to share your paper in a more formal setting. Political science conferences are the venue at which most academics choose to present new research that has not yet moved to the publication stage. The largest political science conference is hosted by the American Political Science Association (APSA) every year on Labor Day weekend; it attracts thousands of scholars from around the world. While undergraduate students sometimes present their work at the APSA conference, a more suitable venue for your work is likely to be hosted by a regional political science association. These regional conferences are often much more accessible for students aiming to present papers, and many of these conferences set aside space on the program specifically for undergraduate research papers. For example, the 2013 Midwest Political Science Association (MPSA) devoted an entire section on its program to papers written by undergraduate students. The MPSA even gives an award each year to the best paper written by an undergraduate student.

If attending a regional or national political science conference is not within your reach, there may be other venues to consider instead. For example, many states have political science associations that hold annual or bi-annual meetings and these meetings would provide another venue where you could present your research. Many universities also host conferences dedicated to undergraduate research, which would provide an even more proximate venue for you to present your work. Seek out advice from your professors and advisers who will typically know about many of these options and can suggest the best one for you.

9 Gary J. Miller, *Managerial dilemmas: The political economy of hierarchy* (Cambridge, UK: Cambridge University Press, 1993).

Box 8.1: A Listing of Regional and State Political Science Organizations that Hold Conferences

Regional Associations

Midwest Political Science Association
National Conference of Black Political Scientists
New England Political Science Association
Northeastern Political Science Association
Pacific Northwest Political Science Association
Southern Political Science Association
Southwestern Political Science Association
Western Political Science Association

State Associations

Alabama Political Science Association
Arkansas Political Science Association
Florida Political Science Association
Georgia Political Science Association
Illinois Political Science Association
Indiana Political Science Association
Kentucky Political Science Association
Louisiana Political Science Association
Michigan Conference of Political Scientists
Minnesota Political Science Association
Mississippi Political Science Association
New York State Political Science Association
North Carolina Political Science Association
Ohio Association of Economists and Political Scientists
Oklahoma Political Science Association
Pennsylvania Political Science Association
South Carolina Political Science Association
Tennessee Political Science Association
West Virginia Political Science Association
Wisconsin Political Science Association

Note: This list comes from APSA. We only included associations when we could discern that they had held (or planned to hold) a conference in 2012 or 2013.

Step 2: Publishing Your Research

Once scholars have written a paper, presented the research at a conference (or at multiple conferences), and incorporated feedback from peers who have read the work, the next step is typically to seek publication for the research. This is obviously an important step for any research project for a number of reasons. First, most professors work at academic institutions where they are expected to publish a certain amount of research if they are to be retained, tenured, and ultimately promoted. However, even if one's career does not rely on publishing research, it is still important to publish your work in some way so that your study will add to the body of knowledge on a particular topic. Only by making your research available to other social scientists will it add to the discipline's body of knowledge.

Traditionally, scholars have presented their work either in books or in academic journals. Academic journals provide the most common outlet for paper-length research studies. Most academic journals operate on what is called the peer-review system. When a scholar submits a paper to a journal, the editor begins by looking briefly over the submission to determine whether (1) the research is a good fit for the research focus of the journal and (2) whether the paper seems to be of sufficient quality to merit a full review. If the paper satisfies both of these conditions then the editor will select several other scholars in the discipline to whom she will send the paper. At most political science journals, the review is double-blind; this means that the reviewers will not know who wrote the paper and the author will not know the names of those scholars who provided the reviews. The impetus behind the double-blind peer-review system is to avoid a system where certain "famous" political scientists are favored over others. The double-blind system is thought to maximize fairness because reviewers are left to evaluate the work itself, not the individual who produced it.[10]

After what is typically several months, the reviewers will return their assessments to the editor. These reviews will typically recommend one of three possible outcomes for the paper—accept, reject, or revise and resubmit. The editor will then choose from among these outcomes based on the reviews and his own reading of the work. It is very rare for a paper to be accepted for publication on its first submission to a journal. From 2006 to 2010, only 0.8% of papers submitted to the *American Political Science Review* (APSR) were accepted for publication after the initial round of reviews.[11] Indeed, the most common outcome is that a paper is rejected for publication.

---

10 In a single-blind peer-review process, the reviewers know the identity of the author of the paper, but the paper's author does not know the identities of the reviewers. This system is rare in political science but more common in other social science disciplines like economics.

11 Ronald Rogowski, "Report of the editors of the *American Political Science Review*, 2009–2010," *PS: Political Science & Politics* 44 (2011): 447–449.

The third possibility for a paper is the "revise and resubmit" decision. For papers that are eventually accepted for publication at a journal, the first decision they typically receive is a revise and resubmit. The revise and resubmit decision is given when reviewers and the editor(s) generally like a paper, but would like to see the authors make some changes. Essentially, the reviewers and editor are asking the authors to make revisions to the paper and then resubmit the paper to the journal for a second round of reviews. The changes required to satisfy a revise and resubmit typically vary in magnitude; in some cases, the authors may only need to expand their discussion of some of the literature on the topic, or tweak the conclusion section of their paper. In other cases, authors may need to make significant changes to the analysis of their data, or even bring new data to bear on the question. These more significant revisions are generally requested when reviewers have concerns about whether the findings reported in the paper are robust. In other words, reviewers may worry that by analyzing the data in a different way or by analyzing an entirely different data set the authors would not reach the same conclusion.

Once an author has finished making revisions, she will resubmit the paper to the journal and the editor will often send the paper back out to at least some of those scholars who reviewed the initial submission. These reviewers will now be evaluating whether the changes the author made satisfy their concerns about the piece. Just as with an original submission, a paper that is resubmitted to a journal may be accepted, rejected, or offered a second opportunity to revise and resubmit. Typically, if the author has faithfully addressed the reviewers' concerns, the paper is accepted for publication. In fact, the APSR reports that over 85 percent of papers that are initially granted a revise and resubmit are eventually accepted for publication.

By now, you should be getting the sense that it is challenging to get your research published in a political science journal. Indeed, the peer-review process is designed to play a gate-keeping role—only research that scholars believe was well designed to yield strong inferences can typically make it into print. For the top journals, a remarkably small percentage of research is ever accepted for publication. For example, the APSR, the discipline's top journal, reports an acceptance rate of less than 10 percent—which means that fewer than 1 of every 10 papers submitted to the journal is eventually published in that journal. That acceptance rate may not seem particularly low for the discipline's top journal, but consider that most scholars do not even consider submitting to the APSR unless they think that the paper is particularly strong. Thus, the APSR publishes less than 10 percent of what are already an unusually strong pool of papers.

Many of the other top journals in the discipline also have acceptance rates between 10 percent and 15 percent. Journals like the *American Journal of Political Science*, the *Journal of Politics*, and the *British Journal of Political Science* are very competitive publication venues. Fortunately, however, the discipline has a deep pool of journals and most strong papers eventually find a home in one of those. Many of these journals are specific to a particular area of research. For example, there are journals specifically for papers focusing on public opinion (*Public Opinion Quarterly*), political parties (*Party Politics*), women and politics (*Politics & Gender*), legislative politics (*Legislative Studies Quarterly*), state politics (*State Politics and Policy Quarterly*), religion and politics (*Politics and Religion*), international affairs (e.g. *International Organization*, *International Studies Quarterly*, etc.), comparative politics in general (e.g. *World Politics*, *Comparative Political Studies*, etc.), and even for studies focusing on specific regions of the world (e.g. *China Quarterly*, *Post Soviet Affairs*, *Journal of Latin American Studies*, etc.).

Academic journals are a useful venue for publishing research because the peer-review process they follow helps to ensure a certain level of quality for what appears in those journals. The tradeoff, however, is that the peer-review process can take quite a while to play out. Consider that it typically takes three to six months to receive a first decision from a journal. Assume that, as is typical for most papers, your paper is rejected at the first journal you send it to. Even though the paper was rejected, you will probably want to address the critiques from the reviews you received before sending the paper to another journal. Even if you work quickly, that might still take another month or two. It has already been eight months since you first submitted your paper. Now assume that you send your paper to a second journal and, six months later, receive an invitation to revise and resubmit your paper. Even if you work relatively quickly, it will probably take you two more months to make the revisions and resubmit the paper. You will then likely wait another three to six months before hearing back on the second round of reviews. Thus, even if you are lucky and your paper is accepted by the second journal, it has now been at least a year and a half since you submitted your paper to the first journal. And once it is accepted, you still must wait for the paper to go through the publication process, which can often take another six to twelve months.

What the peer-review journal process has to offer in terms of quality control it lacks in terms of expediency. Once you are ready to send a paper off to a journal, it is typically reasonable to expect that you will not see that paper in print for at least two more years. In the modern high-speed world, this often seems like far too long a wait for many authors. Thus, the modern academic environment is one in which papers are typically "published" informally on-line before they are truly published in academic journals. While professional academics often post their pre-publication papers on their own websites, there are many other public venues where anyone can post their research. One such site that attracts heavy traffic is the Social Science Research Network (SSRN, www.ssrn.com). Individuals can create an account with SSRN and then post their papers to the site. Once papers are posted there, they will be accessible through a variety of search engines and authors will be able to easily monitor when their paper has been viewed, downloaded, and cited by other scholars. Other sites such as Academia.edu and ResearchGate provide similar venues for posting papers and monitoring how much interest your work is attracting from others.

Even if you never intend on submitting your paper to an academic journal (and it is a simple fact that few undergraduates do submit their papers to journals), there is significant value in "publishing" your work through one of these on-line venues. As we noted before, the process of building knowledge is an important one and every piece of research that adds to what we know can be useful for other scholars. Your study can help scholars as they embark on their own research by allowing them to learn what has been done to answer a particular question and what they can do to improve on previous work. To the extent that your work helps others as they conduct your own research, it should also be given due credit, and by posting your work in one of these archives it becomes easier for scholars to cite your research and direct other scholars to it as well.

Step 3: Archiving Your Data

Once you have published your work in an academic journal or on a website like SSRN, it is your responsibility to publish the data you used or collected in order to conduct your research. One of the key tenets of science is that the findings from any study should be replicable, and the methods and data used to produce those findings should be public. Put simply, if you publish a particular finding, you should provide other scholars with the data and methods they would need to reproduce that finding. The reason we do this is two-fold. First, providing access to our data and methods ensures the integrity of the research process. While extremely rare, there have been cases where scholars have fabricated their data to obtain a desired result. One of the most famous recent instances of this phenomenon involved a Dutch psychologist who was found to have fraudulently manufactured the data behind more than fifty of his published research studies in order to demonstrate support for his theories.[12] And while the intentional manufacturing of data is relatively rare, far more common are inadvertent mistakes that produce incorrect results.[13]

12 Ewen Callaway, "Report finds massive fraud at Dutch universities," *Nature* 479, November 3, 2011.
13 William G. Dewald, Jerry G. Thursby, and Richard G. Anderson, "Replication in empirical economics: The journal of money, credit and banking project," *American Economic Review* 76 (1986): 587–603.

Box 8.2: "Meet the 28-Year-Old Grad Student Who Just Shook the Global Austerity Movement"

By Kevin Roose, Nymag.com (http://nymag.com/daily/intelligencer/2013/04/grad-student-who-shook-global-austerity-movement.html)

Most Ph.D. students spend their days reading esoteric books and stressing out about the tenure-track job market. Thomas Herndon, a 28-year-old economics grad student at UMass Amherst, just used part of his spring semester to shake the intellectual foundation of the global austerity movement.

Herndon became instantly famous in nerdy economics circles this week as the lead author of a recent paper, "Does High Public Debt Consistently Stifle Economic Growth? A Critique of Reinhart and Rogoff," that took aim at a massively influential study by two Harvard professors named Carmen Reinhart and Kenneth Rogoff. Herndon found some hidden errors in Reinhart and Rogoff's data set, then calmly took the entire study out back and slaughtered it. Herndon's takedown—which first appeared in a Mike Konczal post that crashed its host site with traffic—was an immediate sensation. It was cited by prominent anti-austerians like Paul Krugman, spoken about by incoming Bank of England governor Mark Carney, and mentioned on CNBC and several other news outlets as proof that the pro-austerity movement is based, at least in part, on bogus math.

[. . .]

Herndon, who did his undergraduate study at Evergreen State College, first started looking into Reinhart and Rogoff's work as part of an assignment for an econometrics course that involved replicating the data work behind a well-known study. Herndon chose Reinhart and Rogoff's 2010 paper, "Growth in a Time of Debt," in part, because it has been one of the most politically influential economic papers of the last decade. It claims, among other things, that countries whose debt exceeds 90 percent of their annual GDP experience slower growth than countries with lower debt loads—a figure that has been cited by people like Paul Ryan and Tim Geithner to justify slashing government spending and implementing other austerity measures on struggling economies.

Before he turned in his report, Herndon repeatedly e-mailed Reinhart and Rogoff to get their data set, so he could compare it to his own work. But because he was a lowly graduate student asking favors of some of the most respected economists in the world, he got no reply, until one afternoon, when he was sitting on his girlfriend's couch.

"I checked my e-mail, and saw that I had received a reply from Carmen Reinhart," he says. "She said she didn't have time to look into my query, but that here was the data, and I should feel free to publish whatever results I found."

Herndon pulled up an Excel spreadsheet containing Reinhart's data and quickly spotted something that looked odd.

"I clicked on cell L51, and saw that they had only averaged rows 30 through 44, instead of rows 30 through 49."

What Herndon had discovered was that by making a sloppy computing error, Reinhart and Rogoff had forgotten to include a critical piece of data about countries with high debt-to-GDP ratios that would have affected their overall calculations. They had also excluded data from Canada, New Zealand, and Australia—all countries that experienced solid growth during periods of high debt and would thus undercut their thesis that high debt forestalls growth.

Herndon was stunned. As a graduate student, he'd just found serious problems in a famous economic study—the academic equivalent of a D-league basketball player dunking on LeBron James. "They say seeing is believing, but I almost didn't believe my eyes," he says. "I had to ask my girlfriend—who's a Ph.D. student in sociology—to double-check it. And she said, " 'I don't think you're seeing things, Thomas.' "

[. . .]

When Herndon and his professors published their study, the reaction was nearly immediate. After Konczal's blog post went viral, Reinhart and Rogoff—who got a fawning New York *Times* profile when their book was released—were forced to admit their embarrassing error (although they still defended the basic findings of their survey).

[. . .]

Now that he's left his mark, Herndon says he's coping with the effects of academic celebrity—getting a new publicity head shot taken, receiving kudos from his professors and colleagues, handling interview requests. He says he's gotten extensions on some of his papers in order to handle his quasi-fame, but that he hasn't been popping Champagne yet in celebration. "I'm going to celebrate this weekend," he says. "But for now, I have a really gnarly problem set."

Social scientists everywhere have been shocked and dismayed at these stories of the fraudulent manufacturing of data or inaccurate conclusions produced by inadvertent mistakes in the data analysis (see Box 8.2 for a notable recent example). Fortunately, these episodes have provided an impetus for reflecting on what the various social science disciplines can do to minimize the extent to which this happens in the future. Indeed, many academic journals are beginning to embrace a system where scholars are required to post their data online before their work will be published. Social scientists who draw largely on experimental work have also started registries where scholars are encouraged to archive their experimental designs and protocols before they execute the experiments, thereby providing even more transparency to the process.

A second reason for providing access to your data and methods is that doing so allows other scholars to question or build on your findings. In some cases, scholars may wonder whether your findings would be robust to other approaches taken to analyzing the same data. For example, perhaps another scholar thinks that you have omitted an important variable from your analysis and he wishes to re-construct your analysis with that new variable included. Archiving your data can also draw more attention to your own research. We discuss the importance of promoting your research below. Thus, it will suffice to simply note here that when scholars can access your data, it greatly increases the probability that they will cite your research as well.

There are a number of different locations where anyone can archive the data from their study. Traditionally, political science scholars made use of the data archive at the Inter-university Consortium for Political and Social Research (ICPSR), housed at the University of Michigan. This remains an excellent location to archive data sets, but the process can sometimes be a bit time-consuming. Data submitted to ICPSR must often be checked and processed by staff before it is posted on-line, though ICPSR has created a way to streamline that process considerably.

A newer open-access location for archiving data sets is the Dataverse at the Institute for Quantitative Social Science at Harvard University. Archiving data at the Dataverse is relatively straightforward and can be very rewarding. Any researcher can create an account at Dataverse and after doing so can archive her data on the site. Researchers can provide as much or as little information about the data as they wish, but the more information provided, the more likely it is that others will find your data set and use it. One nice feature of the Dataverse is that it tracks how many times your data has been downloaded; thus, you will know when other scholars are using your data set. In addition, Dataverse provides a recommended citation for each data set in its archive; this citation should make it relatively easy for you (or others) to find papers where other scholars have used your data.

If your study is more qualitative in nature, then you may not have a single simple data set to archive on-line. Recall from Chapter 7 that qualitative data can include a wide variety of different items such as notes from interviews, field notes, news articles, government documents, or other related materials. These documents tend to not be stored in one single data file, but rather as a variety of different documents, including word-processing documents, PDFs, and even audio and video files. Additionally, qualitative data often contains sensitive information that must be carefully redacted by the researcher. For these reasons, scholars have not typically archived qualitative materials with anywhere near the same frequency with which they have archived quantitative datasets.

However, there is increasingly a push in political science to archive these materials, and political scientist Colin Elman is currently engaged in a project to create the Qualitative Data Repository (QDR) for researchers. This repository will be to qualitative researchers what ICPSR and Dataverse provided for those doing quantitative work. QDR will allow scholars to archive materials in a variety of digital formats, including documents, audio recordings, video recordings, and photographs. Additionally, QDR staff will be able to digitize documents that researchers only have in hard-copy form. QDR promises to be a significant advancement for qualitative scholarship, which had drawn criticism from some scholars for having a bit of a "black box" character to it. QDR will provide a venue for scholars to open up that black box, providing others with an opportunity to examine the documents compiled by investigators and determine whether they would have reached the same findings based on the same evidence.

It should be clear by now that it is easier for scholars to make their data publicly available today than it has ever been before. Likewise, it is easier than ever before for researchers to access data that others have archived from their own studies. This increased accessibility to replication data has both increased the integrity of social science research and also enhanced the ability of scholars to build on existing research.

Step 4: Promoting Your Research

Once your paper is published, either in a journal or at one of the websites mentioned above, the final step to consider is promoting your research. There are many ways to go about doing this, but the best place to start is to ask your professor about whether this makes sense for what you have produced. Almost all universities have a media relations office that specializes in pitching stories about research studies to the news media. The faculty or staff in your department may be able to put you in touch with these individuals. Even if you do not take that step, anyone can use social media to draw attention to their work. Doing so can be relatively easy; for example, simply posting a link to your paper on Facebook may draw some attention to what you have produced. And if your Facebook friends decide to share your link, attention to your work can spread fast. You can also link to your work on Twitter. And perhaps someone at your university runs a blog that might be interested in having you write a guest post that summarizes your findings.

Political scientists have become increasingly attentive to gaining publicity for their research not only from other scholars, but also from the mainstream media and the general public. Because politics is a topic that is of great interest to most people, many of our studies produce findings that even our friends and family will find interesting. We are ultimately engaged in the research process to add to what we know about society and make the world a better place, but, if our results are hidden from view, it is impossible to make even a modest contribution to the body of knowledge.

ABOVE ALL ELSE: REMEMBER THE *CHALLENGE* OF INFERENCE

The fundamental principles underlying solid research practices that we described in this book underscore the ways in which researchers can maximize the chances that their research contributes to the foundation of knowledge on a subject. These are: asking good questions, reading prior scholarship on

Box 8.3: Confirmation Bias as a Challenge to Inference

Humans tend to be prone to a variety of biases when it comes to how they process information. One of the most prevalent of these biases is **confirmation bias**—the tendency of humans to privilege information that is consistent (and discount information that is inconsistent) with their existing beliefs about the world. For example, political scientists have found that even when people are encouraged to treat political information even-handedly, they still succumb to giving more weight to the information that favors their preferred political party or candidate and less weight to those items that would otherwise undermine their pre-existing preferences.[a]

As scholars, we are not immune to confirmation bias and it poses a significant challenge to our ability to make valid inferences. In his article on this subject, Nickerson writes, "It is true in science as it is elsewhere that what one sees—actually or metaphorically—depends, to no small extent, on what one looks for and what one expects."[b] Nickerson makes note of a variety of ways in which confirmation bias affects human reasoning, even among scientists:

- Tends to draw our attention mostly toward our favored hypothesis.
- Leads us to give preferential treatment to evidence that supports what we are expecting to find.
- It causes us to seek out cases that prove what we already believe.
- It causes us to see in the data support for what we expect to find.

By now, you can probably imagine a variety of ways that confirmation bias might affect how you engage in the research process. In a qualitative study, you might shy away from selecting cases that you expect will undermine your hypothesis or you may highlight the interview or document data that is most supportive. In a large-n quantitative study you may try estimating different regression models until you find one in which your favored independent variable yields the result you expected. And if you are constructing an experiment, you may do so in a way that will tip the balance toward finding a result or you might find fault with an experiment that did not work as you expected.

Any of the above are natural reactions given our human instinct to favor confirmatory evidence and discount information that runs counter to our beliefs. But these tendencies pose a significant threat to making valid inferences, and we must be conscious to fight these impulses as researchers.

a. Charles S. Taber and Milton Lodge, "Motivated skepticism in the evaluation of political beliefs," *American Journal of Political Science* 50 (2006): 755–769.
b. Raymond S. Nickerson, "Confirmation bias: A ubiquitous phenomenon in many guises," *Review of General Psychology* 2 (1998): 175–220, p. 182.

your topic and deciding how you can contribute to it and move it forward, considering the pros and cons of different methodological approaches, clearly defining and consistently using the important terms (or variables) you will be focusing on, considering alternative theories and explanations as you create a research design and ponder your findings, being thoughtful and transparent about your decisions—about cases, definitions, variables chosen, survey question wording, data sources, documents used, interviews conducted, etc.—and how your choices may have introduced potential sources of bias in your study. At every step this means being attentive to the challenge of inference—if we forget or ignore the challenge, we risk producing work that simultaneously fails to provide satisfactory answers while being over-confident in its conclusions.

It is important to remember that social scientific research does not seek to prove anything. Rather, it seeks to understand phenomena. To test hypotheses. To answer questions. To understand why, when, how, or under what conditions certain events take place, a researcher must frame an appropriate question, determine the appropriate method or methods to employ, and carefully document each step of her research process. And the researcher must also be careful to describe the limitations of the analytic strategy selected and the tradeoffs made by selecting one approach over another. Ultimately the researcher must be forthright and clear about the confidence (or lack of confidence) with which she can draw conclusions about the subject matter.

Anyone can write a paper that answers a political question, but to craft a political *science* answer to that question requires attention to the process by which you formulate your answer. This not only means paying careful attention to the approach you use to answer your question, but it also means being open to whatever answer your process produces. Too often students and scholars alike have strong expectations about what the answer to their research questions should be, and when their methods produce unexpected results they consider this a failure of their study. But this can also be an opportunity for discovery. It is true that even a well-crafted research design may produce an inaccurate result, but stronger designs reduce the chances of obtaining a wrong answer and we may just find that our unexpected answer is the right one. When that happens, it means making a truly significant impact on our existing knowledge of the subject.

Of course, some might wonder, given all the challenges of inference, whether it is possible to "know" anything. We do not maintain that something like the "truth" is discoverable—but we do believe that, with many scholars working around the world tackling diverse questions and employing a wide variety of methodological approaches, we can improve our understanding of social and political life (past, present, and future) more accurately and more efficiently. We do argue that adhering to certain conventions in the conduct of scholarly research enhances the likelihood of producing useful, interesting, and influential work. And we believe that anybody is capable of producing such research as long as he maintains an appreciation for, and is motivated by, the *challenge* of inference.

KEY TERMS

confirmation bias   222

mixed-methods approach   206

within-case analysis   207

Index